SECOND PRINTING

Edward F. Snyder
with
Wilmer A. Cooper
Stephen L. Klineberg
Joe Volk
Don Reeves

Edited by Tom Mullen

Witness in Washington

Fifty Years of Friendly Persuasion

Witness in Washington
Fifty Years of Friendly Persuasion

Copyright © 1994 Friends United Press, Richmond, Indiana 47374. All rights reserved. No part of this book may be reproduced in any form whatsoever, except for brief quotations in reviews, without written permission from the publisher.

This second printing, 1995, corrects typographical errors and modifies the format. There are no material changes in the text.

Printed in the United States of America

Cover artwork by Jeffrey S. Dowers,
adapted from *Fortieth FCNL Anniversary Poster*

Library of Congress Cataloging-in-Publication Data
Witness in Washington : fifty years of friendly persuasion
/ Edward F. Snyder . . . [et al.] ; edited by Tom Mullen.
   p.   cm.
  Includes bibliographical references and index.
  ISBN   0-944350-34-8
  1. Friends Committee on National Legislation (U.S.)--History.
2. Society of Friends--United States--Political activity.
3. Lobbying--United States--History--20th century.
I. Snyder, Edward F.   II. Mullen, Thomas James, 1934-
BX7748.C5W58   1996
261.7'08'8286--dc20   95-41908
                                                                         CIP

Copies available from bookstores and
FCNL Education Fund
245 Second Street NE
Washington, DC 20002
(202) 547-6000

Table of Contents

In Appreciation
   Senator Mark Hatfield   vii
Preface
   Tom Mullen   viii
Acknowledgments   x
Sources   xi

Part I

Introduction: Toward the Next FCNL Jubilee
   Don Reeves   1

FCNL in Historical Perspective
   Wilmer A. Cooper   6

Part II

FCNL's First Fifty Years - A Personal Perspective
   Edward F. Snyder

The Context: Anti-communism, Secularism, Pacifism   27

1. Is FCNL naive about the real sources of power on public policy issues?   36

2. Does FCNL speak for all Friends?   46

3. Can a pacifist organization be relevant on national security issues?   70

4. Has FCNL been faithful to Quaker beliefs in the power of love and nonviolence, the indwelling of God in each person?   108

5. Have we put too much faith in the United Nations and other international organizations to achieve peace?   134

6. Have we had the right approach to helping people in the developing world help themselves?   145

7. Is FCNL pursuing effective policies to end poverty and build livable communities in the United States?   165

8. Has FCNL been "effective" on public policy issues?   180

Part III

FCNL—In the Moment or Of the Moment
Joe Volk   197

Envisioning the *Next* Fifty Years: Six Revolutionary Trends
Stephen L. Klineberg   207

1. Demographic Revolutions   208
2. The Transformation of the American Family   212
3. The Shift from Resources to Knowledge   215
4. The Rise of the Global Economy   217
5. Identity and Governance in a More Unstable World   219
6. The Environmental Challenge   220

Appendixes

Friends Committee on National Legislation Officers   223
FCNL Employees, Jan. 1, 1975 - Dec. 31, 1993   224
FCNL Witnesses Before Congressional Cmtes 1944-93   231

Index of Persons   239

Index of Subjects   247

In Appreciation

Please convey my greetings and congratulations to those who have gathered in Richmond to celebrate a half century of accomplishment in speaking out on issues vital to the public interest. In my Baptist training I was warned about the sin of pride, but I think Quakers can be forgiven for feeling very pleased with the impact you have made on national policy issues.

In the early days of FCNL, the sole concern of the organization was the war and its aftermath. Since then, however, the agenda of FCNL has been nearly as broad as that facing the Congress itself. I know of numerous instances in which your voice has been heard, but the benefits of your work extend beyond its direct impact on legislation. It is just as significant that you have continued to educate your constituency, providing meaningful, thoughtful analyses of the complex issues being debated in Washington. Your success in producing a clear-thinking, well-informed body of people across the country may be your most important achievement.

Your staff and volunteers have been a great help to me in the past in sorting out complex issues, and I look forward to continuing to work with you in the future. Together we can progress toward our shared vision for a better world.

U.S. Senator Mark Hatfield of Oregon

(read by Lon Fendall at the FCNL Jubilee gathering in Richmond, IN, June 26, 1993)

Preface

Witness in Washington is a companion volume to *Uphill for Peace* by E. Raymond Wilson published in 1975. That book essentially covered the first thirty years of the Friends Committee on National Legislation. This one celebrates fifty years of FCNL but does not repeat the work that Raymond did.

Ed Snyder is the primary author of this volume. His many years of experience on the staff of FCNL, especially during 1962-90 when he was Executive Secretary, provide a unique background for his reflections and insights. Ed steps back and asks—and also answers eight important questions about FCNL. He does more than report the history of the past fifty years. With refreshing candor and obvious passion, Ed invites us to evaluate where FCNL has succeeded and where it has not.

Wil Cooper, a former Administrative Secretary of FCNL and respected teacher of Quakerism, provides historical perspective for Quaker involvement in politics. He reminds us that "Friendly persuasion" has been a concern of Quakers since the time of George Fox and William Penn.

Stephen Klineberg, Professor of Sociology at Rice University, served seven years on the FCNL Policy Committee, four as clerk. His chapter looks into the future, as we know that issues around peace, human welfare, and social justice will beg for resolution as long as there is a future. Steve's chapter is prophetic.

Joe Volk, with editorial help from Stephen McNeil, focuses on a central concern of FCNL—peacemaking. Joe, the current Executive Secretary, provides a look at the way FCNL struggles with difficult issues. He shows how the staff anguishes over such matters as using the military to deliver humanitarian aid to Somalia.

Don Reeves, Clerk of the General Committee, introduces this Jubilee volume from his own perspective of long-time involvement in the work of FCNL. That *Witness in Washington* happens to be written on Don's "watch" is a coincidence, but it is a happy one. He, too, has helped make the history the book covers.

Witness in Washington is, in some ways, a book for "insiders." It names scores of persons, most of whom will be familiar to those hundreds of Friends who have walked the walk with FCNL. Indeed, if every person whose name is mentioned buys a copy, the book will be a best seller!

Such recognition is intentional. The book wants to celebrate the people and events which have sustained a Friends Witness in Washington for over fifty years. It's good to look back, draw a deep breath, and remember where we've been.

But there's another good reason for this book. Abraham Lincoln said, "If we could first know where we were, and wither we are tending, we could better judge what to do, and how to do it." The *next* fifty years will be as crucial as the first half-century of FCNL.

The hope is that some readers of this book will be inspired by the persistence and faithfulness of the hundreds of women and men who have been and are The Friends Committee on National Legislation. During the *next* fifty years, a fresh band of recruits will be needed for the Lamb's War. They, like those mentioned in this book, will be called to walk uphill for peace and witness in Washington.

Tom Mullen

Professor at Earlham School of Religion,
Editor of the 50th Anniversary Volume

Acknowledgements

In addition to the primary authors of this book, other persons have played important roles in its creation. Barbara Grant Nnoka coordinated efforts to keep the project within its limits. She succeeded, and working with Quakers scattered about the country by phone, fax and mail tested but did not defeat her patience, persistence, and good humor.

The 50th Anniversary Steering Committee, clerked by Binford Farlow, was prompted in October of 1993 by Wallace Collett to create this book.

Substantive research help was provided by Jean Jones, Laura Nell Morris, Aline Autenreith, Deb Smucker, Stephen McNeil, Barbara Grant Nnoka, and Ed Snyder.

Several others served as consultants, readers, technical advisors, and content checkers: Don Reeves, Wilmer Cooper, Linda Coffin, Ed Bronner, Gretchen Hall, Kathy Guthrie, Laura Petroff, Ruth Flower, Nancy Nye, Bob and Susie Fetter.

Certain persons functioned as facilitators for the project. They kept communications open, delivered messages, or provided comfort: Kathy Guthrie, Gretchen Hall, Bob and Susie Fetter, mentioned above, shared facilitator roles with Victoria Stanhope, Amy Mast, Shawn Downey, and Barbara Ginsburg.

Sources

Unless footnoted at the end of the chapter, most of the documentation for material in Ed Snyder's section can be found in the appropriate FCNL Bound Volumes. He has usually given the year in which the item appeared in order to direct the researcher to the appropriate volume. Bound Volumes may be found at FCNL's Washington office, at the Swarthmore College Peace Collection, and at the libraries of Earlham, Guilford, Haverford, Whittier, William Penn, and Wilmington Colleges, and Harvard University, as well as at the Hoover Institution of War, Revolution and Peace in Stanford, California, and the offices of the Friends Committee on Legislation of California in Sacramento.

In general, FCNL Bound Volumes contain the *FCNL Washington Newsletters,* the FCNL *Memo* when published, minutes of most FCNL committees, the variously entitled Annual Report/Legislative Summary/Legislative Report, as well as testimonies, documents, letters of advocacy, etc, plus state legislative material. Researchers may find especially useful FCNL's annual legislative summaries prepared by FCNL staff at the end of each calendar year to inform General Committee members of FCNL's legislative activities. After 1972, these Reports also include reports from FCNL administrative and finance personnel, who provide the absolutely essential undergirding for all of FCNL's legislative activities.

In addition, the Swarthmore College Peace Collection is the depository for much of FCNL's correspondence, subject files, and communications with Members of Congress.

FCNL's Washington office has files for recent years, as well as copies of most of the Congressional hearings at which FCNL witnesses appeared. These give the context of the testimony and include the dialogue with Congressional committee members; the Bound Volumes contain only the testimony as submitted.

FCNL enlightenment on degenderized language occurred primarily in 1974. Documents are quoted here as they originally appeared.

Wilmer Cooper, then acting FCNL Executive Secretary, and Ed Snyder, Legislative Secretary, in 1956 in front of the U.S. Capitol

Introduction:
Toward the Next FCNL Jubilee

In Leviticus, God declared that every 50th year should be a jubilee: a time to be "hallowed," during which "you shall proclaim liberation in the land for all its inhabitants." The jubilee year begins as a time for restoring right relations with God. But many of the instructions for keeping the jubilee focus on social institutions through which people relate to the land and to each other — redistribution of property, rest for the land, forgiveness of debt, release of bondservants. Hundreds of years later, Jesus began his ministry by repeating the same call.

As Friends celebrate 50 years of FCNL's Quaker witness in Washington, we hold up the promise of the jubilee: "Observe my statutes, keep my judgments and carry them out; and you shall live in the land in security." FCNL's witness has been effective because it has grown from the spiritual life of Friends. It will continue to prosper only as it reflects the life of the Spirit. Our mission, as from the beginning, will be to shape the nation's institutions and policies for the well-being of God's children and the rest of creation.

When FCNL was founded during World War II, its work was largely directed to war-time problems. Much of our life and work since then has been dominated by the Cold War. But all along, while resisting militarism, coercion, and injustice, FCNL has paid increasing attention to the positive work of reconciliation among nations and peoples, and to developing human resources. Towards these positive ends, FCNL has supported the United Nations and Law of the Sea; civil rights; self-determination of Native Americans; restoration of confidence in government; economic and employment opportunities; and more adequate housing, education, and health care.

–from the Clerk's Call for FCNL 50th Anniversary Jubilee

During the recent months of FCNL's Jubilee celebrations and capital campaign, as during 36 years of engagement with FCNL, I have been inspired by the steadfastness of FCNL in three respects: the centrality of worship and waiting on the spirit; the persistence of witness on core issues; and the constancy of participation and support from a broad spectrum of Friends and like-minded people.

Worship is a central feature in the life of FCNL's committees, particularly the General Committee; for many, worship is the high point of the Annual Meeting. This year, during the revision of the Policy Statement, nearly 200 Friends Meetings and meeting committees have participated in the process of review and comment leading to the final statement to be considered by the General Committee. We expect, after intense discussion, to find unity on a new policy statement during meetings for worship for business at Annual Meeting. But we will almost certainly stand aside from statements on several issues of great concern to many Friends, but about which we experience different leadings. We intend that FCNL continues to be a place where all Friends feel safe to share their own experience and interpretation of God's presence in their individual and corporate lives. Part of our steadfastness is loving respect, and confidence that Christ's spirit will lead us to greater clarity over time.

During the interview for my present job at Bread for the World, I asked about BFW's "success expectation ratio." The response was that BFW selected and shaped issues so that they might expect to "win" at least partially, 75 - 80 percent of the time. I said that I might need to be reminded occasionally, since I'd had my training among Quakers, where many campaigns are for a decade or two or five. General and complete disarmament has been on FCNL's agenda since the beginning. Winning redress for Japanese Americans incarcerated during World War II took more than 40 years. The peace tax fund was on our agenda for twenty years before its first major Congressional hearing, and may be only slightly nearer passage than Ed Snyder's 1975 prediction of "another 10 to 15 years." Resolution of Middle East tensions has engaged Friends since before the creation of Israel in 1948; we take heart at recent progress, but expect peace in that region to be on Friends' agenda for some years hence.

Since 1975 FCNL, with assistance from Mennonites and others, has had the only full time staff person on Native American concerns among the non-Indian religious community in Washington. The ability to persist on core issues is one fruit of constant waiting on the Spirit.

A glance at the staff and committee lists in the Appendix confirms the persistence of engagement. We can name several dozen families with second generation participation, and a handful of three-generation FCNL families. Samuel Levering served on FCNL's General Committee continuously throughout its first half century. Bob and Susie Fetter, on several occasions, selected youngsters to blow out FCNL's 50th birthday candles who might be active at the time of our Centennial. Barbara Grant Nnoka, without whom this report would not have come to pass, began her FCNL service as a research assistant in 1947.

Many FCNL staff have also served for long periods. At our jubilee, only our third Executive Secretary, Joe Volk, is still relatively "new," having begun service in 1990. Like Raymond Wilson, Joe comes to FCNL with a background in peace education with the American Friends Service Committee. From his engagement with the Vietnam War, he brings yet another generation's personal witness to the futility of violence. He also brings a delightful sense of humor, often expressed as Volk's jokes.

E. Raymond Wilson came to FCNL at its beginning, having helped generate the "need" for FCNL through long service as a peace educator for the American Friends Service Committee. His tenure as Executive Secretary was nearly 20 years, from 1943 until 1962. He was a *very active* Executive Secretary Emeritus for another 20 years. While I was on FCNL staff during the late 1970s, we all held our breath as Raymond almost daily maneuvered his rattletrap old car to Capitol Hill from Sandy Spring to pursue his enduring concerns. Readers who are not already familiar with his account of FCNL's first 30 years may enjoy *Uphill for Peace,* now out of print, but widely available among Friends and in Friends libraries.

3

Edward F. Snyder served FCNL 35 years, as Legislative Secretary from 1955 until 1962, then as Executive Secretary until 1990. Ed's recollections and reflections on FCNL's first 50 years, which constitute the heart of this report, reveal Ed's great spiritual depth, and his gentle but resolute leadership. During his tenure, he helped shape FCNL as a trusted instrument of a wide spectrum in the Religious Society of Friends.

At the risk of naming too few, other long-serving staff include: Jeanette Hadley, administrative assistant for 29 years, from the beginning until 1972; Alice Stout, bookkeeper and administrative assistant for 24 years; and Frances Neely, associate and legislative secretary for 27 years. Among current staff, Ruth Flower, legislative secretary since 1981, following service with the California Friends Committee on Legislation, is among the most highly respected lobbyists on domestic issues on Capitol Hill; Nancy Nye, legislative secretary, was formerly FCNL field staff, following several years service in Friends School at Ramallah, Jordan with Friends United Meeting; and Alison Oldham leads our legislative action program among Friends and others, after serving as a regional field staff. Floyd Voris was the longest-serving volunteer staff, assisting regularly in the mailroom for 18 years, until age 95.

One risk of steadfastness is that it may settle into habits of complacency, self-righteousness, or just plain contrariness. Much peacemaking requires standing in opposition to bad policies. But seeking "a world free from war and the threat of war" implies much more than *conscientious objection, disarmament, or tax resistance*. True security requires creating "a society with equity and justice for all," "a community where every person's potential may be fulfilled," and "an earth restored" from the quatrain created by Lilian Watford, Field Secretary for FCNL, 1980-82.

Sustained work to shift U.S. federal budget priorities from military spending to human and social needs has given FCNL a leadership role in religious and other coalitions. Health care reform and new international trade arrangements have challenged committees and staff to reexamine core issues. And the disintegration of communities, evidenced by crime, drug use, and dysfunctional families, press us to reexamine underlying values.

It may be that in a post-Cold War era, FCNL will be able to devote more of its resources to building structures of enduring peace and security. Part of steadfastness in worship is openness to fresh winds of the Spirit, expressed through wide participation in FCNL policy and priority-setting. I am convinced that long-lived FCNL campaigns rise from being led to bold visions of the future.

Some freshness of Spirit comes from young people. FCNL has just appointed its 24th class of interns—three young people who for one year work closely with FCNL lobbyists. About a dozen of the 75 alumni of this program are engaged in FCNL committees.

In his report, Wilmer Cooper places FCNL, as a "divine lobbyist," within an historical spectrum of Friends relationships with governments ranging from full participation to abhorrence. Wil was associate and administrative secretary for FCNL from 1952 until 1959, before he helped establish the Earlham School of Religion.

Joe Volk, with editorial assistance from Stephen McNeil, gives a glimpse into the effort to adapt Friends peace testimony in the post-Cold War era when nearly all current conflicts are civil strife, rather than international wars. This is part of who we are becoming in this moment.

Stephen Klineberg's essay, which reflects discussions by FCNL Futures Committee and groups of Friends during FCNL's jubilee celebrations, outlines trends which are reshaping the world: changes in population and family life; the shift toward a global, information-based economy; a renewed emphasis on ethnic or other community identity; and growing pressure on the environment. These shifts imply likely changes in FCNL's witness in Washington, and more broadly, in the character of the Society of Friends itself.

New insights based on Quaker values and continued openness to God's leading will be required as people everywhere search for security in their communities and their world in this new era. FCNL invites all Friends, and others, to join us in envisioning a rightly ordered world and the role of Spirit-led Friends in its creation.

Don Reeves

Clerk of FCNL General Committee, July 1994.

FCNL in Historical Perspective

by Wilmer A. Cooper

> The Friends Committee on National Legislation is, in a sense, an institutionalization of the age-old Quaker practice... of the divine lobbyist ...If anyone thinks the techniques of the FCNL are a modern innovation, he knows little of Quaker history.
>
> *Frederick B. Tolles*
> *Ward Lecture*
> *Guilford College, 1956*

Each generation of Friends needs to see itself in light of its history, which goes back to the middle of the seventeenth century. This longer view is especially important as we commemorate the 50th Anniversary of the founding of the FCNL. There is historical precedent for these fifty years of Quakers attempting to influence legislation and governmental policy.

In 1956, about a decade after FCNL's beginning, Frederick Tolles, one of Quakerism's most respected historians, gave the Ward Lecture at Guilford College with the title, "Quakerism and Politics." This classic summary of Friends involvement with government was published in pamphlet form and later became a chapter in Tolles' book, *Quakers and the Atlantic Culture*, 1962. In this opening chapter to FCNL's 50th Anniversary volume we shall refer in some detail to his insights and history of Quaker attempts to influence government.[1]

Early Quaker Precedents

In 1656, George Fox visited Oliver Cromwell, the Lord Protector of England, at Whitehall. Concerning this visit Fox reports, "the power of God riz in me, and I was moved to bid him lay down his crown at the feet of Jesus." Tolles says that "Fox would have him make England a kind of pilot project for the Kingdom of Heaven... Fox was a revolutionary. He had no patience with the relativities and compromises of political life. The absolute demand he made upon Cromwell...stands as one pole of Quaker thought on politics."[2]

Fox's contemporary and companion in the ministry, William Penn, was his opposite number in political outlook. When Penn established his "Holy Experiment" in the Pennsylvania colony in 1682, he did so "on the proposition that government was 'a part of religion itself, a thing sacred in its institution and end.'" But "neither he nor his successors had pretended to maintain George Fox's absolute witness." Thus Fox and Penn represented what Tolles calls "two poles of Quaker political attitudes and behavior," the absolutist and relativist, whose paradoxical positions have "oscillated" since the beginning of the Quaker movement.[3]

It is generally supposed that early Quakerism was little influenced by the Calvinist and Puritan traditions because of Fox's opposition to Calvin's doctrine of election as the basis for salvation. But politically speaking, the Puritan soil that nurtured Fox also strongly believed in transformation, namely, that the world does not have to be the way it is and can be transformed into what it ought to be. The Quakers, like the Calvinists of Geneva and the Puritans of England, held that government can be a vehicle for the fulfillment of God's will in the world. They also shared what Tolles calls "the apocalyptic excitement, the zeal for social action, the identification of politics with religion."[4] Fox believed that it was by the spiritual power of God that transformation takes place. Although Penn was of like mind, he also believed that the means by which it takes place was through political processes and institutions of government. This amalgam constituted the seedbed for the radical

7

belief of Friends that "government was a part of religion itself" and can serve to implement God's will in human affairs.

Although incredible to the Quaker mind today, in 1659, near the end of the interregnum years, the Rump Parliament became so desperate that it proposed that Quakers be asked to help with "a sweeping reorganization of the Commonwealth government," giving judgeships and commissioners of the militia to Quakers and those sympathetic with their views. The French ambassador verified that "the hard-pressed government was relying on its support from the Quakers." But before this "rule of the Saints" could take over, the "unsaintly Charles II" was restored to the throne.[5]

The Middle Period of Quakerism

Following the restoration of Charles II to the English throne in 1660, the dominant mood of Friends was "aloofness and neutrality" with respect to politics.

After enduring several years of persecution and imprisonment, they began to work for religious freedom and toleration. To achieve this end, Tolles says that "Friends engaged in a certain amount of electioneering and lobbying ... but in the long run lobbying was for Friends a more congenial method of influencing politics ... " He continues:

> Quakers had been engaged in lobbying–that is to say, in seeking to influence legislators by personal visits–ever since 1659, when a hundred and sixty-five Friends went to Westminster Hall and sent into the House of Commons a paper offering to lie "body for body" in jail in place of their imprisoned and suffering fellow Quakers ... The Meeting for Sufferings [of London Yearly Meeting] coordinated the work. The weightiest Friends in England, including George Fox and William Penn, busied themselves buttonholing Members of Parliament and appearing at committee hearings. The Yearly Meeting even

rented a room in a coffee house hard by the House of Parliament for a headquarters--a kind of Friends Committee on National Legislation office.[6]

As a result of this lobbying campaign, Parliament passed in 1689 the famous Act of Toleration which brought some relief to dissenters, including the Quakers. Another concession was made to Friends when the Act of Affirmation was passed in 1722, which permitted the Quakers to make an affirmation in place of a formal oath in the courts. They were also guaranteed certain rights of citizenship enjoyed by others, such as the right to sue in courts and to vote in elections. But their right to hold public office did not come for another century.[7]

With the coming of the eighteenth century, the age of Quietism influenced the mood and activity of Friends. Friends tended to withdraw from public life and to fence in their communities from the world around them. Their objective was to maintain the purity of their religious testimonies and practices undefiled by the ways of the world. Although Friends maintained control of the Pennsylvania Legislature until 1756, their power and influence waned with their quietistic withdrawal from the world around them. Late in the eighteenth century, the developing mood of Quaker Quietism counseled Friends not to vote. By 1820, Thomas Shillitoe, an example of this extreme view, advised his fellow members:

> Friends, let us dare not meddle with political matters .... Endeavour to keep that ear closed, which will be itching to hear the news of the day and what is going forward in the political circles.... Avoid reading political publications, and as much as possible, newspapers.[8]

With the passage of the English Reform Bill of 1832, Friends were free to stand for Parliament by taking an affirmation in place of the usual oath of office. As a result Joseph Pease was the first Quaker to be elected to Parliament in 1833. A decade later one of the most distinguished British statesmen of the nineteenth century, the Quaker John Bright, served not only in Parliament but also was a member of Gladstone's cabinet. He finally resigned, however, over the British bombing of Alexandria in 1882. John Bright served in public office conscientiously, although not always with as much consistency as his fellow Quakers wanted. Beside Pease and Bright, many other Quakers served in Parliament in the late nineteenth and twentieth centuries, and still larger numbers held offices in local government. A notable parliamentary example in the twentieth century was T. Edmund Harvey, who served as a Quaker M.P. during both World Wars.

Contrary to the admonition of Friends at the turn of the nineteenth century to free themselves from political involvement, London Yearly Meeting through its 1911 Book of Discipline was advising Friends not only to accept positions of public service but intentionally to prepare themselves for such responsibilities. At the same time, writes Frederick Tolles, "the experience of Quaker M.P.'s suggests that the path of a religious idealist in practical politics is not an easy one."[9] Compromise was always a temptation, and sometimes Friends gave way to it even though they intended to remain faithful to their Quaker principles.

On the American side of the Atlantic, Quakers held a number of important governing posts in addition to the most notable of all— Penn's "Holy Experiment" with government in Pennsylvania, 1682-1756. In Rhode Island during a period of nearly a hundred years (1672-1768) ten Quakers held the position of governor for a total of 30 years. For the last quarter of the seventeenth century, West Jersey was essentially a Quaker colony. And in North Carolina a respected Friend, John Archdale, distinguished himself as governor of that colony.

In spite of this formidable record of public service, some Friends "grew adept at the politics of shuffle and evasion."[10] In response to this and the Quaker abdication of control of the Pennsylvania legislature in 1756, Philadelphia Yearly Meeting began advising Friends not to accept any government service which would compromise their Quaker peace principles. Thus Tolles concludes, "The pendulum had swung sharply away from political participation, and

I think it is fair to say that American Friends have tended almost from that day to this [1956] to avoid direct participation in politics, at least in the sense of seeking elective office."[11] In some places Friends were threatened with disownment if they engaged in political activity. This shift by American Friends is remarkable when British Friends in the nineteenth century were again encouraging members to assume greater political responsibility. By the twentieth century, however, American Friends reversed course again by encouraging greater involvement in government. Philadelphia Yearly Meeting in 1927, and again in 1955, and the Five Years Meeting of Friends in 1945, minuted their support of Friends who accepted active roles in government.

To sum up this vacillation of Friends between compromise on the one hand and sticking to their principles on the other, Tolles quotes Rufus Jones concerning the ambivalence of Friends:

> There has always been in the Society of Friends a group of persons pledged unswervingly to the ideal. To those who form this inner group compromise is under no circumstance allowable. If there comes a collision between allegiance to the ideal and the holding of public office, then the office must be deserted. If obedience to the soul's vision involves eye or hand, houses or lands or life, they must be immediately surrendered. But there has always been as well another group who have held it to be equally imperative to work out their principles of life in the complex affairs of the community and the state, where to gain an end one must yield something; where to get on one must submit to existing conditions; and where to achieve ultimate triumph one must risk his ideals to the tender mercies of a world not yet ripe for them.[12]

Frederick Tolles concludes:

> If anything is clear from our quick historical survey, I think it must be this: that there is no one Quaker attitude

towards politics. Historically, Quakers can be found practicing and preaching almost every possible position from full participation to complete withdrawal and abstention. Rufus Jones has isolated for us, in the passage . . . just quoted, the two polar extremes. I would just underline the dilemma implicit in his description. If a concerned Quaker... decides to enter practical politics in order to translate his principles into actuality, he may achieve a relative success: he may be able to raise the level of political life in his time, as John Bright did, or maintain a comparatively happy or just and peaceful society, as the Quaker legislators of Pennsylvania did. But he can apparently do it only at a price–the price of compromise, of the partial betrayal of his ideals. If, on the other hand, he decides to preserve his ideals intact, to maintain his religious testimonies unsullied and pure, he may be able to do that, but against a price–the price of isolation, of withdrawal from the main stream of life in his time, of renouncing the opportunity directly and immediately to influence history.

Let me call the two positions the relativist and the absolutist. And let me suggest that perhaps each one needs the other. The relativist needs the absolutist to keep alive and clear the vision of the City of God while he struggles in some measure to realize it in the City of Earth. And conversely, the absolutist needs the relativist, lest the vision remain the possession of a few only, untranslated into any degree of reality for the world as a whole. Which position an individual Friend will take will depend, I suppose, on his temperament....[13]

Tolles' conclusion that "there is no one Quaker attitude toward politics" is an understatement. The rank and file of Friends in this century have ranged from very conservative to very liberal, including all political parties across the board. Although only a few in the United States have run for elective office, there have been Paul

Douglas in the U.S. Senate, a Democrat, and two Republican Presidents, Herbert Hoover and Richard Nixon, who acknowledged Friends membership even though some Quakers have been reluctant to claim them.

As Friends have moved through the twentieth century, Frederick Tolles' final conclusion seems prophetic in terms of Friends finding their niche in the political process. It is this role which seemed most appropriate in the founding of the Friends Committee on National Legislation. Tolles says:

> I should like to suggest . . . that if there is any distinctive Quaker posture *vis a vis* politics, it is one which I might describe as the prophetic stance or the role of the divine lobbyist. [After citing a number of examples of such lobbying in Quaker history, Tolles says:] All these, like the prophets of Israel, have felt a divine call to "speak truth to power," to lay a concern upon those who are charged with the governing of men. The Friends Committee on National Legislation is, in a sense, an institutionalization of this age-old Quaker practice.
>
> There are grave perils and responsibilities in this role. There is the peril of hiding a selfish motive behind a facade of religious concern: a Quaker lobby must never fall to the level of the lumber lobby or the oil lobby. There is the peril of mistaking a personal impulse, no matter how altruistic, for a divine call, or becoming a mere busybody, troubling harassed legislators with trivial or irresponsible demands. And there is the responsibility of "earning the right" by a consistent pattern of religious dedication and service to speak to those who bear the heavy burden of political power. This kind of prophetic mission to the rulers of men is a distinctively Quaker approach to politics.[14]

Redefining Friends Role Toward Government

With the coming of the twentieth century and the agony over two world wars, Friends felt the need more than ever to make their concern for peace visible in specific and concrete ways. The founding of the American Friends Service Committee in 1917 was an effort to carry out significant programs of relief and reconstruction, not only to heal the wounds of war and violence but to help lay the foundations for peace. As Friends pursued these efforts, they increasingly discovered that there were political dimensions to peace building which called for a more active Quaker peace witness in Washington and at the United Nations in New York. Services of love and expressions of good will were important to help establish the right climate for peacemaking, but structures and foundations for enduring peace required that governments play a major role. So how should Friends position themselves to work effectively on Quaker concerns regarding peace and justice?

Concurrently Friends became increasingly exercised about the growing power of government and the military over the lives of people. They believed that the possibility of universal military training was a serious threat which had to be addressed. These and other peace and social concerns caused Friends to explore how they could more effectively witness to these concerns in places where it would make a difference.

At the same time, it was becoming clear that the American Friends Service Committee could not work in the political arena without endangering its tax exempt status, which was essential to the rest of its humanitarian and educational work. Thus this background led Friends to explore the establishment of a Washington office. Such an office would be independent of the AFSC and would be recognized as a non-tax-exempt lobby attempting to influence legislation.

The Founding of FCNL

As a forerunner of FCNL, the Friends War Problems Committee was formed in Philadelphia in 1940, soon after the beginning of World War II. Between then and 1943, it met fifty times to deal with Friends growing concern about conscription and how to advise conscientious objectors who were facing the draft. For extended periods of time, Raymond Wilson and Paul French worked as a team in Washington to secure legislation which would provide for conscientious objection to military service. Concerning this work Raymond has written:

> Before it was expanded to form the Friends Committee on National Legislation in 1943, the main thrust of the War Problems Committee was for the rights of conscience in legislation proposed in Congress. Of particular concern was the original draft measure--the Burke-Wadsworth Bill--which finally became law on September 16, 1940. Their second objective was opposition to a whole string of proposed conscription bills, including total mobilization, draft of labor, draft of women and draft of 18 and 19-year-olds. None of these proposals became law during this prewar and early U.S. war era, but they were actively promoted by their supporters, and presented an almost constant threat during that period.[15]

Arch Street and Race Street Meetings in Philadelphia were the most active in this effort, but by July of 1940 a National Conference on the draft was called in Richmond, Indiana which drew Friends from twenty-two of the twenty-five Yearly Meetings in the U.S. Thus through the efforts of the Friends War Problems Committee, serious thought was given to forming a Friends office in Washington to represent Quaker concerns to their Representatives in Congress.

In the midst of World War II, on June 11-12, 1943, fifty-two Friends from fifteen U.S. Yearly Meetings met at Quaker Hill,

Richmond, Indiana to lay plans for the establishment of the Friends Committee on National Legislation. The aim was to seek as wide support as possible among Friends, both for appointment of Yearly Meeting representatives to FCNL and for their financial support. The Richmond meeting released the following statement regarding the establishment of a Washington office:

> Friends have a responsibility to contribute... to the shaping of wise and right legislation in those areas in which our principles and the causes we believe in are most closely affected.... These critical times... are bringing home to us acutely the sweeping role which government is playing in shaping life, both national and international.[16]

Raymond Wilson, the first Executive Secretary of FCNL, played a major role in its success during its early years, but he was not present at the organizing meeting in Richmond, Indiana. Nevertheless, Raymond Wilson had been a staff member of the AFSC's Peace Section, and he worked with Paul French under the auspices of the Friends War Problems Committee to try to defeat the first peacetime draft legislation in Congress in 1940. Raymond had also been active in the previous discussions in Philadelphia about the need for Friends' representation in Washington, so it was natural for the Richmond Conference to ask him to head the new work in Washington.

On November 3, 1943, the FCNL's first office was opened in the basement of the Florida Avenue Friends Meetinghouse in Washington. Joining Raymond were Jeanette Hadley as Office Secretary, and John Kellam as an office assistant. Five years later, in 1948, the office was moved to larger quarters halfway across the city at 1000 Eleventh Street. In the autumn of 1952 the office was moved again, this time to Capitol Hill diagonally across the street from what is now the Russell Senate Office Building. Through the assistance of the Friends Meeting in Washington, a row house at 104 C Street N.E. was purchased and renovated for office purposes, including some office space to rent. By 1958 the Capitol expansion program condemned FCNL's new home in order to provide parking for the new Dirksen Senate Office Building. It was FCNL's good fortune to find a new location less than a block away at 245 Second Street N.E., immediately across from the more recent Hart Senate Office Building. A row house and grocery store on the corner of N.E. Second and C Streets were bought, renovated and merged. With further remodeling, this same building has served as the strategic location of FCNL since occupancy in 1959.

As Raymond Wilson and his colleagues took over this important Quaker assignment in 1943, he later reflected on this experience:

> "We ought to be under no illusion," I said in my letter of acceptance, "that many of the ideals of the Society of Friends will be fully acceptable in the period of hate and disillusionment which follows such a tremendous war as the one in which the world is now involved. We ought to be willing to work for causes which will not be won now, but cannot be won in the future unless the goals are staked out now and worked for energetically over a period of time." I told the Committee that we should not expect many legislative victories in the first ten years if we were working on the fundamental issues that the Society of Friends ought to be working on.[17]

Raymond Wilson had a clear and realistic assessment of the hard road ahead for FCNL, and in many ways continues to be as true today as it was in the 1940s.

FCNL's Relationship to the Religious Society of Friends

One of the distinctive features of the Friends Committee on National Legislation has been its attempt from the beginning to remain close and accountable to its parent body, the Religious Society of Friends. Friends' polity is such that voluntary groups have

17

considerable freedom to come into being, providing they can gain the interest and support of enough people to make the enterprise viable. In fact, one of the problems that often plagues Friends is that the amount of freedom such groups have can become unwieldy and counter-productive if they do not remain close and accountable to the larger body of Friends. In FCNL's case the leadership, beginning with Raymond Wilson, made every effort to cultivate such a supportive and working relationship. For example, wherever Yearly Meetings or important Friends conferences have been held, staff and/or Committee members have tried to be present and make reports, display FCNL literature, and engage individuals and groups in conversation about the work of the Committee. The positive effect of such efforts over extended periods of time have served FCNL well when the Committee has taken positions on issues which were not always popular with the cautious and conservative members in the Friends' constituency.

In spite of FCNL's attempt to represent fairly the views of Friends supportive of the Committee and its policies, it has at times been severely criticized by Friends who do not share its views. In response Raymond Wilson observed:

> If a criticism was justified, and many of them were, we have sought to remedy the situation. If it was an honest difference of opinion, we have sought to recognize and respect it, even if contrary to the policy established at our annual meeting. Where an agreement could not be reached, it was a matter of regret to the staff and meant considerable emotional strain on them. We tried to recognize that no policy of the FCNL should be above review, debate or criticism, and that there was vast room for improvement of its work.[18]

Criticisms have come primarily from Friends. Members of Congress may disagree with positions taken, but almost never have criticized the way in which they were approached by FCNL representatives. The author remembers an especially difficult time when

Raymond Wilson was feeling pressure and stress from Quaker critics of FCNL's position on certain issues. One Sunday afternoon the Wilson and Cooper families, joined by Frederick Libby (that indefatigable Quaker head of the National Council for the Prevention of War) went picnicking in Rock Creek Park in Washington. Sitting in the sunshine on the fresh green grass, Raymond soon shared some of his frustrations concerning criticisms he was receiving from dissatisfied Quakers across the country. In response Fred Libby, with his "fatherly wisdom," said: "Raymond, you know, you never kick a dead body!" In other words, if you're doing something worthwhile you are bound to be criticized, whereas if you aren't doing anything worthwhile no one will bother to criticize. That was wise counsel, especially for Raymond, a prophetic idealist who wanted to achieve world peace and solve all the world's problems in his lifetime.

FCNL's Organizational Structure

The organizational structure of FCNL begins with the General Committee. About 160 representatives are appointed by 26 Yearly Meetings and approximately 8 other Friends organizations. Another 80 members are appointed at large by the Nominating Committee of the General Committee. The Committee's first responsibility is to meet annually in Washington and formulate legislative policies which guide the Committee and staff in their work with Congress. The basic Statement of Legislative Policy is revised every five to six years based on input from many Friends Meetings and study and recommendations by a Policy Committee appointed by the General Committee. These recommendations are then thrashed out at the Annual Meeting, using the Quaker method of business procedure. Occasionally, the Annual Meeting for FCNL is unable to unite on a particular position, such as the case of abortion in recent years. In such cases FCNL delays taking a position, which in turn prevents the staff from working on legislation pertaining to that issue. That FCNL has been able to achieve

19

as much consensus as it has on a broad range of issues, both domestic and foreign, is amazing.

A second responsibility of the General Committee is to select those legislative priorities on which the staff and Committee will work during the forthcoming two-year legislative session. The Committee's Nominating Committee also appoints an Executive Committee, whose responsibility it is to meet with the staff periodically and give closer direction to their work. Annual Committee members also keep in touch with their Friends constituencies back home and feed legislative information to them as well as seek their financial, moral and political action support for the work in Washington. FCNL is a grass roots organization in that it is not a top-down enterprise run only by the staff, but an organization where policy is determined by the Committee representatives. It is then the task of the staff to implement the policies of the Committee through its work on Capitol Hill, and its legislative educational work with Friends throughout the country.

A third responsibility is to adopt the annual budget, to work to underwrite it, and to give general oversight to the administrative and personnel work of the staff. Most of this, however, is handled by the Executive Committee and other subcommittees. Over the years the staff size has grown from its original three to twenty or more, including volunteers, student interns, field secretaries, and the "Friend in Washington" program. During the same time period, the budget has increased from a few hundred thousand to a million dollars a year.

The very nature of FCNL lends itself well to this kind of shared responsibility and accountability, because the issues on which it works require not only lobbying in Washington but also grassroots lobbying in the states and congressional districts. This means involving as many Friends and others as possible in contacting their Representatives and Senators with letters and personal calls. In addition to this aspect of its outreach, FCNL is not financially heavily endowed but depends largely on modest contributions from those interested in its work. Although FCNL is seeking to strengthen its financial base with reserve funds, its aim is not to become dependent on an endowment base for its yearly operation. Its main source of support will continue to be its annual fund appeal to its Friends constituency.

This combination of factors makes FCNL basically a healthy organization, congenial to and responsive to the democratic spirit of Friends. Even though FCNL has broad and general support from Friends, it by no means represents all Friends. Whenever its staff or representatives testify before Congressional Committees, a disclaimer is given at the opening that the testimony is on behalf of the Friends Committee on National Legislation rather than the entire Society of Friends. It is thus registered with the U.S. Congress, so that its operations are open to any Congress person who wants to know what FCNL is and who it represents. We might wish that FCNL could speak for and be supported by the entire Society of Friends, but given the diversity of Quaker faith and practice and the broadly based structure of the Society of Friends, this would be impossible.

If one looks at FCNL's decision-making process which governs its legislative policies and work, there has been a noticeable evolution from the early days to the present. In the beginning, the General Committee and supporters of FCNL tended to follow the experienced lead of Raymond and the staff in Washington. If one attends the Annual Meeting today, where legislative policies and priorities are hammered out, one is impressed with the increasing formative role of the General Committee and its subcommittees. The shift to a more grass roots controlled organization, with less emphasis on staff counsel, came during Ed Snyder's Executive Secretaryship, 1962-90. This gradual movement toward democratic control has been conscious and has strengthened FCNL's accountability to the Society of Friends.

FCNL's Philosophy and Method of Work

The way FCNL goes about its work to influence legislation and government policy is quite different from most special interest groups and lobbies. Although FCNL may utilize the principles of other effective lobbying groups, its approach is distinctive and perhaps unique. FCNL and its staff have not publicized this side of its work nor those human interest stories which dramatize FCNL's work and make it both interesting and fascinating.

FCNL's approach has been to minimize the pressure tactics of many lobbying groups. In the first place it does not have the kind of financial resources and political clout that pressure groups are so often able to bring to bear on legislation. When the FCNL was first established by the representative meeting of Friends in Richmond, Indiana in 1943, they were careful to speak to this point.

> The Committee "is not expected to engage in lobbying of the pressure-group character. Its purpose is rather to work by methods of quiet influence through personal contacts and persuasion to win the assent of reasonable minds and enlist sympathies with the objective sought."[19]

This methodology is clearly "friendly persuasion," appealing to the reason and moral sensitivities of Congress men and women, and other government officials. This approach is nourished by the religious and spiritual basis of FCNL's political endeavors.

Several important principles of legislative action have characterized FCNL's approach. One is not to go-it-alone in Washington but to support coalitions of like-minded persons and organizations who are working on similar legislative issues. This may entail common work on issues which church and public interest groups are addressing.

Another principle is for FCNL to provide research on a broad spectrum of legislative issues which the constituency needs for action. At the same time, FCNL is an important source of information for Congress and various public interest groups. FCNL maintains a staff of four college interns who do research for the lobbyists who work on Capitol Hill. Increasingly, the information they turn up is made available not only through FCNL's *Washington Newsletter* and special action bulletins, but also through direct mail and telephone recordings. Each week the staff updates a telephone tape which provides the latest information on particular pieces of legislation, including action suggestions. Recently, the weekly updates have been posted on electronic networks.

An important ally of FCNL has been William Penn House on Capitol Hill where legislative seminars and special groups are housed and accommodations provided for meetings. FCNL services many of these groups with legislative information needed for lobbying Congress. The seminars range from student and youth groups who want to learn more about their government to adult and older groups who focus on special legislative concerns. William Penn House was established in 1966 and sometimes hosts a hundred groups a year.

In the beginning Raymond Wilson and his small staff spent much of their time "learning the ropes" in Washington and winning the friendship and confidence of those with whom FCNL wanted to work. This confidence building was very important to the future effectiveness and success of the staff work. FCNL lobbyists have gained a reputation in Washington for being factual and objective with their information, and they have demonstrated "technical competence" when disseminating and using this information to effect legislative change. After fifty years they have now been in Washington long enough to be known and trusted by a wide variety of congressional offices and public interest groups, whether or not they agree with FCNL's point of view.

Finally, it is the objective of FCNL to practice integrity in all its work and dealings, and it tries to place this within a framework of Quaker religious concern. Staff try to act out of moral conviction as they join legislative know-how with the political realities of Washington. FCNL endeavors to reflect William Penn's belief that government is "a part of religion itself, a thing sacred in its institutions and end."

Summary

As we look at the first fifty years of FCNL, we can discern three periods with three different Executive Secretaries. The first was the Raymond Wilson period, 1943 to 1962. The second was that of Ed Snyder, 1962 to 1990. And the third is that of Joe Volk, 1990 to the present. Raymond Wilson recorded FCNL's history (1943-1975) in *Uphill for Peace*, published in 1975. Now in this book, Ed Snyder gives an overview of fifty years of FCNL's work. And Joe Volk, the current Executive Secretary, provides a link with the present, while Stephen Klineberg projects something of the future into which FCNL must live.

William Penn's famous words, often quoted by FCNL, exemplify the vision of all three Executive Secretaries during the Committee's first fifty years: "True godliness does not turn men [and women] out of the world, but enables them to live better in it, and excites their endeavors to mend it." The sails of FCNL are clearly set into the winds of Washington politics determined to help move our world toward the common goal of humankind–peace and justice for all sustained by the spirit of love and good will. FCNL has an important story to tell and this 50th Anniversary volume provides a voice.

Reference Notes

Cooper, Wilmer A. ed. *The FCNL Story*. Washington, DC: Friends Committee on National Legislation, 1958.

Tolles, Frederick B. *Quakerism and Politics*. Ward Lecture. Guilford College, NC, 1956.

Wilson, E. Raymond, *Uphill for Peace: Quaker Impact on Congress*. Richmond, IN, Friends United Press, 1975.

Notes

1. Another important treatment of Quaker influence on politics in England in the seventeenth and eighteenth centuries is Norman Hunt, *Two Early Political Associations: The Quakers and the Dissenting Deputies in the Age of Sir Robert Walpole*. Oxford, England: Oxford University Press, 1961.
2. Tolles, *Quakerism and Politics*, p.4
3. Ibid. pp. 4-5
4. Ibid. p. 6
5. Ibid. p. 7
6. Ibid. p. 10
7. Ibid. p. 11
8. Ibid. p. 12
9. Ibid. p. 15
10. Ibid. p. 17
11. Ibid. p. 18
12. Ibid. p.13, 20-21
14. Ibid. p. 20-22
15. Wilson, *Uphill for Peace*, p. 9
16. Cooper, ed., *The FCNL Story*, p. 5
17. Wilson, op. cit., p. 16
18. Ibid. p. 363
19. Cooper, op. cit., p. 7

FCNL Staff and Legislators

Following Quaker delegation's visit to President John F. Kennedy, May 1, 1962. Left to right: David Hartsough, Dorothy Hutchinson, Henry J. Cadbury, Edward F. Snyder, Samuel R. Levering, and George Willoughby.

FCNL 20th Anniversary Dinner at Earlham College in Richmond, Indiana, in 1963. Left to right: Edward F. Snyder, Executive Secretary; Samuel R. Levering, clerk, FCNL Executive Council; behind the flowers is Senator Ralph Flanders (R-VT); Sumner Mills, chairing the occasion; Miriam Wilson and E. Raymond Wilson, Executive Secretary Emeritus.

The FCNL 20th Anniversary Dinner in 1963. Edward F. Snyder, Executive Secretary, and Senator Ralph Flanders (R-VT).

Senator Hubert H. Humphrey (D-MN) and E. Raymond Wilson, Executive Secretary Emeritus, discuss issues.

1965 White House signing of the Arms Control and Disarmament Agencies (ACDA) Extension Act. Left to right: George Bunn, ACDA council; Victor Reuther, UAW; Edward F. Snyder, FCNL Executive Secretary; Paul Walter, UWF; Senator J. W. Fulbright (D-AR); Vice President Hubert H. Humphrey; Adrian Fisher, Deputy Director, ACDA; William Foster, Director, ACDA; and President Lyndon B. Johnson.

In 1966, Edward F. Snyder, Executive Secretary, and Senator George McGovern (D-SD) share a light moment.

In 1966, three FCNL representatives talk with Senator Paul Douglas (D-IL), a member of 57th Street Meeting in Chicago, about civil rights and military spending. Left to right: E. Raymond Wilson, Executive Secretary Emeritus; Stuart Innerst, FCNL's Friend in Washington 1960-1961; Senator Paul Douglas; and Edward F. Snyder, Executive Secretary.

Senator Mark Hatfield (R-OR) inscribed this picture to Edward F. Snyder: "A co-worker for peace and special neighbor." (photo taken from Senator Hatfield's 1983 office showing the FCNL Building in the background!)

Gerald Clifford, Coordinator of the Black Hills Steering Committee, South Dakota and Cindy Darcy, FCNL Native American Advocate, 1989.

In 1992, Representative Dante B. Fascell (D-FL) receives Nuclear Test Ban Leadership Award from members of the Arms Control Community. Left to right: Joe Volk, FCNL Executive Secretary; Representative Dante B. Fascell; David Barton and Ivo Spalatin, staff members for the House Foreign Affairs Committee.

In 1994, Press Conference on Code of Conduct for Arms Sales.
Left to Right: Senator Mark Hatfield (R-OR); Representative Cynthia McKinney (D-GA); Holly Burkhalter, Director, Human Rights Watch; and Joe Volk, FCNL Executive Secretary.

Ed Snyder and George Bliss. George was FCNL Associate Secretary for Finance and Promotion, 1967-1980.

On the occasion of Jeanette Hadley's retirement from FCNL. Jeanette was Administrative Assistant 1943-1972.

FCNL's First Fifty Years
A Personal Perspective

By Edward F. Snyder

THE CONTEXT

In November 1943, the world was locked in the catastrophe of total war. Civilian, military, and cultural casualties were immense. The Nazis, in control of most of Europe, were countering Soviet offensives in the Ukraine and battling an allied toehold in Southern Italy. The Normandy invasion was still in the early planning stages. Alaska's Aleutian Islands had recently been retaken; and sea, land, and air battles raged in the South Pacific. At the

* * * * * * *

My portion of this 50 year review could not have been completed in the time allotted without the research help of Stephen McNeil, Jean Jones, and Barbara Grant Nnoka, and the invaluable editorial comments and advice of Don Reeves, Robert C. Schultz, Linda Coffin, Richard W. Taylor, Wilmer Cooper, Laura Nell Morris, Stephen Klineberg, William Snyder and Gray Cox, and the advice, forbearance and understanding of Bonnie Snyder during the past eight months. We are all indebted to Barbara Grant Nnoka for her advice, counsel, patience and persistence. Without her this volume would never have seen the light of day. The sins of commission and omission in the text are solely my own.

I regret that space limitations have prevented me from recognizing all the FCNL interns and the many colleagues in other organizations who have been full partners in the enterprises mentioned here. Nor is it possible to pay tribute to all those unsung heroines and heroes—FCNL's support staff and volunteers—who keep the office running, raise the money, keep the records, answer the phones, type, print, and mail.

Nor is there mention in this text, which concentrates on issues, of the many Friends and friends who have given generously and even sacrificially of their resources, time, and expert financial advice to keep this Quaker witness alive on Capitol Hill for 50 years.

end of the month, Roosevelt, Churchill, Stalin, and Chiang Kai-shek met in Teheran.

In that same month, a group of Quakers, marching to a different drummer, concluded an extensive discernment process and opened a Quaker lobbying office in the basement of the Florida Avenue Meeting House in Washington. The next month, at the first meeting of the FCNL Executive Committee on December 14 in Philadelphia, Raymond Wilson, FCNL's Executive Secretary, described action on three legislative issues on which he was working—conscientious objectors, feeding the hungry in Europe, and repeal of the poll tax. The treasurer reported a balance on hand, after all bills were paid, of $89.06.

During the following 50 years FCNL worked in the thick of three unprecedented developments in human history:

1. a cold war which divided the world into two hostile and dangerous armed camps, each seeking allies and opportunities to extend their power and control around the world;

2. the advent of nuclear weapons capable of destroying human civilization; and

3. a dawning recognition that planet earth is indeed "one world", a global village, and that affluent groups and nations have a practical obligation as well as a moral responsibility to find ways to "help others help themselves."

The next eight chapters seek answers to these questions: can a Washington-based, religious, pacifist, lobbying organization be relevant and credible to those making decisions of tremendous consequence for the future of the world?   If so, can it simultaneously bear faithful witness in a spirit of love, nonviolence and justice?

During FCNL's first five years the United States emerged from the second world war as the world's preeminent superpower—militarily, economically, and politically. Washington controlled the United Nations, set Western Europe's agenda, reconstructed Japan in its image, and began a massive nuclear weapons research and production program. Middle and upper class citizens entered a golden age of affluence unlike any the world had ever known.

As FCNL sought to communicate with Washington policy makers in this context, three factors complicated our task: a climate of anti-communism, intimidation, conformity, and chauvinism, especially in the first 20 years; an increasingly secular culture; and the low esteem of pacifism in the postwar world.

Anti-communism: It is hard to reconstruct today the pervasive fear, mistrust, and suspicion that swept the country during FCNL's first 15 years. FCNL's 1949 report to Iowa Yearly Meeting Conservative noted "this period of near hysteria on international relations." In October 1951, Raymond felt it necessary to consult the Executive Committee about the wisdom of accepting an invitation to Miriam and himself to attend a November 7 reception at the Soviet Embassy. One committee member "expressed the hope that [he] would feel free to stay away in good conscience" since AFSC representatives had also been invited.

The escalating cold war, the hot war in Korea and McCarthyism made civil liberties one of FCNL's four priorities in 1950. FCNL's 1953 midyear report noted that "In the area of civil liberties there is a growing fear to exercise our basic freedoms of thought, speech, and assembly." Concern across the Society of Friends culminated in a called meeting of Friends at Scattergood School in Iowa in

> Risk for risk, for myself I had rather take my chance that some traitors will escape detection than spread abroad a spirit of general suspicion and distrust, which accepts rumor and gossip in place of undismayed and unintimidated inquiry. I believe that that community is already in process of dissolution where each man begins to eye his neighbor as a possible enemy, where non-conformity with the accepted creed, political as well as religious, is a mark of disaffection; where denunciation, without specification or backing, takes the place of evidence; where orthodoxy chokes freedom of dissent; where faith in the eventual supremacy of reason has become so timid that we dare not enter our convictions in the open lists to win or lose....
>
> U.S. Court of Appeals Judge Learned Hand, quoted in FCNL Statement of Legislative Policy 1953-54

April 1954. In the same month FCNL's Executive Committee approved a detailed statement on civil liberties, but noted parenthetically: "Two members of the FCNL General Committee have registered dissent on portions of this statement."

FCNL witnesses at congressional hearings testified against wiretapping in 1954, 1955 and 1962, opposed the Mundt-Nixon bill in the House Un-American Activities Committee in 1950, urged protection of the privilege against self incrimination in 1954, and opposed expansion of the federal security program and challenged proposed antisubversion legislation in 1959. Winslow Osbourne told a House Judiciary subcommittee in 1956 of the Post Office practice of impounding literature sent from England to the New England AFSC office for inclusion in their "peace packets." Post Office officials said leaflets entitled *The H-Bomb and You*, *Indochina and World Peace*, *China and the United Nations*, "followed the Communist line and were questionable for mailing."[1]

Friends across the country felt this oppressive atmosphere as they confronted loyalty oaths in schools and other places of employment, travel restrictions, and security checks, as well as controversies within their own Meetings. Kathleen Lonsdale, British Quaker, scientist, and member of the Royal Academy of London, ran afoul of U.S. visa requirements when she tried to visit U.S. Friends.[2] Edward Condon, Director of the U.S. Bureau of Standards and later Director of Research for Corning Glass Works, was hounded out of the first position and unjustly denied a security clearance for the second in a highly political attack.[3] In December 1962, the House Un-American Activities Committee subpoenaed members of Women Strike for Peace on the rationale that "in today's world, intense peace propaganda and agitation in non-Communist nations obviously serves the aggressive plans of world Communism."[4] In 1965, the announcement of a Justice Department investigation into Communist influence in peace demonstrations prompted my critical reaction which the Washington Post printed October 21.

FCNL's Executive Committee spent considerable time in 1958 considering whether, and under what conditions, FCNL should sell its literature to Communist organizations, literature which would be distributed by them. It developed a policy to help staff respond to FBI agents who were making security checks on former FCNL employees applying for government or other positions. FCNL itself was targeted in 1956 when an army private, apparently under the impression that FCNL was a Communist organization, broke into the office one weekend and threw books, papers, correspondence, clippings, and furniture out the second story window.

Congressional hearings were used to badger and intimidate witnesses, leading to proposals for reform. Wilmer Cooper's testimony to a Senate Rules subcommittee on July 6, 1954 in favor of just and uniform Congressional procedures was reported in the *New York Times*. Wilmer noted that "our great nation is in a sorry state of affairs if its chief lawmakers are unable to govern themselves in the process of governing the rest of us."

Secularism: The FCNL is a firmly based religious organization in an increasingly secular culture. Despite the apparent growth of church membership in the immediate postwar years, religion has been consistently marginalized in favor of corporate, scientific, and materialistic values. Many members of Congress, traveling on their own spiritual journeys, were breaking out of the confines of a narrow, sectarian upbringing. While they often received delegations of religious leaders courteously and attended religious services regularly, they tended to discount the claims of faith based groups as not particularly relevant to the "real world" issues with which they were required to deal.

In addition, many fundamentalist church leaders and TV evangelists were being wooed and won by well financed right wing, military oriented groups. The widely publicized pro-military views of these religionists further diminished the claims of faith based groups like FCNL, which claimed loyalty to a power beyond the nation-state.   In drafting testimony and other public presentations, FCNL representatives were constantly evaluating how to present our views in a way that touched an inner chord in listeners, rather than turning them off because of semantics.

One event which ameliorated this image of irrelevancy for FCNL was the award of the 1947 Nobel Peace Prize to the American Friends Service Committee and the Friends Service Council of London.

No matter that the AFSC and the FCNL are entirely different organizations. To the public, Quakers are an undifferentiated—though small—mass. (FCNL representatives are accustomed to being identified as being from "The American Friends Service Committee on National Legislation.") So FCNL reaps the benefits—and sometimes pays the price—for the general reputation of Quakers. Fortunately for FCNL, that reputation is overwhelmingly positive, thanks to the good works and active, constructive citizen action of countless Friends in communities across the country and worldwide.

Pacifism:[*] Applicants for conscientious objector status often confronted prevailing attitudes and misconceptions when Draft Board members challenged them: "But what would you do if somebody broke into your house and started to rape your grandmother?" Members of Congress might, or might not, be more polite. But their message to Quakers was often the same: "This is a dangerous and violent world. War and preparation for war are necessary evils. Our cause is just. We will defend your right to hold your pacifist beliefs. But don't ask us to adopt them as public policy. Even if we agreed, we need to represent the views of the overwhelming number of our constituents (if we expect to be reelected.)"

Henry Cadbury testified against military aid to Greece and Turkey in 1947 as chairman of the AFSC. He had a number of thoughtful exchanges with members of the House Foreign Affairs Committee. But two members demonstrated different approaches to discrediting the pacifist position.

Representative Robert B. Chiperfield, Republican of Illinois, took the soft approach:

> **Mr. Chiperfield:** Does your membership believe in bearing arms in time of war?
>
> **Mr. Cadbury:** Our official position since the origin of the society in 1650, uncontradicted by any official statement since, has been that killing in war is contrary to the principles of the Christian religion.

[*] See discussion on "pacifism" in chapter 3, pp. 70-2

Mr. Chiperfield: I am not at all critical, I simply wanted to know the fact. I know that your organization does wonderful work in other fields, but I just wanted to know whether that was a fact or not.

Mr. Cadbury: That is quite the fact.

Mr. Chiperfield: I have no other questions, thank you.[5]

Representative John Davis Lodge, Republican of Connecticut, took a different tack:

Mr. Lodge: You say we should be patient with the Russians. Whether you feel that we have been or not, I do not know; but let us assume that a bunch of gangsters come into Washington and start looting, raping and pillaging, all over the place, how long should we wait before taking action? How patient should we be about that?

Mr. Cadbury: I think something depends upon the cleanness of our own hands and about the probability of results outside that area.

Mr. Lodge: Do you mean we have to have a utopia here before we can defend ourselves against such evils?

Mr. Cadbury: No; but I would like to think that we could exercise other initiatives besides this action, and may I say that we should have exercised it long ago.

Mr. Lodge: Let us assume you are a mayor of a great city and you are faced with a situation where babies are being dropped out of 10-story windows and young women are being raped in the public parks, and people are getting murdered behind fences.
   How patient would you, as mayor of the city, feel you have to be before you took some effective police action to try to put a stop to that state of affairs?

Mr. Cadbury: If I took effective police action and made so little effort to analyze what the ultimate cause of that behavior was I would feel I was derelict in my duty and no matter how justified I felt in the police action, I would count myself as an accomplice in crime.[6]

The role of a pacifist organization in Washington is not easy. It seeks to "speak truth to power" in a world of nation-states deeply committed to war as legitimate and necessary. Ironically, but perhaps usefully, all three FCNL executive secretaries and an acting executive secretary during the first 50 years were U.S. military veterans—Raymond Wilson in the first World War, Ed Snyder and Chuck Harker in the second, and Joe Volk in the Indochina war.

At the end of FCNL's first 50 years, the U.S. government and public are in a much different place than they were in the mid-1940's. With the end of the Cold War and the demise of the Soviet Union, the U.S. is the sole surviving superpower. But economically it is only one among many contenders. It no longer controls the UN which is much more representative of the world as a whole. Domestically the change has been even more dramatic. The struggle against racism and poverty has become a major part of the national agenda. The public has moved from optimism about the future and unity against a common enemy to disillusionment, cynicism, and division. In pursuit of the mirage of "national security," the nation's best and brightest lied to the public and led the country into the Indochina war, Watergate, and Iran-Contra. They plotted through the CIA to assassinate foreign leaders, and performed extensive radiation experiments on unsuspecting citizens. By the early 90's "government" had become the enemy for many people. Demagogues, and even sitting presidents, ran against "the mess in Washington." Taxes, the price we pay for civilization, had become a dirty word. "No new taxes" was a constant refrain, hamstringing efforts to build a better society for all.

Notes

1. FCNL MEMO No. 37, July 10, 1956.
2. FCNL MEMO No. 9, November 10, 1954.
3. E. Raymond Wilson, (1975) Uphill for Peace, (pp. 121-126), Friends United Press, Richmond, Indiana.
4. FCNL MEMO, No. 114, Dec. 14, 1962.
5. House Foreign Affairs Committee, Hearings, Assistance to Greece and Turkey, April 3, 1947, p. 236.
6. Ibid. pp. 243-2449

1. Is FCNL Naive About the Real Sources of Power on Public Policy Issues?

FCNL has a sound understanding of the legislative process and a defensible view of the underlying political, economic, social, and psychological forces at work. Our faith that there is a spiritual dimension to reality which has power and effect is, admittedly, a minority view. But if this is true, who is naive?

It is clear that FCNL representatives are not naive about the political process in Washington. Staff and key committee members are lawyers, government administrators, state and local elected and appointed officials, business people, farmers, educators, economists, journalists, social workers, scholars and scientists.

FCNL publications about the political process, including the "How-to" series,[1] have been widely used. Operating in the Washington maelstrom for 50 years has been an intense learning experience, and FCNL judgments on strategy and tactics are often appreciated by others.

My own personal perspective on the political process in which FCNL works is this: British historian and philosopher Lord

> **We must come to see that human progress never rolls in on wheels of inevitability. It comes through tireless efforts and persistent work of men willing to be co-workers with God, and without this hard work time itself becomes an ally of the forces of social stagnation.**
>
> Martin Luther King, *Letter from a Birmingham Jail*

Acton was right: "Power tends to corrupt, and absolute power corrupts absolutely." The "Founding Fathers" were Divinely inspired to have drafted a Constitution based on the separation and balance of powers.

Of the three branches of government, Congress is the most accessible to the people, and therefore the most appropriate focus for citizen action. FCNL publishes detailed information about the members of Congress, their voting records, committee assignments, bill sponsorship and statements in committee and on the floor. FCNL *Newsletters*, action mailings and phone calls are filled with bill numbers and legislative timetables. The names of key decision makers to whom letters, phone calls and visits should be directed are identified.

But Congress is not a pioneering institution. It reacts—to the President, to the public, to the media, to big contributors, to relatives of young men coming home in caskets. And in the resulting compromise among contending interests, legislators find a politically viable middle ground. In this traditional and mechanical view, the policy making process can be viewed as a funnel. The more of one's own proposals, positions, letters, and votes one can press into the mix at the large end, the more likely the product emerging at the small end may bear some resemblance to one's original concept. There is validity in this view, but it leaves a small role for tiny organizations like FCNL.

Our experience suggests another valid way to view the process. Much legislation is designed to solve problems, as perceived by the general public. Lasting solutions are more likely to be founded on creativity, ingenuity, and insight than on a majority view, even if tempered by compromise. Time and again, small pioneering groups like FCNL, working with a relatively few courageous and farsighted members of the House and Senate, have provided the vision and leadership to bring about constructive change. I estimate that only about 5% of the public—left, right and center—are actively engaged in the political process in the U.S., so groups like FCNL have a much greater influence than their small numbers suggest. We can help create the seedbed and the political space for new concepts and policies to be tested and refined.

Our experience also clearly demonstrates that "government" and the political process are not monolithic. There are many available points to insert perspectives and proposals into the decision-making process. And there is a community of likeminded citizens—in government and out of government, in churches, corporations, labor, academia and elsewhere—who are working together for common goals. These people, often unknown to each other but motivated by a shared vision, are mutually supportive as they ask questions, refine proposals, discuss them with policy makers and educate other citizens.

The power and reach of the President is tremendous. He proposes budgets and policies to which Congress must respond; he can veto Congressional initiatives. But his very power makes him less accessible to small organizations like FCNL. But the President's appointed officials in the executive branch are approachable and their recommendations often filter up to the Oval Office. Our work to achieve acceptance of the goal of general and complete disarmament (GCD) bore fruit in the late Eisenhower and early Kennedy administrations. Our efforts to establish the Peace Corps and the Arms Control and Disarmament Agency required close cooperation with the Kennedy administration. We worked with Johnson administration officials on civil rights, with the Carter administration on human rights, and with various officials in the Nixon, Ford, Carter, and Reagan administrations on the Law of the Seas.

FCNL's work with the Judiciary has been infrequent, although occasionally we have joined in *amicus curiae* briefs to the Supreme Court. But some of our work in Congress has sought to prevent the Congress from overturning Supreme Court decisions which we believed to be sound policy, for example, the 1959 anti-subversion bills, and bills on school prayer, and abortion.

But beyond these formal structures, there is the question of who really commands the levers of power. Are elected officials merely pawns, and the entire political process basically a charade which masks the real holders of power? Having watched the Washington scene, we would indeed be naive to deny the inordinate power and influence of economic forces: high priced lobbyists for big corporations, for multinationals, for the military-industrial-academic complex, for foreign governments. These people often determine the outcome before most citizens are aware of the issue.

And we would be naive to underestimate the ability of clever people, for their own nefarious purposes, to manipulate nonrational and irrational human emotions and to stimulate fear, racism, sexism, classism, and all sorts of myths and stereotypes.

The Supreme Court in its "one person-one vote" decision[2] opened the way for the United States to become a truly participatory, democratic society if people would take their citizenship responsibilities seriously. But even now, Quakers and many others are still searching for ways to help ourselves and our fellow citizens identify and effectively express our own real interests. When we do that, a good society can begin to be built. But today most citizens are sleepwalking through one of the most exciting and dangerous periods in human history. We are drugged by the mass media, advertisers, the siren call of the shopping mall, and status quo special interests which encourage us, at every turn, to avoid or deny reality.

My experience has been that FCNL supporters are unwilling to grant that these powerful overt and subterranean forces in our society must inevitably control. We basically believe people have the power, and, with the right perspective, can construct a good society. If this be naivete, we should make the most of it. In some ways the very powerlessness of Quakers is an advantage. We may gain a readier reception by not presenting a political or economic threat to decision makers, by not carrying a secret agenda, by not looking for credit or public acclaim.

But FCNL is acutely aware that congressional campaign finance reform is essential if democracy is to work. It is not working today.

Money talks. Congressional decisions are now up for sale to the highest bidder. FCNL has participated in major coalitions led by Common Cause on this issue. We have been less ready than many to compromise on the goal of public financing of campaigns. In 1974 one of FCNL's priorities was campaign finance reform; intern Cliff Mesner of Nebraska devoted months to the effort. Twenty years later we are still working for meaningful reform.

Nonviolence

There is one other area where Friends are often charged with naivete, with being unrealistic "do-gooders," with utopianism. Representative John Davis Lodge challenged Henry Cadbury at the 1947 congressional hearing with it: Friends simply do not understand the power of evil in the world, and the necessity to use violence to resist it.

The first part of the charge—that Friends don't understand the power of evil—sounds strange to a group that labored in a Europe devastated after two world wars, that helped to harbor refugees from Naziism, that spent years making artificial limbs for Vietnamese at Quang Ngai (near which was a village called My Lai,) that sought to conciliate the passions of the Arab-Israeli conflict and the Indo-Pakistan war, and that has worked for centuries in prisons in this country and abroad.

The second part of the charge is true. The Quaker peace testimony as generally interpreted rejects the view that violence is necessary, at times, to resist evil. This is usually the basis for the charge of naivete. In seeking to live in this Spirit, Friends may be charged with being "fools for Christ." Acts of injustice, violence, and hatred arising from past experiences, from our basic human nature, from wherever, are the reality that confront us daily as we pass through this life. But our response need not be of the same kind.

> **In our era, the road to holiness necessarily passes through the world of action.**
> UN Secretary General Dag Hammarskjold, *Markings*

Instead, nonviolence, forbearance, patience, and loving kindness—and in the end, a willingness to sacrifice life itself—are the appropriate answer. We can only hope and pray that we will be given the strength to respond in that way if challenged. George Fox recognized the reality of an ocean of darkness and death. But he also saw an ocean of light and love overflowing it. Followers of Jesus believe that evil is not overcome by evil. Evil is overcome by good.[3]

In the final analysis, FCNL's most important contribution to the national debate on public policy issues may be our implicit, and at times, explicit assumption that there is also a spiritual, religious, and moral power at work in the world. We seek to understand this power and to help channel its energy into the Washington policy making process. If, indeed, we correctly perceive an additional dimension of reality, who then is naive?

This is not an easy teaching. The following statement, revised slightly over the years, has appeared in every FCNL Statement of Legislative Policy since it was first adopted in December 1956:

> We favor, as the Christian course of action, immediate and complete disarmament by the United States together with constructive and far-reaching revision of its foreign policy. We are prepared to accept the risks involved in this course because, in our view, the present policy holds greater risks, disregards the sacredness of human life, and is contrary to God's will. In the absence of such a national policy we believe any substantial first steps toward disarmament by the United States government will help increase international trust and goodwill and thus improve the chances for world disarmament.

The 1963-64 Statement of Legislative Policy in the section on disarmament called for a "Commission to Study Non-Violence":

> A public Commission should be created to study and report on non-violence as a way of achieving freedom, justice and peace. Friends also should continue to study and experiment in this field.

Henry Cadbury was confronted directly by this issue in the midst of a lengthy interrogation by Senator Bourke Hickenlooper of Iowa during FCNL testimony against Senate approval of NATO in 1949:

> **Sen. Hickenlooper:** Do you advocate the United States giving up substantially all of its armaments before any other nation does likewise, as a gesture of good will?
>
> **Dr. Cadbury:** I think we can afford to go ahead of other nations, and I would only recommend the more radical proposal if I thought the United States had the spiritual backing behind it which that would require. I wish it had.[4]

At various times FCNL staff and committees have explored the concept of nonviolent resistance, and the applicability of the work of Gene Sharp, Adam Roberts, Stephen King-Hall and others. An AFSC working party in 1967, published *In Place of War,* an inquiry into the feasibility of nonviolent national defense. A *Washington Post* article by Jonathan Powers, "Nonviolent Resistance—Alternative to the Present Bankrupt Policy" was widely distributed by FCNL. Unfortunately, the response on Capitol Hill to such views was even less receptive than at the Pentagon, where thoughtful policy makers recognized the danger of the nuclear arms race.

Vision

Where there is no vision, the people perish.

Proverbs 11:14

Vision, sometimes denigrated as "utopianism," is another essential ingredient of sound public policy. Vision helps us escape the trap of the sterile status quo. It enables us to conceive a better way and motivates us to act for radical change. Vision and hope have been constant themes throughout FCNL's history. Since 1977, FCNL's policy statements have included four goals—the four "we seeks." They have been used on a widely distributed poster, decals, greeting cards, and on a huge, colorful staff-created banner which graced a number of major Washington demonstrations in the 80's and drew admiring comments. These proclamations continue to express succinctly FCNL's vision for our nation and the world:

- We seek a world free of war and the threat of war.

- We seek a society with equity and justice for all.

- We seek a community where every person's potential may be fulfilled.

- We seek an earth restored....

Judgment and Mystery

Abraham Lincoln, shortly before he was assassinated, spent much of his Second Inaugural Address seeking to discern a Divine purpose for the carnage of the Civil War. He asked whether the institution of slavery had been so offensive in the sight of God that "every drop of blood drawn by the lash shall be paid by another drawn by the sword." Lincoln believed "The Almighty has His own purposes," and "The judgments of the Lord are true and righteous altogether."[5]

If we believe there are moral laws in our universe which we transgress at our peril, we must tremble for our country. Can we walk away, scot-free, from the consequences of our acts of violence in Indochina, in Central America, in the Persian Gulf, in our urban ghettos, in relations with Native Americans? Is our present national travail in some way related to our collective transgressions?

Such thoughts about consequences can only increase humility, lessen self righteousness, and renew determination to proceed with malice toward none and charity for all. Doubts are swallowed up in mystery and wonder at the channels of action which open before us as we seek to follow the leadings of God in our personal lives. Hesitations are swept away by experiences of prescience and synchronicity.

"Above all," asserts the 1988 Statement of Legislative Policy, "we depend on God's guidance to help us chart our way." We rejoice when a sense of clarity, order, and guidance gently invades our staff and committee meetings for worship.

Friends at FCNL annual meetings often pluralize the third verse of "Amazing Grace" and sing with special fervor: "Through many dangers, toils and snares, we have already come: 'Tis grace that's brought us safe thus far, and grace shall lead us home."

> **Close your ears to John Woolman one century and you will get John Brown the next, with Grant to follow.**
>
> English historian George M. Trevelyn

Notes

1. How-to: Write a Letter to the Editor; Work in Politics; Visit a Member of Congress; Write Members of Congress and the President; Work for the Congressional Candidate of Your Choice; Organize an Action Network; Adopt a Member of Congress.

2. *Gray v. Sanders*, 372 U.S. 368 (1963) "The conception of political equality from the Declaration of Independence, to Lincoln's Gettysburg Address, to the Fifteenth, Seventeenth, and Nineteenth Amendments can mean only one thing—one person, one vote." p. 381. See also *Baker v. Carr*, 369 U.S. 186 (1962)

3. See discussion in "Epilogue," pp. 195-206, Robert O. Byrd, *Quaker Ways in Foreign Policy*, University of Toronto Press (1960)

4. Senate Foreign Relations Committee hearings, North Atlantic Treaty, May 11, 1949, p. 768.

5. See my article, "Some Thoughts on Consequences," *Friends Journal*, March 1992, p. 14.

2. Does FCNL Speak for All Friends?

Over the years, FCNL has attempted to make clear it does not speak for all Friends. This is done through disclaimers in testimonies, the *Newsletter* and otherwise. The Policy Committee has developed a process to solicit Friends' views when policy statements are drafted and priorities chosen. Mutual understanding has been increased by staff travel, "area meetings," field secretaries, seminars, and staff interaction with local activists.

> **Mr. Snyder:** We appreciate the opportunity to appear before [the Senate Internal Security Subcommittee] to present testimony on bills relating to the national security....
>
> This committee of the Religious Society of Friends seeks to represent many of the concerns of Friends, but does not claim to speak for the whole society, whose democratic organization does not lend itself to official spokesmen and whose members reserve to themselves their right to speak on issues of importance....
>
> **Senator Keating [N.Y.]:** I commend you for the statement that you don't speak for all the Friends. We so frequently hear people come in and say, "I speak for 10 million people," or "I speak for 100,000 people."
>
> Of course, anyone in a legislative hearing knows it is inaccurate because any organization worth its salt permits democratic procedures and we all know that there is no unanimity amongst all of them.
>
> I wanted to get that into the record because it is so refreshing to hear a statement like that.

> **Senator Dodd [Conn.]:** I think we can add that when there is such unanimity, we are suspicious.
>
> **Mr. Snyder:** I must say that the Friends cherish their right to hold their own opinions and so we very specifically make this statement.
>
> I might point out that our committee is widely representative and there are members appointed from almost all the yearly meetings of the Society of Friends in the United States.... [1]

One of my earliest experiences on Capitol Hill was attending a hearing on bills to liberalize the Refugee Relief Act of 1953. A witness for the national office of the American Legion testified in opposition. He was followed in the witness chair by a representative of another veterans group who took the exact opposite position. The impact of the first testimony was effectively diminished. The point was driven home to me that credibility on the Hill requires organizations to maintain close contacts with the constituency they purport to represent.

Developing FCNL Policy

From its beginning FCNL has recognized the fundamental importance of respecting the wide differences among Friends on public policy issues. The first FCNL "Statement on Policy" was "discussed in detail" at the January 29, 1944 General Committee meeting and approved, after editing, at the March 7, 1944 Executive Committee meeting. It stated "As to Reaching Decisions and Speaking for Others:"

> It is understood that the Committee shall not take action, or issue any statement in the name of any other organized bodies of the Society of Friends, such as Yearly, Quarterly or Monthly Meetings, without the prior approval of such bodies.

> In reaching decisions or assuming positions with reference to legislative issues, the General Committee or the Executive Committee shall consider carefully the state of mind and opinion among Friends supporting the Committee and shall apply to the best of their ability the principle of the sense of the Meeting. This implies a responsibility resting not only on the Committee but on Friends generally to weigh their positions and to test their attitudes not merely by common thinking and conventional standards but by deeper insights and spiritual sensitivity.
>
> With respect to important issues regarding which there is clearly a divided mind among Friends, the Committee shall recognize its responsibility to groups whose attitudes on such questions may differ. There will be times when the Committee may find that it is not justified in taking a position one way or the other. There will be, however, the obligation to report information and to promote an eager search for common unity and common purpose.

After 1944, Statements of Legislative Policy were issued annually from 1947 through 1954 and biennially from 1955 through 1966. Multiyear statements were issued in 1967, 1972, 1977, 1982, 1988, and 1993. Each included a statement to the effect: "This is not an official statement of the Society of Friends."

Statements on specific subjects have also been issued.[2] This provides a way to delve into complex issues in more depth. Often such statements are condensed in subsequent overall Statements of Legislative Policy, but the more detailed policy statements, unless outdated by later statements or events, are available to guide the staff and future Policy Committees as new situations arise.

The Policy Committee

Until 1955 policy decisions were made by the General and Executive Committees. The Reorganization Plan adopted in January 1955 set up a Policy Committee focusing on seven substantive areas. From 1955 to 1967, Samuel Levering chaired this committee as well as the Executive Council, and later the Administrative Committee. These individuals were looked to for leadership in specific areas:

Disarmament and Conscription	Lyle Tatum
United Nations Affairs	Richard Abell
redefined in 1956 as Conscription and Militarism	George Willoughby, later Byron Haworth, then Arlo Tatum, then Chester Graham
Disarmament and UN Affairs	Dorothy Hutchinson, later Elton Atwater
Foreign Economic Affairs	Stacey Widdicombe, later Emile Benoit
Immigration and Refugees	Kathleen Hanstein, later Richard F. Smith, then William Maxfield, then James Read
Civil Liberties	William Rayhill, later Oliver E. Stone, then John Rounds, then Ralph Rudd

Civil Rights/Race Relations   David H. Scull, later
                                   Mary Cushing Niles, then
                                   George Sawyer

Domestic Issues   C. Edward Behre, later
                                   Peter Forsythe

In 1970, the practice of identifying individuals with specific areas was discontinued.

Farsighted clerks have served the Policy Committee over the years. Mary Cushing Niles, who chaired the committee from 1967 to 1974, gave dynamic leadership during an era when it was breaking new ground on economic and social issues. Lilian Watford, co-chair in 1977, knew FCNL intimately as clerk of the Executive Committee, field secretary with her husband Clyde, and early lobbying colleague of Raymond Wilson when she represented the Northern Baptist Convention. Miriam Levering, co-chaired first with Lilian Watford and then with Bill Fuson from 1978 to 1980. Miriam gave gentle, probing, sensitive leadership; she also served on the staff as Friend in Washington with Sam on the Law of the Seas issue. Bill Fuson's merciless way with superfluous verbiage gave clarity and coherence to FCNL's major policy revision of 1981. Dorothy Mason of North Carolina in 1981 and 1982 helped Friends to be more sensitive to conservative viewpoints during the 1981 policy revision process. Barry Hollister, 1983 to 1985, brought his years of Friends' experience at the UN, with AFSC, FGC and many other Quaker and non-Quaker organizations. From 1986 through 1989 Steve Klineberg's unassuming expertise and listening skills led FCNL through the 1987 Policy Statement revision. Since then Stephen McNeil has chaired the committee steadily and sensitively as it worked with the staff on the end of the cold war and the advent of a new administration in Washington.

Policy Committee membership is one of FCNL's most interesting assignments. It provides an opportunity to work with Friends of different political, economic and theological persuasions; and to share with staff the challenging task of applying general principles to hard legislative realities.

In addition to drafting periodic revisions of the Statement of Legislative Policy, the Policy Committee in each election year proposes for General Committee consideration FCNL's *legislative priorities* for the next two year session of Congress. Over the years the process of determining FCNL policy and selecting FCNL priorities has been refined to include more and more Friends at the local level. Typically, the Policy Committee circulates to all General Committee members and FCNL local "meeting contacts" an open-ended questionnaire. Recipients are urged to discuss the questions with their local meeting in formal and informal sessions. Based on responses the Policy Committee develops a first draft which is then recirculated. Those responses are considered, and another draft, or even two, may be circulated prior to the annual meeting. Final action is taken in plenary sessions, often interspersed with small group discussions and late night meetings of the Policy Committee. Computers and copy machines make it possible to produce extensive revisions overnight, ready for further action the next day.

By the time this process reaches fruition, much listening, learning and sensitizing has taken place. Staff members find these sessions especially valuable in interpreting the nuances and hesitations behind the bare words of the statement. Often the final sessions concentrate on one or two issues on which Friends have deep differences. FCNL clerks of these sessions have often shown great skill and sensitivity in reaching a decision. At times no resolution is possible. Then, the committee clerk may explicitly note the failure to reach consensus. Or the issue may be referred back to the Policy Committee for further work, or put on the list of unresolved "Challenges to the Society of Friends."

The Search for Unity

In examining those issues on which agreement has been difficult to reach, I find three categories:

One, issues where Friends' clear testimonies collide with community standards of the time. Usually the strength of the testimonies enables FCNL to adopt policies which are perceived as quite radical by the general public, for example, anti-militarism and unilateral disarmament. But the dissents noted in FCNL statements on Civil Liberties and on recognition of the People's Republic of China indicate there are issues on which some sensitive Friends found it difficult to depart from the world's ways.

Two, issues about which Friends' testimonies are unclear, absent, or in the process of further development, and on which Friends have deep and strongly held personal views. I include abortion, sexual orientation, substance abuse, and pornography among these. The first two of these have occasioned the most controversy at FCNL annual meetings in the past two decades.

Three, economic issues on which Friends have no clarity and on which existing testimonies on peace, justice or simplicity provide insufficient guidance. Friends differ widely in this area. And these are the issues which have aroused the most opposition to FCNL over the years. This debate spilled out into wider Quaker circles in the late 1950's. The Policy Statements adopted in 1953 and 1955 began, tentatively, to move into national domestic economic issues which were beyond the traditional concerns of civil rights and liberties, American Indian, and immigration. This new venture was complicated considerably because of the "Condensed Statement of Policy" issued for the 1955-1956 and 1957-1958 Statements. These were widely distributed, "popular," simplified, two page summaries developed to give inquirers a quick overview of FCNL concerns. But their bold assertions of policy conclusions without the tentative qualifiers, cautions or differentiations made in the original statements raised the eyebrows of many Friends. And the presentation gave no indication of actual FCNL legislative priorities. FCNL did *no* significant legislative work at all on the 13 issues identified in the "Economic Life" and "Health, Education and Welfare" sections which occupied nearly 20% of the 1955-1956 text!

During the late 1950s, extensive correspondence and meetings took place in an effort to listen to and to deal with some of the criticisms.[3] No further "Condensed Statements of Policy" ever appeared. And the staff and committee were sensitized to the strong feelings held by many Friends about government "interference" in economic affairs. FCNL's careful statements in the early 1970's on taxation, jobs and assured income, welfare, farm labor, and health did not arouse similar opposition, primarily because of the wide consultative process which had been adopted. Recent policy language on "Economic Life" is carefully crafted to deal with the differing political views of Quakers–which include Republicans, Democrats, Socialists, and Independents.

There is also the question of the level of agreement needed before a policy statement may be attributed to the General Committee. The issue arose at the 1957 annual meeting when a Friend asked for clarification. He felt that a position on which there was general agreement, but not unanimity, had been left out of the Policy Statement. The next Executive Council meeting at Haddonfield, N.J. in March minuted: "The Council recommends to the next Annual Meeting that FCNL operate on the basis of *substantial agreement.* There was a general feeling, however, that the staff should circulate in advance as many as possible of the proposals that are to be considered by the Committee, to give absentees a chance to participate in the decisions."

Spreading the FCNL Word

The FCNL probably would never have reached its 10th birthday without Raymond Wilson. Raymond, by temperament and training, was more of an educator than a lobbyist, and this served FCNL well in its formative years. He knew how to go directly

---

Notice on box of Raymond Wilson's
historical material at FCNL:
"Do not destroy. ERW"
Graffiti added by unknown author:
"ERW is indestructible."

to critics, to listen nondefensively, to search for areas of agreement, and to summarize fairly an opposing view before stating his own. He had a keen mind and prodigious memory. The sheer volume of facts which he could cite invariably impressed and often overwhelmed listeners. He was in his element organizing FCNL agricultural seminars and disarmament and civil liberties conferences.

Raymond was probably the most widely traveled Friend in his generation. He insisted that other FCNL staff also spend many weeks each year outside Washington, attending yearly meetings, quarterly meetings, monthly meetings, conferences, institutes, weekend retreats–wherever Friends would have us. And we were advised to stay during the whole session–not just in for the report and leave. That way we could visit with Friends in cafeteria lines, at meals, in the dorms, and after sessions, listening and sharing. This continuing FCNL presence over the years accounts for much of FCNL's acceptance today. Friends may not always agree with all FCNL policies, but they are convinced that FCNL representatives have a deep religious motivation, a willingness to listen, and the ability to present FCNL positions fairly and competently to policy makers.

Supporting and advising Raymond was Jeanette Hadley, who had been with FCNL from its first day in Washington. Jeanette was also integrally involved in Five Years Meeting, later Friends United Meeting, and was my irreplaceable colleague and tutor, along with Wilmer Cooper, on Quaker esoterica when I came to FCNL in 1955.

Raymond also supported legislative action at the state level. And he found a number of Friends taking the initiative there, especially in California where legislative committees were formed in both the northern and southern parts of the state. The California FCL launched in 1952 is still very much alive, with an active lobbying program at Sacramento. Some local Friends legislative groups work only on state issues; others have worked on both state and national issues. When they worked on both, as in California and Illinois-Wisconsin under the leadership of George Watson, George McCoy, Chester Graham and others, they were and are important action arms for FCNL. Ultimately, the burden of Washington oversight of state-level personnel, finances, administration, and relations with local Friends became too much for the Washington office to manage. A 1964 FCNL decision made the state committees autonomous, but assured a continued close working relationship with FCNL.

An ambitious FCNL Reorganization Plan adopted at the January 1955 annual meeting was a significant effort to broaden FCNL participation beyond the Philadelphia-Washington axis which had dominated the early years. Twenty two "areas" across the country containing significant numbers of Friends were identified. Each monthly meeting would, hopefully, appoint an "FCNL Liaison Worker." These liaison workers plus General Committee members in that area would form a committee headed by an area vice chairman, able to devote at least two weeks a year to FCNL, with expenses paid. While this ambitious plan never got off the ground, it provided the seedbed for two later FCNL programs–meeting contacts and field secretaries.

The plan also contemplated moving FCNL business and policy sessions around the country. This innovation continued from 1955 through 1961. It was a major tool in raising awareness of FCNL among Friends, but it failed to provide continuity in the conduct of FCNL business and was ended in 1962. During this period, "area meetings" involving staff and committee were held in Richmond IN, Philadelphia PA, Hartford CT, Moorestown NJ, Barnesville OH, Guilford College NC, Germantown PA, Chicago IL, New York NY, Haddonfield NJ, Indianapolis IN, Cambridge MA, Muncie IN, Ridgewood NJ, Wilmington DE and OH, Virginia Beach VA, and Yellow Springs OH. Other FCNL business meetings have been held outside Washington in Wichita KS, Atlanta GA, and Cape Cod MA.

When George Bliss retired in 1980 as FCNL's widely traveled Finance and Development person and field secretary, he proposed dividing the country into four regions to be served by experienced, usually retired Friends willing to work for FCNL on a part time, low budget basis for up to two years. He proposed financing the project by dividing his salary in quarters. Over the years since then, "field secretaries" have contributed immensely to the growing awareness of FCNL in the Society of Friends. The quality of the persons who took on this labor of love was a major factor in its success, with people like Ted Neff, Clyde and Lilian Watford, Marguerite and Richard Tirk, Paul Goulding, Alison Oldham, Franklin and Mary Clark, Catherine and Robert Wahrmund, Della Walker, Stephen Angell, Jr., Herbert Foster, William and Helen Fuson, Lowell and Lena Mills, Ralph Blankfield, Sandra Gey, Jim Johnson, Martin Cobin, Cameron Satterthwaite, Robert Hinshaw, Ardith Tjossem, Nancy Nye, Harry Tischbein, and Marge Schlitt.

The job description for "field secretaries" was continually under discussion among staff and committees. Was their chief priority fund raising, or education about FCNL, or stimulating grass roots action? They were expected to do it all, and their priority often depended on their own interest and experience. Some found themselves in a pastoral role when they visited isolated Friends in small meetings and listened to personal, meeting, or community concerns.

"That Yellow Sheet"

FCNL Washington Newsletter number 571 was published December 1993 at the end of FCNL's 50th Anniversary year–an average of more than 11 per year since the first issue November 9, 1943. The *Newsletter* has been the major vehicle of communication with Friends, other supporters and members of congress and their staffs. Its familiar yellow, now off-white, color has distinguished it from the piles of white paper on the desks of many busy people. Its mass of statistics, bill numbers, lists of sponsors, committee assignments and voting records has been a bane to some readers, a delight to others. Staff and committee members are continually suggesting ways to make it more readable. Lobbyists are continually asking for more space to give more facts, to explain the complexities of a legislative situation. Raymond Wilson's call for an 8 or 16 page *Newsletter* was never heeded. My suggestion to Friends who complained the *Newsletter* was too technical was to imagine they were looking over the shoulder of FCNL staff members who were writing to persuade key people on Capitol Hill, where it was widely read.

A smiling Congressman stopped me in the Capitol one day to say he had just received a $10 contribution from an FCNL supporter. He didn't know the person, who was not a constituent of his. The donor had explained that she was sending a contribution to every member whose votes agreed perfectly with FCNL's position in its voting record. I don't believe she went bankrupt on one of the most effective FCNL support efforts I ever heard about. In 1969, FCNL urged supporters to send contributions to the UN Development Program via their Representatives as a way of expressing concern for congressional cuts in funding. The August FCNL *Memo,* reported that $686.19 had been received by the UN.

Voting records can easily be manipulated to give false impressions. In the early years FCNL joined with other religious groups in publishing a voting record, but decided that the issues selected did not adequately serve FCNL readers. FCNL voting records have sought to give a fair presentation of views and to avoid a simple "right-wrong" or percentage score. In the early days our presentations were so low key and factual that readers were confused about the meaning of "a vote to table an amendment to the amendment" and other such complicated legislative maneuvers. Consequently we adopted the current practice of putting the symbol for the vote in bold type if it agrees with FCNL's position. This makes it much easier to understand a member's general political orientation as well as his or her vote on a particular issue. We were gratified when the House Republican Research Committee in analyzing interest group voting records in 1980 stated:

> In [FCNL's] style of presentation, there are no misleading, or misdirecting figures or rubrics. Only objective information is included with which readers can easily see where a Member's position varied or coincided with the FCNL's position. The Research Committee commends the FCNL on such reasonable methods of representation.

Since 1960 FCNL *Newsletters* have compared presidential candidates. They have generally received high marks for their accuracy and fairness. Data gathering is much easier if the candidate has served in Congress, as most have. Votes on tough issues are often more informative than policy pronouncements. But the task is still daunting, given the partisan emotions which often run high. We were pleased in 1976, when President Ford's campaign manager commented on our comparison of Ford and Carter: "Your *Newsletter* is both fair and informative and provides a commendable service to your members."

The process may also disclose previously unknown information. Our 1964 comparison of Johnson and Goldwater on repeal of the self-judging amendment to U.S. adherence to the World Court treaty turned up the fact that Johnson refused to support its repeal, though the 1960 Democratic platform did. The 1972 August/September *FCNL Newsletter* comparing McGovern and Nixon had the largest circulation of any in our history—some 100,000. The *Newsletter* was a dispassionate comparison, but in the latter days of the campaign, people across the country realized it cut through the campaign rhetoric and supplied solid factual information.

Seminars

Public education is the foundation on which any effective legislative program is built. Coming to FCNL from AFSC's Peace Education program, Raymond Wilson found a new arena for his educational skills. In the 1950's the AFSC maintained a staffed seminar program operating out of FCNL's office which used FCNL resources. Raymond, the frustrated Iowa farmer, also organized two Agricultural Seminars, recruiting from among the hundreds of Quaker farmers he had come to know over the years. The seminars dealt with the morality of U.S. surpluses in a hungry world as well as the technicalities of price supports and commodity agreements.

FCNL also conducted joint seminars for many years with the Five Years Meeting of Friends, later Friends United Meeting. The

Quaker Leadership Seminars, promoted especially by Herbert Huffman, acquainted many Friends pastors with the complexities of applying morality to Washington politics. Seminar participants listened to and questioned experts, and then talked with their own Senators and Representatives. Youth Seminars brought together young people from across the country and gave them never-to-be-forgotten first impressions of their government in action.

In the early 1960's FCNL's legislative pace increased geometrically, and the task of organizing seminars, finding speakers, and arranging appointments, housing, meals, and literature became increasingly burdensome. I returned from serving on the Quaker Team at the UN in 1964 convinced that Quakers should have a house on Capitol Hill similar to Quaker House in New York, close by the United Nations. Over the next two years through the leadership of Raymond Wilson, Ed Behre and others that dream became a reality. The availability of Bob and Sally Cory to direct the William Penn House project made it possible. FCNL's relationship with William Penn House became nearly organic, since it immediately took up the educational role FCNL had been performing. FCNL's lobbying role could expand, but the essential educational work continued, with FCNL in an advisory and resource role. Over the years William Penn House has made a major contribution to the Quaker presence in the nation's capital.

Interns and Coordination

Two additional programs play a major role in communicating with Friends, thus helping assure that FCNL represents Friends fairly, even though it does not purport to speak for all Friends.

The FCNL intern program began in the turmoil of the Vietnam war. Many young Friends were disillusioned and frustrated with the options for relevant action. They asked FCNL to set up a program through which they could focus on Congress as a relevant way to end the war. Ever since, young people, often just out of college or graduate school, work for 11 months as legislative and research assistants to one of FCNL's lobbyists. They rejuvenate

FCNL staff annually; they effectively augment FCNL's work on the Hill. And they have gone on to use their experience in a variety of national, international and local work. Often these are young Friends who return to their own meetings or join other Friends meetings, bringing with them intimate knowledge of FCNL and the legislative process.

By 1984, FCNL had a strong legislative program in Washington with experienced lobbyists, able interns and strong financial backing. But the approach to Friends and others around the country was uncoordinated. A lobbyist working on his or her issue might call a Friend in a key district to ask for action only to find that another FCNL lobbyist had just called requesting action on another issue. Fortunately, the right person and sufficient funds arrived simultaneously to resolve the problem. Alison Oldham, who had just completed three years as FCNL's East Coast Field Secretary, became FCNL's Legislative Action Coordinator. She knew how Friends at the local level regarded FCNL and the Congress. And she knew which tools to provide them for their effective action, while also helping FCNL's lobbyists coordinate their work more effectively. Her editorial skills soon made her indispensable in the production of the FCNL *Newsletter* and other publications, including *Visions of a Warless World*.[4]

FCNL and Electoral Politics

From the outset FCNL viewed its work as legislative, not politically partisan. *Newsletters* identified members by name and state, but left out party affiliations whenever possible. Friendly contacts were sought and maintained with both Republicans and Democrats. Testimony was presented to the platform committees of both parties at conventions to select presidential candidates. Raymond Wilson helped organize and participate in religious delegations to meet with candidates Eisenhower, Stevenson, Kennedy, Nixon, and Humphrey on policy issues.

But unlike FCNL, most of the people we deal with on Capitol Hill have one–or both–eyes on their constituents and the next election, rather than fundamental principles and values. Our efforts to focus attention on substantive issues through circulating "Questionnaires for Candidates," sending issues papers to candidates and similar devices have been frustrating. Regrettably, the political process is increasingly dominated by personalities, partisanship, big campaign contributors, ad hominem arguments, negative campaigning, single issue groups, sound bites, spin doctors, and a manipulated and manipulating mass media. Nevertheless, the outcome of particular elections can determine whether FCNL's policies and priorities will be favorably received. Thus, FCNL's "How to Work in Politics" makes the strong case for active participation in the political party of one's choice. And FCNL's voting records help readers determine which candidates to support.

The advent of "peace candidates," beginning in the late 1950s, blurred even further the line between legislative and electoral action. Such candidates were Democrats, Republicans and Independents, running in primary and general elections. A number were Quakers, conscientious objectors, or colleagues in related organizations. In 1958, Quaker Bill Meyer of Vermont and Fellowship of Reconciliation member Byron Johnson of Colorado were elected to the House. In their two years in Congress, they won the respect of fellow members and helped to publicize FCNL and other peace concerns. In 1962, FCNL cooperated with other organizations to identify "peace candidates." That year, peace oriented Senator Joseph Clark was being challenged for his Senate seat from Pennsylvania by Representative James VanZandt, a former Veterans of Foreign Wars commander. In cooperation with Turn Toward Peace, a coalition in which FCNL actively participated, FCNL circulated to *Newsletter* readers in Pennsylvania the Senatorial candidates' responses to a questionnaire on war and peace issues.

FCNL electoral activity escalated in 1966, under the impact of the Vietnam war. In June, some 400 Friends were asked to circulate a questionnaire to local candidates. In October, an Action Bulletin called upon approximately 3,500 recipients to become involved in the election process. It suggested discussing issues with friends, neighbors and the press; setting up meetings for the candidates and encouraging other church and community groups to do the same; and helping candidates with fund raising and literature distribution. FCNL mailed background material on the Vietnam war to approximately 1100 candidates and circulated extra copies of the

October Voting Record *Newsletter.* David Hartsough visited Friends and others in Delaware, Pennsylvania, Ohio, New York, Connecticut and New Jersey identifying candidates who stressed a peaceful settlement in Vietnam. The FCNL *Memo* of October 14 reported, however, that David Hartsough and Charles Harker "found that Friends and others are hesitant to become involved in local election campaigns, even where there are candidates reflecting Friends' views"

In 1970, with the war spreading throughout Indochina, public concern was intense. FCNL organized an "elections desk," assigned one intern full time to it, circulated questionnaires to candidates and received 150 responses, prepared and sold 61 copies of a 140 page *1970 Electioneering Handbook* containing FCNL analyses of issues, voting records, and campaign materials. The 1970 FCNL Legislative Summary reported: "Of the 136 "New Priorities" candidates identified by FCNL for the U.S. House and Senate, 49 incumbents and 13 new candidates were elected; 4 incumbents and 70 new candidates were defeated leaving a net gain for FCNL views of 9 seats in the House and no change in the Senate."

In December 1970, FCNL conducted a survey of the electoral activity and policy views of FCNL supporters and readers. The results were reported in the May, June, and July 1971 *FCNL Washington Newsletters.* Not surprisingly, responses indicated a strong anti-war, anti-draft position, with considerable division about economic and personal issues. More than two-thirds had voted and contributed to candidates. More than 80% had written at least one of their Senators or Representative; one-third had written a letter to the editor about a particular issue in the past year.

Lobbyists and FCNL Supporters—A Team Effort

I once heard hawkish political scientist, Herman Kahn, author of *On Thermonuclear War*, make the unforgettable remark: "Pacifists are like manure. They shouldn't be piled in one place. They should be spread around." He was warning against an inordinate peace sentiment in Washington if it was not widely supported around the country. One can agree with his point without accepting his simile.

No lobbying effort can be successful without significant Washington grass-roots cooperation. FCNL's history is replete with stories of constituents paving the way for FCNL lobbyists to make constructive contacts with members of Congress and their staffs– and vice versa. Constituent letters and telegrams in response to *Newsletter* items, Action Bulletins, and phone calls from Washington have required Senators and Representatives to learn more about an issue and on numerous occasions, formed or changed their vote. Ever since FCNL began, Friends have come to Washington in delegations, caravans, car pools, and buses to oppose universal military training, the Vietnam war, Central American involvement, and to support world order and many other FCNL priorities. Today Friends are advised to talk to their Senators and Representative when they are at home; it is a more effective and economical way to reach them personally.

> **I see by the morning papers that the Gun Owners of America have subjected you to the scurrilous charge of being a 'do-gooder.' Take heart. If the choice is between 'doing good,' 'doing bad' or 'doing nothing,' it's clear which side we should be on.**
>
> June 1, 1983 letter from Ed Snyder to Senator Ted Kennedy.

Time is often crucial. In the early days, the *Newsletter* was sent by second class mail to save money. This led to great staff frustration because of the length of time between writing an action message and having it received by *Newsletter* readers. Many ways have been developed to reduce the "turn-around" time. FCNL supporters have identified their specific interests and received first class mailings or phone calls on those issues. The telephone has been used more. A weekly telephone tape message is updated each Friday afternoon, giving information and action recommendations on issues in Congress the following week. Now, FCNL updates, analyses and background papers are available to all with access to a computer network. Capitol Hill is increasingly flooded with FAXes and other mass produced communications. But despite all the recent technological innovations, the advice from those who know Capitol Hill is the same as that found in FCNL "How-To's" on Writing or on Visiting your Representative and Senator: a personal visit or letter is still the best and most effective action. FCNL's forte continues to be in the quality of the communications, rather than the quantity.

Some examples:
- Late one Friday afternoon in 1955, General Lewis B. Hershey proposed extensive and adverse changes in the C.O. provision of the draft law. Before the Senate Armed Services Committee consideration of the bill Monday afternoon, FCNL staff, working with other interested organizations, contacted John Oliver in Missouri and Byron Haworth in North Carolina. Their phone calls to Washington paved the way for personal conferences with Senators Stuart Symington and Sam Ervin before the mark up session. The Committee turned down the Hershey amendment.[5]

- An FCNL committee member notified Ruth Flower in 1982 that New York State was referring welfare applicants to military recruiters for possible "job placement." Ruth documented the practice in a letter to the New York congressional delegation. Rep. Joe Addabbo was chairing a Defense Appropriations Subcommittee hearing the day after receiving her letter. During the hearing,

Addabbo secured a commitment from Pentagon officials that they would not cooperate in such a practice. New York abandoned the policy.[6]

• In 1980, Steve Linsheid, joint FCNL-Mennonite Central Committee Indian advocate, sought to oppose the proposed Orme Dam in Arizona which would flood the Ft. McDowell Yavapai Indian reservation. Dan Shaffer, FCNL Executive Committee member and economic planner for the Ft. McDowell tribe provided invaluable support, drafted testimony, visited members of Congress, and prepared a summary of economic alternatives to the dam. Although the Senate had authorized preconstruction funds, the Orme Dam was never built.[7]

• FCNL took the lead in drafting an omnibus U.S.-Soviet "Exchange for Peace Resolution" in 1985 but needed a major Congressional sponsor. Representative Lee Hamilton was identified and Alison Oldham, Legislative Action Coordinator, called Bill Dietz, FCNL committee member and Hamilton constituent. His letter plus staff visits committed Hamilton to champion the measure.

FCNL in the Quaker Rainbow

FCNL provides a channel through which Quaker insights, concerns, and convictions arising among individual Friends, Monthly, Quarterly and Yearly Meetings and other Friends organizations can flow to members of Congress and other policy makers in Washington. If the springs dry up, FCNL will cease to have a creative role. If Friends predominately have feet of clay, so will FCNL. While FCNL may be able to provide early warning of dangerous trends, or identify emerging challenges, or provide a forum for Friends to share their concerns, in the final analysis FCNL cannot move far beyond the common denominator of Friends' concerns. This fact grows out of FCNL's decision making process, based on an effort to reach unity. Thus the ground breaking educational work on emerging issues in the Society of Friends must be undertaken by sensitive Friends and groups with special concerns such as A Quaker

Action Group (on nonviolent direct action,) Peace Brigades International, Friends Committee on Unity with Nature, Friends Committee on Gay and Lesbian Concerns, and the Sanctuary movement of the 1980s. At times the AFSC has undertaken this role. To the extent that these groups educate and sensitize Friends to their concerns at the local level, FCNL is able to act forcefully at the national level.

An FCNL annual meeting provides a significant cross-section of modern Quakerism in the United States, although, regrettably, it is by no means inclusive of the entire spectrum of Friends. Appointees come from 26 Yearly Meetings and Conferences and, currently, seven other Friends organizations.[8] In addition, no more than half the number of yearly meeting and other Friends agency appointees can be appointed at-large. A conscious effort is made to assure that some of these at-large appointees come from Yearly Meetings which do not send representatives. Attenders at FCNL annual meetings come from varied backgrounds—theologically, politically, economically and socially. Worship sharing, small group and plenary sessions are often a mind-opening experience for those present. But all are united in the conviction that Friends' religious faith, however expressed, is deeply relevant to public policy issues in our nation's capital.

The American Friends Service Committee provides a deep reservoir of experience and expertise on which FCNL draws in its work on Capitol Hill. AFSC programs are grounded in relief, education and service work in trouble spots around the world and in urban ghettos, rural slums and Indian reservations at home. AFSC staff and committee members have provided expert testimony for FCNL before congressional committees, shared their experiences in interviews with members of Congress and participated in FCNL committee work. FCNL staff members have worked for the AFSC, been members of AFSC delegations to other countries, and worked closely with the Quaker Team at the UN. FCNL minutes are replete with reports of staff and committee meetings where information is exchanged, plans and priorities reported and decisions made in order to avoid duplication and achieve beneficial coordination where desirable.

Washington has seen hundreds of demonstrations during

FCNL's 50 years. FCNL staff and committee members have marched in some and been speakers and resource persons in others. But FCNL policy has been to co-sponsor and fully participate only in public witnesses sponsored by other Quaker groups. These have included the 1962 Friends Witness for World Order[9] and the 1960 Friends Peace Witness which encircled the Pentagon.[10]

Public witness and civil disobedience can be supportive of sound legislative action, in my experience. The best radical witness can sensitize members of Congress and make them more open to new ideas and creative legislation. I remember a Representative proudly showing me an autographed picture of the crew of the "Golden Rule" among the bank of pictures on his office wall. In May 1958, when word was received of the forced interruption of the voyage of the "Golden Rule" to the Pacific nuclear test area, the FCNL Executive Committee sent this message: "You are very much in our prayers. We send you our love and support you in your deep concern that ending nuclear weapons tests is the first step toward disarmament."

Staff members have felt free to follow their consciences. In 1969 George Bliss and David Hartsough were among those arrested on the Capitol steps while reading the names of men killed in Vietnam. The charges were dismissed and the Capitol steps became an accepted arena for public expression. A year earlier David had been arrested along with 34 other Friends as part of a demonstration and Meeting for Worship organized by Friends General Conference on the Capitol grounds to support the Poor Peoples Campaign.[11] Staff members have also engaged in war tax resistance.

Although FCNL confines its program to U.S. public policy issues, these affect Friends in other countries. FCNL attempts to be sensitive to the situation confronting Friends abroad, including the Middle East, South Africa, Kenya, Japan and Central America. In 1962, at the invitation of the Friends World Committee for Consultation, Raymond Wilson stopped in Kenya on his return from the World Council of Churches meeting in India to share his thoughts on the opportunities and responsibilities for Kenyan Friends in relation to their new government.[12] Thirty years later a personal message was delivered to FCNL from Quakers in Kenya.

In their struggle for democracy, they pleaded for "Quaker influence" in U.S. policies toward their country and others in Africa.[13]

Harold Wilkinson of Australia, who had just completed a period of service with the Friends Service Council in London, visited FCNL in late 1977 and early 1978. He wrote a report exploring the feasibility of creating a similar Friends body in Britain.

In 1985, Jo Vallentine, Australian Quaker and young mother was elected to the Australian Senate as a member of the Nuclear Disarmament Party. Just before a key House vote in Washington, she sent a letter via FCNL to all members of the U.S. House of Representatives opposing the M-X missile project: "Whether we [Australians] like it or not, the people of the entire world are your constituents: Your decision on the M-X missile system affects us all."[14] She visited Washington in 1988 after the UN Special Session on Disarmament, had lunch with several Senators' wives concerned for peace, and was introduced to several Senators. Her youth, her red hair, and her official position in the Australian Senate made quite an impression in the Senate Dining Room and gave increased relevance to her peace message.

Notes

1. Hearings on "Proposed Antisubversion Legislation," Internal Security Subcommittee of the Senate Judiciary Committee, Part 1, pp. 428-429, May 1, 1959.

2. These special policy statements have been issued by the General Committee, the Policy Committee, or the Executive Committee: Dunbarton Oaks proposals, 1/45; Civil Liberties, 4/54; Immigration and Citizenship, 12/55; Civil Defence, 3/57 and 1/62; UN Police Organization, 5/57; Farm labor, 1/62 1/63 and 1/69; Prayer and Bible Reading in the Public Schools, 9/64; Vietnam 9/66; Goals for a Just Society — Jobs and Assured Income, 1/69; Encouraging International Development, 1/70; Population and Family Planning, 1/71; Amnesty, 1/72; Principles of Health Care, 1/74; Taxation and the Distribution of Wealth and Income in the U.S., 1/74; Presidential Impeachment, 1/74 and 8/74; Supreme Court decision on Abortion, 1/75; UN Membership and U.S. Participation, 7/75; Energy and Nuclear Policy, 1/76; Panama Canal Treaties, 9/77.

3. See Raymond Wilson's Chapter 18, "The FCNL and Its Critics" in

Uphill for Peace.
   4. *Visions of a Warless World* was the first major publication of the FCNL Education Fund. This 130-page booklet by Walden Bello and an FCNL advisory committee, published in 1986, discusses how many different traditions and disciplines view "peace". It is a very useful resource for schools, colleges, and study groups.
   5. FCNL *Memo* No. 21, June 14, 1955.
   6. 1982 FCNL Annual Report, p. 16.
   7. 1980 FCNL Annual Report, p. 16; 1981 FCNL Annual Report, p. 20.
   8. Yearly Meetings: Baltimore, Illinois, Indiana, Intermountain, Iowa (Cons.), Iowa (FUM), Lake Erie, Mid-America, Nebraska, New England, New York, North Carolina (Cons.), North Carolina (FUM), North Pacific, Northern, Ohio, Ohio Valley, Pacific, Philadelphia, South Central, Southeastern, Southern Appalachian, Western, Wilmington. Central Alaska Friends Conference, Missouri Valley Conference. Friends Organizations: AFSC, Friends General Conference, Friends United Meeting, California Friends Committee on Legislation, Indiana Friends Committee on Legislation, United Society of Friends Women, Young Friends of North America.
   9. See FCNL *Memo* No. 107, May 16, 1962.
   10. See FCNL *Memo* No. 89, Nov. 15, 1960.
   11. See FCNL *Memo* No. 180, Aug. 16, 1968.
   12. See FCNL *Memo* No. 103, Jan. 17, 1962.
   13. 1992 FCNL Annual Report p. 22.
   14. 1985 FCNL Bound Volume, FCNL Doc. L-501, letter of March 25, 1985.

3. Can a Pacifist Organization Be Relevant on National Security Issues?

Yes. A significant number of people in the United States share FCNL's approach to national security issues, including some members of Congress. This view deserves to be considered in the arenas where national security decisions are being made. An organization committed to this view can help define, refine, and present recommendations to policy makers. An organization with clarity of purpose and longevity can also help provide leadership in forming coalitions of likeminded organizations and individuals.

The past half century has been dominated by ghosts of Munich and Pearl Harbor and their supposed lessons: war came because the U.S. was not sufficiently prepared militarily; peace is maintained by being prepared for war. "Peace is our Profession" was the motto of the Strategic Air Command. President Kennedy's image of the U.S. eagle with talons and an olive branch expressed the sentiments of most. Ronald Reagan's "Peacekeeper" was the incredibly lethal M-X missile.

There are many definitions of "pacifism" and "pacifists," not all complimentary. The Random House Unabridged Dictionary definition is "opposition to war or violence of any kind; the principle or policy of establishing and maintaining universal peace or such relations among all nations that all differences may be adjusted without recourse to war." Those of us who grew to maturity during and after World War II have seen the word used to belittle or dismiss persons, groups, and proposals. FCNL, always concerned to enhance communication and minimize impediments to new ideas, has historically avoided use of the term. The conscientious objector provision in the Selective Service law requires "opposition to war in any form." For many, pacifism does not rule out–and indeed may embrace–nonviolent resistance as a feasible national security policy. Furthermore, the nuclear age created "nuclear pacifists" who vigorously opposed any use of nuclear weapons–as well as most conventional wars which could escalate to nuclear war. And peace oriented "just war" supporters questioned whether any nuclear war could be just and were appalled at U.S. military intervention in small countries.

Faced with the egregious militarism of the last half of the 20th Century, these distinctions blurred and faded as people of good will united to oppose the nuclear arms race, massive military spending, and military intervention. Two social scientists have estimated that some 10 million citizen activists in the mid-1980s attempted to turn U.S. national security policy in a more peaceful direction.[1]

In this fluid situation, FCNL's clarity on policy issues resonated positively with many troubled citizens. FCNL has a broad based approach to peace and "national security" in which the level of arms is only one aspect. We firmly resist those who attempt to pigeonhole us into one-dimensional irrelevancy. I identify five propositions which define FCNL's approach to national security issues:

1. Arms and military establishments must be reduced drastically. The goal is general and complete disarmament. (GCD) Military intervention in the affairs of other countries must cease.

2. International institutions of law and order must be developed to resolve conflicts peacefully and protect the legitimate interests of the parties so they will not feel it necessary to maintain military establishments or resort to war.

3. Peace cannot be assured so long as a huge and growing economic gap exists between the haves and have-nots within and among nations.

4. Peace begins in the minds of people. Reconciliation and forgiveness mark the shortest route. Exchanges of people are a major way to break down barriers and stereotypes.

5. The U.S. cannot become a genuine leader of peace in the world so long as economic, social and racial justice is denied to so many in our own country. One of our best contributions to world peace would be to build a good society here at home.

The problem–or perhaps the saving grace–of this complex and interrelated approach is that it is difficult to popularize or encapsulate in slogans like "ban the bomb," "end nuclear tests," or "freeze." FCNL's broad approach may appear to diffuse our efforts, but plain speech requires recognition of the complexities of the politics of peace. This approach may also enable others to expand their own perspectives when we cooperate on narrow focus campaigns.

Establishing the Goal—GCD

On Monday, March 13, 1961, Raymond Wilson, Elmore Jackson of the Quaker UN Program, and I were ushered into the office of John J. McCloy. President John Kennedy had been in office less than two months but he had already tapped McCloy, a Wall Street lawyer from the heart of the "Establishment," as his "Special Adviser to the President on Disarmament" to sort through the issues of nuclear testing and disarmament. Sixteen years before, Raymond had visited McCloy, then Assistant Secretary of War, in his paneled Pentagon office. At that time, Raymond had been successful in securing War Department opposition to the Starnes Rider, which was aimed at punishing conscientious objectors. [2] Now, we urged a four-fold U.S. declaration: 1) that the goal of the United States is general and complete disarmament, 2) that a realistic timetable for disarmament be formulated, 3) that the UN should be strengthened and progress be made toward world law and an

> **The United States has today tabled at Geneva an outline of every basic provision of a treaty on general and complete disarmament in a peaceful world....This outline of a treaty represents the most comprehensive and specific series of proposals the United States or any other country has ever made on disarmament."**
> President John F. Kennedy, Press Conference,
> April 18, 1962

international police force, and 4) that studies be initiated on the economics of disarmament.

Little did we realize then that in just six months McCloy would play the principal role in furthering one of FCNL's lifelong goals. On September 20, 1961, the United Nations unanimously endorsed a U.S.-Soviet, "Joint Statement of Agreed Principles for Disarmament Negotiation" thereafter known as the McCloy-Zorin Agreement.

The goal was to achieve agrements which ensure:

- that disarmament is general and complete and war is no longer an instrument for settling international problems;
- is accompanied by the establishment of reliable procedures for the peaceful settlement of disputes;
- is implemented from beginning to end under such strict and effective international control as would provide firm assurance that all parties are honoring their obligations....

Raymond Wilson wrote the book on general and complete disarmament, literally. His chapter "Dare the World Disarm?" in *Uphill for Peace* modestly hints at his role in this cause which consumed so much of his creative energy. He was the key person in organizing seven national conferences on disarmament between 1953 and 1961. He was the leader in the Disarmament Information Service, a clearinghouse which held 28 meetings between 1957 and 1963, bringing together leaders in the disarmament field and representatives of national organizations. He took the lead in drafting the 1959 joint appeal to Eisenhower, Macmillan, and Khrushchev and in organizing the 1960 Campaign for Disarmament.

Raymond worked effectively with colleagues who shared the same goal, people like Homer Jack and Sandy Gottleib of SANE, Betty Goetz Lall, Senator Humphrey's key aide on the Senate Subcommittee on Disarmament, Annalee Stewart, Washington lobbyist for the Women's International League for Peace and Freedom, Quaker Charles Price, once head of the Federation of American Scientists, and Sandy Persons of the United World Federalists.

His solid reputation brought him into contact with government officials working on this issue in the White House, the State and Defense Departments, and the Arms Control and Disarmament Agency, including Harold Stassen, Edmund Gullion, James Wadsworth, William Foster, Adrian Fisher, and Arthur Barber. Thus it was no fluke that we were able spend an hour with John McCloy as he began his duties for President Kennedy.

Raymond was well respected by Senators Ralph Flanders of Vermont and John Sparkman of Alabama whom he encouraged to take the lead in sponsoring the 1953 Senate Resolution on enforceable, universal disarmament. He worked closely with George McGovern on disarmament, in addition to food for peace issues.

Raymond was a personal friend and counselor of Senator Hubert Humphrey, the leading Senate champion of disarmament during the Eisenhower and Kennedy administrations. Raymond told me that after Humphrey became Vice President and an apologist for the war in Vietnam, Raymond met him in a receiving line. Humphrey's famous smile froze; his stricken look seemed to acknowledge he had fallen short of the high expectations of a respected friend.

My sense is that in the long light of history, FCNL's work to establish the goal of general and complete disarmament may be its most important accomplishment. This can be said in spite of the fact that almost from the beginning, that goal has been ignored, rejected, or denigrated by those committed to the status quo and the nation-state system. But references to the goal of general and complete disarmament are found in the major arms control treaties of the past 30 years: 1963 limited test ban, 1968 nonproliferation, 1972 anti-ballistic missiles, 1979 SALT II offensive arms.[3]

FCNL has spent considerable effort since 1961 defending the concept of disarmament. Even selection of the name of the Arms Control and Disarmament Agency in 1961 was controversial. The

House wanted to call it the "Arms Control Agency" Fortunately the Senate insisted the word "Disarmament" be included. In the 1960's we opposed bills to abolish the Agency. We urged that it have permanent status and that it be adequately funded. And, in 1981 when the House of Representatives voted to delete the word "Disarmament" from the name of the U.S. Arms Control and Disarmament Agency, we led a successful effort in the Senate to retain the title.

This has not meant we were uncritical champions of the ACDA. Far from it. In its first year, the agency made a serious effort to develop an actual treaty moving toward the goal of GCD in appropriate stages.[4] For its pains it came under serious attack from the right wing. This experience inhibited ACDA officials, and, soon after, we found some officials in the Department of Defense more ready to lead on disarmament issues than officials in the ACDA. In 1993, FCNL again went to bat for the ACDA; along with colleague organizations, FCNL successfully opposed the new Clinton administration's effort to fold ACDA into the overall State Department.[5]

FCNL's disillusionment with government sponsored peace agencies which could be used to rationalize military initiatives made us slow to endorse early proposals for a Peace Agency. We felt the Departments of State and Defense should be peace agencies. Thus, even when Kenneth and Elise Boulding strongly supported creation of a Peace Academy, we hesitated until we were reasonably sure measures had been built into the proposal to insulate the agency from political pressures to the maximum extent possible.[6]

Congress created the U.S. Institute of Peace in 1984. Despite some misgivings about the legislation, FCNL worked for passage of the bill. Thereafter, FCNL sought to keep the Institute alive and growing.

Long Term vs. Short Term

Among the dilemmas FCNL faces constantly is how much

effort to put on establishing goals and how much on next steps. At the September 1957 Area-Executive Council meeting at the 15th Street Meetinghouse in New York City, the issue was the relationship of disarmament to the burgeoning public clamor against nuclear weapons tests. Raymond Wilson made the point: "The FCNL should work on the total questions of disarmament and political settlements, and to take nothing less than that as a major goal. It is easy to rally public sentiment *against* something (as we did with UMT.) But this may be at the price of building positive things that need to be built." Raymond tells how Senator Flanders called him in for a dressing down for failing to give adequate support to Flanders' proposal to end the war in Korea. Raymond was in the final stages of the successful battle against UMT, but he "acknowledged that the criticism was well deserved."[7]

The conflicting priority claims between disarmament and nuclear weapons testing continued until the 1963 limited test ban treaty was signed. Other conflicts which have created tensions have been: conventional arms control and arms sales vs. nuclear arms control; ending the Vietnam war vs. changing national priorities; arms control vs. human rights. The problem of competing priorities will never end, given limited staff, numerous issues, and the breadth of Friends concerns. FCNL's priority setting process is the most valuable way to sort through these questions.

Unilateral Initiatives

General and complete disarmament requires all nations to agree before it can come to pass. Unilateral disarmament calls for one nation to make major reductions in its military establishment with the hope others will respond. Both are FCNL policy; neither is politically likely in the near future. The concept of unilateral initiatives bridges the gap. These are conciliatory steps taken by one nation with the hope, but not the certainty, that they will be reciprocated. One noted proponent of this process, Charles Osgood, dubbed it GRIT, for Graduated Reciprocated International

Tension-reduction measures. Every FCNL Statement of Legislative Policy since 1956 has carried a list of proposed first steps toward world disarmament.

Much FCNL staff effort has been expended to gain acceptance of the concept of unilateral initiatives. Among the initiatives advocated at one time or another have been:

- stop testing nuclear bombs;
- stop producing fissionable material for nuclear weapons;
- stop testing intermediate and intercontinental ballistic missiles;
- end transfer of U.S. nuclear weapons information or materials to other countries;
- reduce military spending 10%;
- end the draft;
- destroy all chemical and biological weapons;
- renounce first use of weapons of mass destruction;
- withdraw U.S. troops from foreign bases; and
- phase out U.S. participation in military alliances and overseas bases, cease supplying military training and weapons to others, and encourage all other supplying countries to do the same.

Clearly, much on this list remains to be done. Regrettably, the progress which has been made has not come about through the magnanimity or vision of U.S. policy makers. Sometimes it has come through popular pressure, as with the end of conscription and production of chemical and biological weapons. Moratoria on nuclear weapons testing, usually initiated by the Soviet Union, helped bring about the limited test ban and may yet produce a comprehensive test ban treaty. Some troops are being brought home and some foreign bases are being closed, often due to local pressures on the host government.

The success of the process of unilateral initiatives was

finally proven, not by the United States but by the Soviet Union. President Mikhail Gorbachev recognized the danger and futility of the nuclear arms race and the need to concentrate on domestic priorities because of its deteriorating economy. He moved so decisively in a series of steps in Eastern Europe, suspension of nuclear weapons tests, and in intermediate nuclear arms negotiations that even the hawkish Reagan administration could do nothing but agree. The end of the cold war came so fast, as the process unfolded, that experts were stunned. The lesson should not be lost for future policy makers.

The Nuclear Factor

> **The advent of the atomic bomb has changed everything—save our modes of thinking—and thus we drift toward unparalleled catastrophe.**
>
> Albert Einstein

It was Monday, October 22, and David Hartsough and I were driving back to Washington from a week full of FCNL meetings in North Carolina. Walls of yellow, orange and red mountains, highlighted by the warm October sun, greeted us as we negotiated the sharp turns on the Blue Ridge Parkway. The rest of the week also had near perfect fall weather. It was not a time to contemplate the end of civilization as we knew it.

The radio on Dave's ancient VW bug carried increasingly ominous reports of an impending presidential speech about the Soviet presence in Cuba. We knew something about that. FCNL's October *Newsletter,* which we had just distributed at our North Carolina meetings, carried a long story about congressional pressures on the president to blockade or invade Cuba. Congress had passed a resolution to that effect. We stopped to telephone Frances Neely at the office about the content of telegrams to the President and senators. We were still on the road when the President spoke. I was stunned by his rock hard ultimatum to the only other superpower in the nuclear age. Gandhi had taught that one always left an opponent an honorable way out of a serious confrontation. But the Soviet Union had no alternative; it must turn its ships carrying nuclear missiles around and retreat.

Many books have been written about that week. All agree that one misstep could have carried the world over the brink into nuclear catastrophe. Some people were hardly aware of the danger. But most in Washington were. I knew because several years earlier I had been on a Washington radio talk show describing what would happen if a megaton bomb went off over the White House. In midweek I attended an emergency meeting of parents and school officials at the College Park Elementary School. The mood was one of near panic as parents saw the dark, underground room in which children would be herded if the sirens blew. We had sent a note the previous year opposing our children's participation in the school's civil defense drills and we had authorized our daughter and son to leave school and walk home if such a warning came. Saturday, a knowledgeable friend who worked for a senator on the Foreign Relations Committee drove circuitously to New Jersey with his family on back roads hoping to minimize the danger.

What does a small pacifist group do when the dinosaurs trample the earth? We sent telegrams to President Kennedy and Senators Fulbright, Humphrey and Mansfield urging negotiation and opposing unilateral action. We called Friends and concerned organizational representatives around the country. We sent an Action Bulletin to 1446 individuals across the country. We consulted extensively with Quaker UN representatives. We talked with contacts in various embassies including the Soviet Union. I talked with Congressional staff and with Senators Frank Church and Hubert Humphrey urging restraint and negotiation. A deeply troubled Humphrey said, enigmatically, "A lot of people are doing a lot of thinking right now." We worked with the Methodist Board of Peace and World Order to call a meeting of church leaders from across the country on Sunday afternoon at the Wesley Theological Seminary. We worked with the UN Association to set up a Monday meeting. Wednesday evening I appeared on a previously scheduled panel on pacifism with Methodists at the University of Maryland. It was a challenging occasion! But most evenings time was set aside to be home, to share memories, to be with four children, to listen to Beethoven symphonies after they had gone to bed, and to sit quietly, to cherish moments of love, and to pray after thinking about how best our basement might provide shelter.

Sunday morning our family returned home from a deeply moving meeting for worship at Adelphi Meeting to learn that the Soviet Union had indeed turned its ships around and retreated. The following week I had a luncheon date with the Soviet diplomat I'd known for several years and with whom I had talked the previous week. It was another beautiful fall day as I met him on the FCNL steps. Perhaps misunderstanding my theological beliefs, he said with a great smile of relief, "Aren't you glad to be walking around down here rather than with the angels up above?" Several years later in Moscow I asked a Soviet official if Khrushchev's fall from power was related to his decision to retreat, a move that would have been greeted with shouts of treason if done by a U.S. President. "Not at all," he said, "it was his agricultural policy."

"Unmitigated Condemnation"

Within two weeks of the dropping of the atomic bomb in 1945, Rufus Jones, Clarence Pickett, and Raymond Wilson joined 31 other religious and educational leaders in communicating to President Truman their "unmitigated condemnation" of the bombing of Hiroshima. They appealed to him "to take immediate steps to discontinue its production and to press for commitments by all nations outlawing the atomic bomb and also war, which has developed the technology of mass destruction."[8]

From that time forward, FCNL was involved in every major effort to slow, reverse, and end the accelerating nuclear arms race.

Testing: In the mid-1950's California Friends brought to FCNL annual meetings their concern for the end of nuclear weapons tests. From then until the present, FCNL has given priority to ending nuclear weapons tests. We played a significant role in legislative efforts leading up to Senate approval of the Limited Test Ban Treaty on September 24, 1963.[9] We questioned the advisability of the Threshold and Peaceful Nuclear Explosions Treaties which would authorize continued testing.[10] In 1994 FCNL continues to work to make a comprehensive test ban treaty a reality.

In 1957 Trevor Thomas, then head of the Northern California office of the Friends Committee on Legislation, took leave to became the first director of the newly formed SANE, the National Committee for a Sane Nuclear Policy. This began a long and close relationship with SANE leaders like Homer Jack and with Sandy Gottleib, who for many years was an FCNL tenant at 245 2nd St. N.E.. Another long time FCNL tenant, Jeremy Stone, directed the highly effective work of the Federation of American Scientists.

Civil Defense: Opposition to the wasteful, futile, and provocative civil defense programs and the so-called "shelter" programs was an FCNL priority in 1957 and again from 1961 to 1964 when the Kennedy administration pushed for a vast expansion of shelters. [11] In 1960, in a consciousness raising effort, I arranged for a showing of the new film, *On the Beach* in the Senate Office Building. FCNL also opposed "clean" bombs and "limited" nuclear war.

Nonproliferation: FCNL's priority on nonproliferation began in 1958 when Representative Chet Holifield CA of the Joint Committee on Atomic Energy appealed to Raymond Wilson to organize public opposition to President Eisenhower's proposal to transfer nuclear weapons information and material to other nations.[12] Clarence Pickett gave eloquent testimony against the proposal in 1959 before a subcommittee of the Joint Committee on Atomic Energy. Our intensive efforts were only moderately successful, but the issue was joined. In 1964, the Johnson administration sought to create a multilateral nuclear force (MLF) in Europe which would give other nations greater access to U.S. nuclear weapons. We believed it would also poison then current disarmament negotiations which aimed to produce a nonproliferation

81

treaty.[13] During the autumn of 1964 I commuted to New York as a member of the Quaker Team at the UN and concentrated on the nonproliferation issue. Conferences with UN, State Department, and ACDA officials and key Senate aides emboldened me to write Vice President Humphrey. I urged that President Johnson speak at the UN calling for an international treaty, and I enclosed some draft treaty language.

On August 17, 1965 the United States submitted a draft treaty. Ironically, over the next several years while the war in Vietnam raged, negotiators from the United States, the Soviet Union and other nations reached agreement. The Non-Proliferation Treaty was signed July 1, 1968 and approved by the Senate March 13, 1969.

As FCNL's first half century ended, nonproliferation was still a live issue. Joe Volk and staff attempted in 1992 to restrict U.S. export of nuclear related materials and technology to countries with unsafeguarded nuclear facilities. In 1993 FCNL endorsed comprehensive legislation to promote a nuclear nonproliferation policy.

Delivery Systems: Nuclear bombs must be delivered to their targets, so FCNL has opposed all proposals to expand the number of bombers, submarines, and missiles carrying nuclear warheads, and to increase missile accuracy, and to reduce the response time. This has meant opposition to the M-X and Midgetman missiles, B-1 and B-2 bombers, the Star Wars Strategic Defense Initiative, Trident subs and Trident II D5 missiles. In 1982 and 1983 we urged House and Senate approval of a "nuclear freeze" resolution; but ultimately it was nibbled to death legislatively.

Treaties: FCNL questioned the adequacy of the Strategic Arms Limitation Treaties, SALT, but endorsed both the SALT I and SALT II Treaties as minimal steps along the way. The July 1979 *FCNL Washington Newsletter*, "SALT II and the Runaway Arms Race" is perhaps FCNL's most comprehensive single statement on the nuclear arms race. It highlights the excruciating dilemma posed for FCNL by the minimalist SALT process, which sought to cap the nuclear arms race *after* further increases in weaponry.

It is difficult today, after the sword of Damocles appears to have been taken away, to recall the desperate perspective of the years from 1948 to 1988.

In 1959 Representative Chet Holifield chaired landmark hearings on "The Biological and Environmental Effects of Nuclear War." The week-long hearings created headlines across the country, awakening many for the first time to the dangers. I thought I was well versed in the facts, but I was overwhelmed by the mind numbing statistics which translated into unimaginable human suffering. The day the hearings concluded, I flew to Boston to represent FCNL at New England Yearly Meeting. Looking out the plane window, I tried to imagine the effects of bombs landing on Baltimore, Philadelphia, New York, Providence, and Boston. During my presentation to the Yearly Meeting, I sought to communicate the horror and terror of nuclear war I had heard at the congressional hearing. At the conclusion there was a period of deep worship. Out of the silence Henry Cadbury rose and spoke briefly. His words (from *II Timothy 1:7*) have sustained me, and I have shared them often since:

"For God has not given us a spirit of fear; but of power, and love, and of a sound mind."

Projecting Power Abroad

FCNL has opposed extension of U.S. military power abroad at military bases, and through military alliances, military intervention, and military aid, training, and sales throughout its 50 years. There have been few victories.

In the early years, as the allied wartime alliance fell apart and the cold war began, FCNL testified and lobbied against military aid to Greece and Turkey in 1947 and the creation of NATO, the North Atlantic Treaty Organization, in 1949.[14]

FCNL has opposed U.S. military intervention in Latin America, Africa, Korea, and the Middle East. Richard Post, as Friend in

Washington, made a special effort to change U.S-Cuba policy in 1973. But no priority consumed us more than the war in Vietnam, and later all of Indochina, during the ten year period between 1965 and 1975. For those who want the FCNL story from 1954 to 1973, I recommend the two chapters on this subject, nearly 50 pages, in Raymond Wilson's *Uphill for Peace.*

I will add only a few personal thoughts. The assassination of John F. Kennedy left me with a deep sense of foreboding, which was only temporarily allayed by the passage of far-reaching civil rights legislation in 1964 and the Johnson-Humphrey electoral victory later that year. During the first year after Johnson bombed North Vietnam and began escalating the war, FCNL worked feverishly to oppose the policy, to galvanize public opinion, to urge U.S. bombing pauses, and to call for U.S. acceptance of UN and other third party negotiating initiatives. In 1965, I helped organize or participate in delegations to talk with three of the key people who met regularly with President Johnson to plan strategy–Vice President Humphrey, Secretary of Defense Robert McNamara, and Secretary of State Dean Rusk.

By mid 1966 it seemed clear to us that the Johnson

> In fact, the *ideals* of the U.S. and the U.S.S.R. are quite similar, if one examines basic documents such as the constitutions of the U.S. and the U.S.S.R. in terms of peace, justice, and human rights. And if one examines the *actions* of each side, one discovers certain similarities in policy in the arms race, in geographical areas like Southeast Asia, in relations with developing countries. Nations, like individuals, like to judge themselves by their ideals rather than by their actions.
>
> Problems arise, however, when nations and individuals judge themselves by their ideals and others by their actions. That is the situation today."
>
> FCNL Washington Newsletter July 1979, p. 5.

administration was committed to some sort of military victory in Vietnam, and was not ready to negotiate in good faith. By the end of the year it seemed apparent that the only relevant way to end the war was for Congress to cut off the funds.[15] That analysis was sound, but we had no idea it would take seven more years of increasing Congressional opposition before a majority was achieved in both houses of Congress to cut off funds–then, the issue was the bombing of Cambodia.

Late in 1966 I had come to the conclusion that the Johnson administration could not be moved and Congress was unwilling to take leadership. Nothing was likely to change for the next several years, so I should take advantage of an AFSC offer to spend two years in Singapore organizing conferences and seminars for diplomats and young leaders. I would also travel in Southeast Asia as a "Quaker International Affairs Representative." Thus for two years, from mid-1967 to mid-1969, our family lived in Singapore and I traveled extensively in the region including South Vietnam, Cambodia, and Laos, and with my colleague Brewster Grace conducted five international conferences–a tremendous learning experience for me!

As for my prediction about nothing changing in the United States, it was the most colossal misjudgment of my career. During that two years, Johnson was basically driven from office, Martin Luther King and Robert F. Kennedy were assassinated, the cities burned, the campuses erupted, the Democratic convention was a nightmare, and Nixon beat Humphrey in the presidential election.

We returned to find the peace symbol was a fashion item, not evidence of treason. Clark Clifford, recently Secretary of Defense, and I shared the platform on Moratorium Day, October 15, 1969, at Sandy Spring Friends School. And the Mobilization brought more than a quarter of a million people to Washington a month later.

The first day I returned to the office, I put on the shelf above my desk a picture that I had taken in Vietnam. It shows three young boys, two on crutches, one in a wheelchair, lounging outside the AFSC Quang Ngai center which made artificial limbs. There are only two whole legs among the three boys. That picture represented to me the cost of our blind obsession with firepower and hegemony that was causing so much suffering for the people of Indochina–and for U.S. service men and women. It was my daily goad to action for the following five years.

FCNL emerged from the Indochina war period with greatly increased credibility on Capitol Hill. One reason was that we had brought a steady stream of people just back from the region into congressional offices. They recounted their personal experiences, how life appeared to the average Vietnamese, the failure of U.S. policy to "win hearts and minds." In the early days, members would challenge our perspectives. "I've just been down to the White House (or State Department or Pentagon) and the President (or Secretary) tells me that just isn't so." But often, in the following weeks, events developed as we had predicted, not as the officials promised. There was no light at the end of the tunnel.

In September 1979, I returned to Cambodia/Kampuchea as part of an AFSC delegation, the first private U.S. relief agency to do so, after Vietnamese military forces had driven the Khmer Rouge from Phnom Penh. We witnessed the havoc wrought by the Khmer Rouge during its four year reign of terror. I hope our testimony before the Senate Judiciary Committee and in various press conferences and articles helped to bring about a more realistic public assessment of what had happened there.[16] Regrettably, the anti-Vietnamese mood in Washington lingered on and caused the U.S. government to support the Khmer Rouge claimants as the official representatives of Cambodia for years.

War Powers: In 1973, reacting to the Indochina War, Congress enacted the War Powers Resolution over President Nixon's veto. It supposedly required Congressional participation in presidential decisions to commit troops abroad. The process has been marginally effective. In 1986 we opposed efforts to weaken or repeal it in order to deal with "terrorism." We urged it be strengthened to require *prior* consultation with Congress.[17]

Central America: The U.S. peace movement was galvanized into action in the early 1980s by the murders of thousands of people in El Salvador by right wing death squads. Many religious leaders were victims, including Archbishop Romero while at mass. Visiting U.S. religious workers and thousands of Salvadoran citizens who were suspected of opposing the repressive military government were also killed. The new Reagan administration saw the struggle in terms of Communist infiltration in the region. It supported the military coup leaders against the growing insurgency. The possibility of direct U.S. military intervention in 1981 was very real and, I believe, was prevented only by the outcry of concerned citizens across the country. But huge amounts of U.S. military aid to El Salvador, as well as to Guatemala and Honduras, continued throughout the decade, despite demonstrated massive human rights violations.

The Reagan administration viewed the Sandinista government in Nicaragua, backed by Cuba, as the major threat–a channel for military aid to the insurgents in El Salvador. It undertook a concerted effort to overthrow the Nicaraguan government. "Contras" were armed and trained, harbors mined, and embargoes put in place.

Throughout the 1980s FCNL opposed U.S. military aid to all parties in the region. It supported the Contadora peace process, an initiative of the presidents of the five Central American nations, which began in 1984. In 1987 Costa Rican President Oscar Arias undertook a major new initiative which FCNL strongly endorsed. The long association of Quakers with Costa Rica through the Monteverde community made FCNL especially supportive of the Arias initiative, which resulted in the 1987 Nobel Peace Prize for the Costa Rican president.

On Capitol Hill, a major coalition of religious, human rights and civic organizations took shape. Alison Oldham and FCNL interns were key players in the Central America Working Group associated with the Coalition for a New Foreign and Military Policy. Strategy sessions were often attended by representatives of Congressional leaders. Religious organizations were especially involved because their colleagues, often Catholics, were being killed in Central America.

By early 1988, while the fragile Arias peace plan was taking shape, the Reagan administration was still working through the Nicaraguan contras to overthrow the Sandinista government; and a majority in Congress was reluctant to challenge this policy. Legislative strategists in Congress were searching for the best way to proceed. They had enough House votes to cut off military aid, but not enough to cut off economic aid to the contras. They looked to the religious community for counsel. We were divided.

In order to win a February 3, 1988 vote against both military and economic aid to the contras, the House leadership had promised an early vote on a Democratic alternative containing only non-military aid to the contras. The question for the religious groups, which were all strongly opposed to any aid to the contras, was whether they would support some economic aid or oppose all. The debate was as intense as any in my experience. FCNL took the position that defeat of the Democratic leadership alternative would very likely be followed by another vote which would authorize military aid, as had happened in a similar situation several years before; this could be a death blow to the Arias plan. Others took the principled position against any aid to the contras—a position strongly supported by religious people around the country who were not acquainted with the arcane legislative situation then unfolding. FCNL's *1988 Annual Report* set forth the lineup:

- **supporting** the Democratic leadership package of "humanitarian" aid to contras and to Nicaraguan civilians: FCNL, Presbyterian Church (USA), Episcopal Church, Lutheran Church, Jesuit Social Ministries, NETWORK, U.S. Catholic Conference;
- **opposing:** American Baptist Churches, Church of the Brethren, Unitarian Universalist Association, United Methodist Church–Office of Church and Society, Witness for Peace;
- **taking no stand:** United Church of Christ, AFSC.

The result amazed everyone. The Democratic package was approved March 3, 215-210. But with the switch of a few votes, the House then rejected it on final passage, 208-216. Moderates were convinced that the Democratic leadership had made a good faith effort to meet their demands. They criticized the Reagan administration for not supporting the bill on final passage–so they did not press a vote on military aid. In the end, *no* aid was approved for the Nicaraguan contras, paving the way for the Arias plan to go forward. All the religious groups felt somewhat justified. Was it serendipity or "Getting to Yes" via a Divine plan?

"Pay Any Price"

John F. Kennedy's eloquent Inaugural Address, credited in considerable measure to presidential assistant and former conscientious objector Ted Sorenson, set forth the standard for judging the appropriate level of military spending during the cold war:

> Let every nation know, whether it wish us well or ill, that we shall pay any price, bear any burden, meet any hardship, support any friend or oppose any foe in order to assure the survival and success of liberty.

Over the years FCNL spent a major portion of time, some might say an inordinate amount, challenging the level of military, not "defense" [18] spending. We did so in testimonies, budget analyses, *Newsletter* articles, and in organizing and sustaining coalitions and rallying grass roots activists. It is not a subject on which the national security establishment gives much credence to Quaker organizations. But we felt we could do no other. And the level of military spending which was proposed annually has been so gross that FCNL has never been forced to confront directly the relevant question: "Well, what level of spending do you believe is necessary?"

Frances Neely, in an attempt to sharpen analysis and clarify issues, raised this question on a number of occasions in coalition

> I would be remiss if I did not remind my colleagues that some of what we buy in the name of defense does not in any way provide for the defense of the country. It may help the economy in a certain area of the country. It may help a certain company, it may help a certain group of employees, but it does not add to our military strength.
>
> Rep. Joseph Addabbo, Chm. Hse Appropriations Subcommittee on Defense, Sept. 15, 1980 House floor.
> (Quoted in FCNL Washington Newsletter Feb. 1981.)

meetings. She was never able to obtain a coherent answer, which may have been inevitable since the coalitions represented both pacifist and non-pacifist organizations. Representative Thomas L. "Lud" Ashley of Ohio pushed me on this question in a 1977 budget hearing:

> It does seem to me that you have raised a number of very relevant questions in particularized areas that I think will be useful to those of us on this committee in the weeks and immediate months ahead.
>
> It is hard to quantify, though, isn't it, Mr. Snyder? You end up urging the committee to make recommendations to the full House for a level of defense expenditure less than that of fiscal 1976. That is somewhat precise, but it is not all that precise. It is hard to quantify, isn't it? At least it is hard for me to get at those levels which demonstrably are justifiable on the basis that they support a level of national security that is imperative in the world in which we find ourselves.
>
> Do you find yourself bothered sometimes by the difficulty in quantifying the precise levels of defense expenditures which you feel are justifiable?[19]

Representative Ashley asked a relevant question, but I would have entered into a thicket of controversy, caught between military experts and Quaker pacifists, if I had named a particular figure. In response, I referred to my testimony which had stressed cuts in nuclear weapons production, in delivery systems, and in the huge costs of maintaining nearly 300,000 U.S. troops in Europe. In my view, FCNL's job is to raise the issues few others do and to challenge policy makers to a broader view of national security, leaving the precise level to the various congressional committees. Throughout this entire period, we felt that we could say in good conscience when we saw their figures: "It's still too much by any reasonable non-pacifist standard."

Over the years our rationale for cutting military spending has varied depending on current events, the most recent studies, administration requests, or congressional priorities. Here are some overall themes–

Survival: The immense power of nuclear weapons and the constant race to increase accuracy and shorten response time demonstrate the need to end the arms race, This is especially true because the Department of Defense admits it cannot defend the country and is forced to rely on deterrence to prevent an attack from taking place. Survival of the country and even civilization are the highest priority; spending on dangerous and provocative weapons should be cut.

But opponents countered by arguing that *more* spending was needed to deter an attack. Eventually, I concluded that this was indeed the real reason for the immensely overblown military budget. There was no rational reason for it; it was just a very expensive way to *communicate resolve* to the Soviet Union that the U.S. was ready to launch nuclear war if necessary. The debate was often simplistically phrased, "I'd rather be dead than red." A widely reprinted Herblock cartoon challenged this false dichotomy. Beneath contending, vociferous demonstrators, one carrying a placard "I'd rather be dead." and another "I'd rather be red," rode a small boy on a tricycle with a sign: "I'd rather be."

Priorities: What are the real U.S. values and priorities? The first place to look is the Budget of the U.S. Government submitted by the President and to the congressional reaction to it. FCNL has stressed the priorities approach consistently over the years in testimonies, *Newsletters,* and lobbying. By stressing how human needs are being denied by military spending, FCNL lobbyists on military and domestic issues could integrate their research and lobbying efforts. Frances Neely for many years was a leader in the Coalition on National Priorities and Military Policy comprised of 37 national organizations.

In 1976, Congress enacted legislation setting up a coherent budget making process. House and Senate Budget committees in one bill now recommend overall national priorities, setting expenditure levels for various categories. This innovation provided a major forum in which we could debate national priorities. The Coalition for a New Foreign and Military Policy, which I co-chaired for a number of years, proposed that an amendment be drafted to transfer funds from the military to various nonmilitary categories. The struggle for passage of a "transfer amendment" continued for years in Congress. It never succeeded on the floor of either the House or the Senate, but I believe the issues it raised in the Budget committees shaped the resolution as it came to the floor, and usually resulted in a House vote on the alternative Congressional Black Caucus budget. The transfer amendment certainly gave local activists a relevant way to relate local needs to military spending and occasioned many local hearings, forums, and city council debates.[20] Regrettably, decisions made on national priorities over the years reflect our national values all too clearly. Despite the efforts of many organizations like FCNL, faith in military hardware to provide security has triumphed over the demonstrated needs of the citizenry and a more comprehensive definition of national security. We have "paid any price."

Economics: A prime axiom of politics is that "people vote their pocketbooks." Another is that specific interests prevail over general interests, organized groups over the unorganized, and short term interests over long range perspectives. Put these together and you have bad news for those who hope to cut military spending. The military-industrial complex is no myth. Workers know where their paychecks come from. Seats on the congressional armed services committees and the military appropriations subcommittees are sought by senators and representatives who want to protect local industries and workers and to assure their own reelection. When amendments to cut weapons programs are on the floor, memoranda will often be circulated identifying by state or district the number of jobs that will purportedly be lost.

FCNL has sought to deal with this reality by explanation and reassurance. The 31 page 1960 FCNL publication gave the facts in "The Big Hand in Your Pocket! Your Taxes, Your Livelihood, and the Growing Power of the Military" Periodically this information is updated in Newsletters and other publications. The pamphlet "Disarmament and Your Job" was prepared by Emile Benoit, Columbia University economist, and Ada Wardlaw in 1958 and updated in 1961. It sought to reassure owners, workers and community leaders that reductions in arms spending do not have to mean loss of jobs. Kenneth Boulding testified for FCNL in 1956 before the Senate Subcommittee on Disarmament calling for more government research on the issue. FCNL representatives pressed the Arms Control and Disarmament Agency to do more studies.

A July 1965 Report by an intergovernmental committee is still the most authoritative official statement. It assures citizens and congress that economic conversion is possible without serious dislocation so long as adequate preparations are made:

> Even general and complete disarmament would pose no insuperable problems; indeed it would mainly afford opportunities for a better life for our citizens.[21]

With the demise of the cold war, this issue became active again for FCNL in 1989, but remains very difficult.[22]

Politicians who believe that "pocketbook issues" are closest to their constituents' hearts are usually right. But when constituents' sons, brothers, and husbands start coming home in body bags and coffins, a new factor enters the equation. Then, lobbyists for peace groups may find more doors open than before. But in more normal times, constituents concerned about ending the arms race, the United Nations, international poverty, other people's children, prisoners on death row, may expect less congressional response than is accorded groups out to protect their bottom line, even though they may receive more respect. One senate aide, obviously emerging from a battering by a special interest pleader, said to me with admiration and relief, after hearing our plea, "Jeez, you guys are on the side of the angels."

International politics: Groups like FCNL, which challenge the balance of power in international affairs, the nation-state system and sovereignty as meaningful concepts in the nuclear-space age, naturally have a jaundiced view of some of the reasons for national security doctrines and their related military spending. Nevertheless, our contrary view needs to be heard, even though it may not heeded. Henry Cadbury and Richard Wood testified for Friends against the proposed military aid to Greece and Turkey in 1947. Henry Cadbury and Raymond Wilson testified against the proposed North Atlantic Treaty Organization in 1949. And a 32 page analysis and critique of NATO prepared by Raymond Wilson and Barbara Grant Nnoka was sent to most Senators, and to key organizations and individuals.

From 1973 through 1975 Frances Neely engaged in an intensive campaign to challenge U.S. foreign policy assumptions and the resulting military equations. Research and lobbying centered on proposals to reduce troops in Europe, close many foreign bases and reduce U.S. arms aid and sales. Floor amendments to reduce U.S. troops in Europe, sponsored by Senator Mike Mansfield and Representative Tip O'Neill, gathered substantial support. In 1973 Mansfield's amendment to cut overseas manpower by 190,000 within three years originally passed, 49-46. It was later rejected 44-51 after frantic lobbying by the Nixon administration. The O'Neill amendment was defeated, 163-240, in 1975. Frances activated a wide variety of organizations on this issue as chair of both the interreligious task force on military spending and the legislative committee of the 37 member Coalition on National Priorities and Military Policy.

FCNL's critique of several particular items of military spending also had political dimensions. Multilateral nuclear forces in Europe would undercut negotiations for a nonproliferation treaty. Star

Wars spending would undermine negotiations on a space treaty.

As FCNL's first half century closed, Joe Volk was taking the lead in a Washington coalition to establish a "Code of Conduct" which would seriously reduce, if not end, the pernicious arms trade which has greatly increased the casualties suffered by innocent civilians in conflicts around the world. This issue has many political ramifications, but it might also have been included in the discussion of economics, above. The chief rationale for arms sales abroad after the cold war is over is purely and simply economic–profits and jobs.

* * * * * *

After surveying FCNL's efforts over the years to reduce military spending, the reader may conclude as staff and committee members often did: Nothing works! And nothing can work until the whole frame of reference changes. Not until "national security" has a broader definition. Not until more effective international institutions of conflict resolution are devised. Not until mutual interdependence is acknowledged.

FCNL's effort described in the next section was being implemented when the cold war ended. Whether that was anything more than coincidental cannot be known. But here are the facts.

Deterrence by Fear or Friendship? A Case Study

> **Since wars begin in the minds of men, it is in the minds of men that the defenses of peace must be constructed.**
> Charter of the UN Educational, Scientific, and Cultural Organization (UNESCO)

The 1980 election of Ronald Reagan on a conservative, promilitary, anticommunist platform caused many FCNL supporters, myself included, to wonder how we had arrived at this point. The fate of the world was at stake. Intelligent and able people were at the negotiating table seeking to reverse the nuclear arms race. Yet it continued to spiral out of control. Weapons and doctrines became more provocative. Leaders vied for public approval by seeing who could be more bellicose; peace was a muffled, minor theme. I was driven back to square one to try to comprehend what was going on.

My legal training had stood me in good stead in communicating with Congress, where many members were lawyers. Legal analysis was helpful on many issues. Legal writing is supposed to be logical and clear, though pedestrian and boring. Such training helped in examining pending legislation and arms control treaties, proposals for improving the World Court, and revising the UN Charter. But it was utterly useless in explaining the irrational forces at work in the arms race.

I began to realize that I had been downgrading too quickly another whole dimension in human affairs–the psychological aspect which could explain some of the irrational and nonrational forces at work in the world. I was helped, indeed driven, to this conclusion by several factors. My wife, Bonnie, had studied for a Masters in Mental Health degree at Johns Hopkins Medical School in the late 1970's and she shared many insights. Even more compelling, our daughter's mental illness as she began her first year of medical school forced me to examine much more closely the insights of modern psychology and psychiatry. (I believe it is no coincidence that one of the most perceptive, able, and articulate members of Congress in this generation, Ron Dellums, is a psychiatric social worker by profession. His training gives him solid insight into the Congress, the military establishment, and the international arms race.)

The writings of Eric Fromm, Jerome Frank, Ralph White and Robert Jay Lifton also took on new relevance and meaning for me. I learned about the International Society of Political Psychology. Suddenly many things began to make sense: avoidance, denial, projection of one's own problems onto others, scapegoating, the corrosive power of fear, "enemies." This analysis translated many basic religious concepts into modern terminology.

Out of these new insights I began to see that the doctrine of nuclear deterrence, the centerpiece of U.S. national security policy, was in fact the engine driving the careening nuclear arms race. The nuclear arsenals held by the British and French could destroy our nation as surely as Soviet weapons could. Why didn't we feel it was necessary to deter them by targeting their cities and launching sites? In the search for answers I circled back to policies which FCNL had supported all along–dialogue, exchange of persons, and intercultural appreciation as the way to escape the trap of fear and misunderstanding. Why not deter the Soviet Union, as we did Britain and France– with friendship rather than fear?

In 1981, FCNL began to implement these insights with the wholehearted support of staff and committee members. Louise Farr, a classmate at Yale Law School who had prepared our report on Indian legislation for four years in the 1960's, researched and drafted a major 40 page document, "Weaknesses of United States Deterrence Policy." This was summarized in our August 1981 Newsletter. This analysis was also the core of a paper, "Why Does Not the Process of Disarmament Begin?" which I gave at the Stockholm conference called by Swedish Quakers and attended by Soviet and East European officials in September 1981. The year's focus on nuclear deterrence culminated in my testimony to the Senate Foreign Relations Committee November 9, 1981 as it considered the foreign policy and arms control implications of the strategic weapons program. Subsequently, I stressed the same theme in testimony before other congressional committees and in an October 1985 article, "Deterrence: From Fear to Interdependence" in the *Bulletin of Atomic Scientists*.

These new insights were in fact old stuff. In 1946, John Nason, then President of Swarthmore College, had filed a statement for FCNL in support of Senator J.W. Fulbright's bill to use the proceeds from the sale of surplus war property for the exchange of students. Gilbert White, then President of Haverford College, had testified for FCNL in 1954 in support of increased funds for international exchanges. In June 1957 an FCNL seminar had examined whether mutual deterrence was the way to peace. British and American Quakers had been some of the first in their respective countries to visit the Soviet Union in the early cold war period–an action that generated considerable controversy. In 1968, Soviet expert and Friend-in-Washington, William Edgerton, sought to interpret the dynamics of communism and Soviet society to members of Congress. And in 1955, in one of my first successful lobbying efforts, Senator Karl Mundt and ten House members had written President Eisenhower, urging him to put exchange of persons on the agenda for the forthcoming summit meeting with Khrushchev. It was included and was the only item on which progress was made in the ensuing five years.[23]

But how to begin in 1981 with this new President, who was riding into town on a wave of anti-communism? We began by drafting a letter to President-elect Reagan and President Brezhnev urging them personally to oversee an exchange of their top aides in the security field (a "timberline" conference, not a Summit.)

> The goal of these dialogues and exchanges would be modest: The goal is not to change the basic views or philosophy of any of the participants. The goal is rather to assure that those who will be making crucial national policy decision in the next few years will make those decisions on the most accurate assessment possible of facts, perceptions, and intentions, undistorted either by unreasonable hopes or irrational fears.

The letter, with an accompanying memorandum drawing on Quaker experience in conferences and seminars, was signed by Asia Bennett of the AFSC, Herbert Hadley of the Friends World Committee for Consultation, and myself. It was delivered to Reagan through transition team member General Edward Rowny and to Brezhnev through Minister-Counselor Vladillen Vasev at the Soviet Embassy.

A March 9 reply from Richard Allen, assistant to the president for national security affairs, doubted the efficacy of dialogues while the Soviet "military buildup and expansion" continued. "It is our belief that before we can enter into meaningful discussions and negotiations with Soviet representatives, we would have to take a variety of measures to strengthen our international positions and to coordinate our security policy with that of our allies."

No specific reply was received from President Brezhnev, but an embassy official called my attention to a February 23 speech, by the Soviet President in which he said: "The international situation depends largely on Soviet and United States policies. The state of relations between these and the gravity of international problems call for a dialogue at all levels. The U.S.S.R. is prepared for such a dialogue. Experience indicates that summit meetings are its decisive element."

Exchanges with the "evil empire." At the November, 1981 FCNL annual meeting, after I had reported our analysis of deterrence and efforts to promote exchanges, a Friend, Walter Felton, approached me with determination and said U.S.-Soviet exchanges were now taking place. He had just been in one. During the next several months, Caroline Packard, my intern, and I gathered information about the range of U.S.-Soviet contacts and summarized them in the March 1982 *Newsletter,* "Seeking Security–Deterrence By Fear or By Friendship?" The *Newsletter,* which was well received, could not possibly carry all the relevant information and documents we had gathered, so they were published in a 36-page backup document which also had wide circulation.

At one point I gave a copy of the *Newsletter* to a Soviet diplomat asking him to share it with Ambassador Dobrynin. Later I learned the ambassador had appreciated it, but thought that "friendship" might be a bit strong. Some others had, too. Our next major *Newsletter* on the subject in May 1983 was entitled "Building Deterrence by Interdependence."

But this was the era of the "evil empire." The Russians were 10 feet tall and stealing our secrets through various scientific exchanges. A compliant Democratic House had voted for the "Findley" amendment to end all U.S.-Soviet long term, scientific exchanges through the State Department or the International Communications Agency after June 30, 1982. We had lobbied against this amendment, and we urged Senate and House conferees to delete it.

What happened next was very significant. The conferees deleted the termination provision, but to pacify its proponents they required the State Department to report on the various scientific and technical exchanges that were taking place and to assess who was benefiting from them. They anticipated the report would prove Uncle Sam was really being duped again into giving away the store to the Russians. The report was delayed many months and after it was submitted to Congress, no one seemed to know just where it was. We finally obtained a copy from the State Department, and we were astounded. The 81-page report was filled with fascinating information and the official assessment indicated there was little risk to the U.S. and much benefit from the exchanges. We made a 10-page summary and circulated it widely. The Jack Anderson column of October 23 summarized it. The August/September 1983 FCNL *Newsletter* gave details:

> It shows how the U.S. and USSR, even after the Afghanistan invasion, have cooperated in such diverse fields as gypsy moth control, artificial heart research, anti-cancer therapies, heart disease and glaucoma research, earthquake predictions, microwave radiation health standards, and Soviet-manufactured atomic technology installed at the Fermi National Accelerator Laboratory.

Pushing ahead, we supported members of Congress who were introducing various proposals to increase U.S.-Soviet exchange programs for students, for high level military leaders, for scientists and technicians.

In November 1983, in cooperation with the Institute for Soviet American Relations, founded by FCNL General Committee member Harriett Crosby, we co-sponsored "Surviving Together." It reported positive aspects of U.S.-Soviet relations, especially scientific and technical exchanges, trade, and arms control. "Surviving Together" was widely read on both sides of the increasingly porous Iron Curtain.

1985, the climactic year. FCNL in 1984 had taken the lead in organizing the U.S.-Soviet Working Group made up of representatives from scientific, religious, peace, and other organization. The group reached agreement on drafting an omnibus "Exchange for Peace Resolution" which set forth a comprehensive list of areas for improved U.S.-Soviet relations. The list was compiled in consultation with senators and representatives and their staffs and with relevant State Department officials. A tactical decision was made to seek State Department comment on the draft resolution before introducing it in Congress. We anticipated favorable State Department comments and this would help us obtain co-sponsorship by middle-of-the-road members.

We needed a widely respected member of Congress to take the lead and settled on Representative Lee Hamilton of Indiana. He was in a key spot as Chair of the House Intelligence Committee and the House Subcommittee on Europe and the Middle East of the Foreign Affairs Committee. He was also a very busy person, so before attempting to arrange an appointment, we asked one of his constitu-

---

Characterizing the U.S.-Soviet Struggle

"Sidney Koretz's letter questions Eric Sevareid's comparison of the United States and the Soviet Union as bullfighter and bull. He prefers two puffed-up frogs in a pond or two scorpions in a bottle.

More realistically, how about two antagonistic family members who, like it or not, have no alternative but to continue to live in the same house. They could then take Ann Landers' advice and seek family counseling.

Sound advice might suggest: stop exaggerating, stop threatening, keep your cool, keep talking, try to understand the other's point of view, and find small, realistic steps to take in order to survive and prosper together."

Ed Snyder's letter to the Washington Post printed Feb. 3, 1985.

ents, Bill Dietz, to write calling his attention to the draft resolution. During the meeting with Hamilton, he agreed to write Secretary George Shultz asking for his views. The draft resolution, plus the 11-page backup memorandum I had drafted were sent in March. Then followed an anxious period of waiting which dragged on and on. Our State Department contacts told us there was no problem at State, but since the Resolution mentioned all the various existing scientific and technical exchanges, plus some possible new ones, the comments of all the relevant departments and agencies had to be obtained.

After the draft had been circulating for seven months in the Executive Branch, we were impatient. We needed a vehicle on which to do congressional lobbying and public education. Our informants in the State Department gave us periodic reports from which it appeared that all the agencies consulted–more than a dozen—had given positive comments. Only the Department of Defense was negative. State had replied to their objections, but Defense had sent back a rebuttal. To resolve the issue the Office of Management and Budget, which was shepherding the process, sent the issue to the CIA.

It was now October. President Reagan's first summit with President Gorbachev, scheduled for November in Iceland, was fast approaching. The possibility of significant progress on pending U.S.-Soviet arms control issues was dim. I called on numerous officials with the Exchange for Peace Resolution in hand. Ambassador Arthur Hartmann was home from Moscow to help prepare the President for the Summit; he listened with interest. The director of political-military affairs of the National Security Council at the White House did likewise. Many State Department officials were already familiar with its content. The Exchange for Peace Resolution had been fully explored during the preceding months while it was circulating in the executive branch.

The draft omnibus Exchange for Peace Resolution we had prepared was never returned from the State Department. It didn't have to be. The Summit communique gave the answer. At Reykjavik, Reagan and Gorbachev had renewed the "General Agreement on Contacts, Exchanges and Cooperation in Scientific, Technical, Educational, Cultural and Other Fields." They also endorsed a broad agreement for cooperation on environmental protection, and series of "exchange initiatives."[24] An article by John A. Nicolopoulos, Greek journalist and former diplomat and historian, in the *Dallas Morning News* of December 18, 1985, credits FCNL for its key role in the process.[25]

During the next three years of Reagan's term, we continued to press this initiative. We worked with Representative Hamilton to arrange a congressional hearing where experts made the case for scientific exchanges and answered criticisms. I drafted an appeal to Reagan and Gorbachev urging them to work together on the two issues crucial to human survival–preventing nuclear war and protecting the environment. William Barton of the London based Friends Service Council accompanied me to Moscow where we presented the appeal to various officials in October 1986. Our U.S.-Soviet Working Group continued to meet, to hear experts, to analyze bills and lobby. "Surviving Together" became the key journal in the nation reporting on various exchanges and cooperative projects. We took the lead in drafting a letter to President Reagan supporting and encouraging expansion of U.S.-Soviet cooperative projects. The April 22, 1988 letter was cosigned by representatives of 26 national organizations. National Security Council Advisor General Colin Powell replied cordially on June 24, noting further positive steps which just been taken at the recently concluded Summit in Moscow.

* * * * *

When the cold war ended, the arguments began over who could claim credit for the beneficial result. Secretary of State George Shultz in his 1988 testimony on the INF treaty stated that "an effective deterrent" was the key. The outcome showed "the importance of negotiating from strength and of being patient, determined, and purposeful at the bargaining table."

In FCNL's February 22, 1988 letter to the Senate Foreign

Relations Committee supporting the INF treaty, we suggested that "such views seem to take a partial and simplistic view of events in this historic period." We suggested that these factors were overlooked:

- There was a growing acceptance by leaders in Washington and Moscow of the fact that there are no winners in a nuclear war and that one should never be fought. This helped immeasurably to create the political will to reach an agreement. This political will was powerfully buttressed by an apprehensive public in the United States and Europe. Frightened by the accelerating arms race and by the bellicose talk of leaders, people took to the streets demanding that U.S.-Soviet arms talks begin and that agreements be reached.

- This view also overlooks the economic pressures being felt by leaders in Washington and Moscow in this period. United States was moving from being the world's largest creditor nation to being the world's largest debtor nation....In the Soviet Union, the picture was far more serious and pressing. The decades-long priority to the military establishment had impoverished the entire non-military sector and encouraged rigid, compartmentalized thinking and bureaucracies....

- But perhaps the most significant element of all, seldom acknowledged in Administration testimony, was the change in Soviet leadership in 1985 which brought Mikhail Gorbachev to power with a different concept of national security. In the new Soviet view of security, the number of bombs is not as important as the country's economic and political strength, and this could not be achieved while the Soviet Union was squandering resources on military technology and outmoded institutions in need of restructuring. This new way of thinking about national security is the only reasonable explanation for the many Soviet concessions which were made in negotiations on the INF Treaty....Certainly U.S. weapons superiority and NATO cohesion in the past had met only unyielding Soviet resistance under different Soviet leadership. It is also important to recall that these concessions came *after* the Reagan military buildup and SDI spending had leveled off, not while it was going up.

Notes

1. Marullo, Sam and Lofland, John, ed. *Peace Action in the 80s: Social Science Perspectives,* Intro., Rutgers State University Press, (1990). I find it impossible to identify the number of "pacifists" in the U.S.. Dennis A. Gilbert in *Compendium of American Public Opinion*, pp. 67-69, Facts on File Publications, NY, NY (1988), cites various polls which lead me to believe that the number might be between 5% and 15%, depending on definitions, world events at the time, and the phrasing of the question. The low end might suggest the number who oppose the use of military force and war under all circumstances. The higher figure might suggest the number of "nuclear pacifists."

2. See Raymond Wilson, *Uphill for Peace,* Chapter 4.

3. See 1981 FCNL Bound Volume, FCNL Doc. G-24.

4. See Department of State Publication 7277, Disarmament Series 5, released September 1961, entitled "Freedom from War, The United States Program for General and Complete Disarmament in a Peaceful World."

5. See 1993 FCNL Annual Report pp. 17-18.

6. See my testimony before the U.S. Commission on Proposals for the

National Academy of Peace and Conflict Resolution, July 22, 1980 in 1980 FCNL Bound Volume, T-12, and my letter to Senator Robert T. Stafford, Chair of the Senate Subcommittee on Education, Arts and Humanities, April 30, 1982, endorsing S. 1889, 1982 FCNL Bound Volume, L-22, and my letter to Senator Stafford the next year endorsing S. 564, 1983 FCNL Bound Volume, L-313. See also "Legislative History of Peace Academy Bills," 1982 FCNL Bound Volume, G-53.

    7. *Uphill for Peace*, p. 273.
    8. Ibid. pp. 217-218.
    9. Ibid. pp. 226-229.
    10. See *FCNL Washington Newsletters*, July 1976, Feb. 1987.
    11. *Uphill for Peace*, pp. 229-233.
    12. Ibid. p. 236
    13. Ibid. pp. 237-238.
    14. Ibid. pp. 246-51.
    15. See James L. Adams, *The Growing Church Lobby in Washington*, pp. 224-225, Eerdmans, (1970)
    16. See my testimony before the Senate Judiciary Committee, October 31, 1979; *FCNL Washington Newsletter* November 1979; 1979 FCNL Annual Report, p. 4.
    17. See FCNL Doc. T-604, letter to Ch. Dante B. Fascell, May 15, 1986. See also *FCNL Washington Newsletter*, May 1986, "Terrorism–Bringing the War Home."
    18. We assiduously try to avoid the term "defense." Semantics are important in framing issues. Since defending oneself is usually viewed as positive, the use of "defense spending" subtly concedes its validity. After the second world war, the name of the "War Department" was changed to the "Defense Department," a major semantic defeat for pacifists. Since the Defense Department concedes it cannot defend the nation against an all out nuclear attack, I have argued it should be renamed the "Department of Deterrence." Certainly U.S. military excursions throughout much of the world are hard to describe accurately as defensive.
    19. Hearings, House Budget Committee, "Fiscal Year 1977 Budget and the Economy," Feb. 2, 1976, pp. 241-242.
    20. For a detailed comparative analysis of three citizen efforts--the transfer amendment, opposition to the B-1 bomber, and opposition to the

Panama Canal Treaty, see Shaw, Catherine E. (1981). "In the Public Interest: Public Interest Groups and American Democracy" (Doctoral dissertation, University of Michigan, 1981) *UMI Dissertation Services* 8116335.)

21. Introduction, "Report of the Committee on the Economic Impact of Defense and Disarmament," July 1965, Gardner Ackley, Chairman.

22. See Ruth Flower's section of FCNL Annual Reports for 1989 through 1993.

23. See FCNL *Memo* No. 23, July 25, 1955.

24. See 1986 Bound Volume, FCNL Doc. G-601.

25. Reprinted in FCNL Doc. R-602, 1986 FCNL Bound Volume.

4. Has FCNL Been Faithful to Quaker Beliefs in the Power of Love and Nonviolence, the Indwelling of God in Each Person?

An earnest effort has been made to honor historic Quaker concerns regarding conscientious objection to military service, the death penalty, and the rights of African Americans, Native Americans and Japanese Americans. There has been extensive soul searching on the legitimate use of force by government, the role of police in an organized society, and the use of economic sanctions in lieu of military action. Faithfulness is always an issue for groups working in the legislative arena where compromise is essential.

Conscription and Conscientious Objection

Most lobbies don't work for altruistic purposes. They lobby for a narrow self interest, usually economic, of their own members and supporters. FCNL's work against the draft, to protect conscientious objectors and to ensure religious freedom meets the classic definition of a "lobby." On these issues, FCNL is working to protect the interests of its constituents, Quakers. In FCNL's early years, during and soon after the second world war, much effort was devoted to

> "Sherman said 'War is hell,' a definition never exceeded in brevity nor excelled in accuracy. War is un-Christian, and nuclear war doubly so."
> E. Raymond Wilson, *Quaker statesman, at the National Council of Churches meeting at San Diego.*
> Item in the Los Angeles Times *Feb. 24, 1968.*

protecting conscientious objection and opposing conscription and universal military training (UMT.)

Raymond Wilson has written about the intensive FCNL efforts to oppose the infamous "Starnes rider," which prevented C.O.'s from doing relief and ambulance service abroad during the second world war. He also tells the story of the "Frozen Fund," the government's breach of faith with C.O.'s when it refused to fulfill its promise to use government funds generated by C.O. labor for war rehabilitation programs. For 15 years, FCNL and others tried unsuccessfully to secure congressional action to fulfill the memorandum of understanding signed by government officials. [1]

For seven years, from 1945 to 1952, Raymond Wilson of the FCNL and John Swomley of the National Council Against Conscription led the legislative effort to prevent enactment of universal military training in the United States. That effort was finally successful after the measure was defeated on the House floor, 236-162 March 4, 1952. A proposal for a compulsory reserve was defeated three years later. But conscription, in the form of *selective* service, continued as a part of the potential future of every young man almost continuously from 1945 to 1973. Draft registration, with only a temporary hiatus in the 1970s, continued through 1993.

FCNL witnesses against UMT and selective service extension over the years included D. Robert Yarnall, J. Henry Scattergood, Raymond Wilson, Sam Levering, Henry Cadbury, Harrop Freeman, Samuel Marble, Clyde Milner, Charles Darlington, Ralph Rose, Lyle Tatum, Ralph Rudd, and Charles Harker.[2]

In opposing the draft, FCNL witnesses stressed different points, depending on their own approaches and then-current events. Friends' religious basis for opposition was usually stressed. Ralph Rose summarized some of the other reasons in his May 1967 statement to the House Armed Services Committee:

> We Quakers oppose extension of the draft because military conscription is alien to American tradition; because the present law is one of injustice, inequity and

discrimination; because the draft violates fundamental civil liberties; because the concept of military solutions including a conscripted army and military alliances is obsolete and the antithesis of peaceful settlement of disputes under world law administered by a strengthened United Nations.

In 1969, Chuck Harker of FCNL and Jim Bristol of AFSC, took the lead in organizing the National Council to Repeal the Draft. NCRD remained the leading anti-draft coalition encompassing organizations across a broad political spectrum until the authority to induct young men into the military finally ended in 1973. The demise of induction authority was due primarily to public outrage over the war in Indochina, and the capricious and inequitable way men were conscripted to serve and often die there. President Jimmy Carter reinstated draft registration in 1980 to demonstrate U.S. "resolve" when the Soviet Union invaded Afghanistan. FCNL's efforts to end registration, to reduce funding and to abolish the Selective Service System have continued through 1993, led by Ruth Flower.

Conscientious Objectors: Eternal vigilance was required to defend existing statutory language protecting CO's, language which FCNL worked on in 1951.[3] In 1955, General Hershey proposed serious last minute changes which were prevented by rapid response from FCNL and related organizations.[4] In 1967, the House Armed Services Committee added a provision to place C.O.'s under military jurisdiction. An intensive effort was mounted and the Committee reversed itself and withdrew the provision when the draft extension bill was on the House floor. Ralph Rose, in his 1967 testimony against the draft, urged recognition of both the sincere nonreligious objector and the "selective objector," who is opposed to a particular war, though he may not be opposed to all war. The Supreme Court's 1970 decision in *Welsh v. U.S.* protected the nonreligious objector. We failed, however, to secure recognition of the "selective objector." Senator Philip Hart's proposal to do this lost in a June 8, 1971 Senate floor vote, 12-50. In 1992, FCNL supported Rep. Ron Dellums' bill to protect members of the armed forces who claim C.O. status, an issue that surfaced forcefully during the Persian Gulf war.

"**National service**" is a subject approached warily by FCNL over the years. The words have sometimes been used as a euphemism for making conscription more popular by adding a civilian component. The key question is whether *compulsion* is an element in the overall program. In 1966, Secretary of Defense Robert McNamara suggested that to remedy draft inequities, every young person be asked to give two years of national service either to the military or to some development work at home or abroad. FCNL made its case against the draft and national service in my letter of October 19 to the National Advisory Commission on Selective Service, chaired by Burke Marshall, a law school classmate. FCNL's November 1966 *Newsletter* stated our position:

> The FCNL has throughout its history taken a position of opposition to compulsory service whether military or civilian, but is in favor of a wide expansion of useful projects at home and abroad under both governmental and nongovernmental auspices and financing, on a voluntary basis.

In 1993, President Clinton proposed and Congress approved a national service program unrelated to military service. It raised the stature of civilian service and was much more consistent with FCNL policy.

Amnesty for Indochina war resisters, which often involved draft law violations, took a significant amount of time for three years, 1973-1976. Harrop Freeman testified in favor of FCNL's position of unconditional amnesty before a House Judiciary subcommittee March 11, 1974 on the basis of FCNL's Statement on Amnesty of Feb. 21, 1972. President Ford's 1974 "earned reentry" clemency was an inadequate halfway measure. President Jimmy Carter's first Executive Order on January 21, 1977 granted a blanket pardon to all Vietnam draft evaders who had not been involved in a violent act. Military deserter and less-than-honorable discharge cases were considered on a case by case basis. Congressional resistance failed to overturn Carter's action.

World Peace Tax Fund

The draft law directly confronts 18 year old men with the question—does participation in the war system violate your conscientious beliefs? What about their elders? Does payment of federal income taxes, a large percentage of which goes for war making purposes, violate their conscientious beliefs? If there is a conscientious objector provision in the draft law to respect freedom of conscience, why can't there be a similar provision in the federal income tax laws?

FCNL has called for some sort of "civilian peace tax" since 1960. The story of how the proposal developed from concern to reality is a classic case of how a Quaker lobby can operate on Capitol Hill. The issue is grounded in a fundamental Quaker concern: refusal to participate in war to the maximum extent possible. It began with one couple, David and Miyo Bassett; it was supported by their Ann Arbor, Michigan, Friends Meeting; they sought and obtained expert assistance from the University community, and brought the issue to FCNL in 1970.[5] FCNL staff helped refine the proposal and sought congressional comment and support. Some saw the issue as one of religious and civil liberties; others saw it as a peace issue. All support was welcomed. The first bill was introduced in 1972 with 10 cosponsors, led by Ron Dellums—another example of how legislators and interest groups can share a mutual interest and work together for a common purpose. Representative Ben Rosenthal and I spoke at a press conference as the bill was introduced on the April tax deadline. In 1977, Senator Mark Hatfield of Oregon, introduced a comparable Senate bill and has been a strong and consistent advocate ever since, joined by several of his colleagues on both sides of the aisle.

In FCNL's 1972 annual legislative summary I opined that, "I

view this as a 10-15 year legislative effort before passage can be achieved." To many that seemed unduly pessimistic, an interminable period in which to wrestle annually with one's conscience at tax time. A significant number turned to tax resistance in various forms but even that did not persuade authorities to grant this concession to the demands of conscience. In 1992, the "Peace Tax Fund" bill, H.R. 1870, had a major hearing before a House Ways and Means subcommittee. FCNL submitted supportive testimony and Ruth Flower, chair of the Peace Tax Fund Campaign's legislative committee, testified on some technical aspects of the bill.[6] Individual Friends and Friends organizations submitted supporting statements. The witnesses who testified demonstrated that support has spread far beyond the historic peace churches and the religious communities to civil liberties and peace circles. The Campaign is ably led by our Mennonite colleague, Marian Franz. Yet more than 20 years after the bill was introduced, we are still waiting for a breakthrough.

Religious Freedom

The oppression of early Friends for their religious beliefs in Britain and the American colonies undergirds Friends current concern for religious freedom. Government imposed prayers in public schools have been opposed, even including a required period of silence.

> We share with the proponents of these constitutional amendments a grave concern over the erosion of moral values in our increasingly materialistic society. But we do not believe the cause of true religion will be advanced by routine prayers in the public schools. A religious activity within the compulsory public school framework which is designed to appeal to all and to offend none makes for spiritual malnourishment, not growth. No child or parent should be encouraged to believe that perfunctory exercises

in the classroom are the substance of religion. The danger is that sensitive and seeking young people may believe this is indeed what religion is all about and turn away. The Constitution rightfully leaves matters of faith and religious education to the family and to the religious institutions, and that is where they should remain.
Excerpt from FCNL March 5, 1984 statement to Senators on proposed Constitutional amendments to permit prayer in public schools.

In 1990, the free exercise of religion guaranteed by the First Amendment was threatened by the Supreme Court's decision in *Oregon v. Smith*, which abandoned the "compelling interest" standard for judging government interference with religious practices. A three year struggle in Congress to restore the traditional interpretation culminated with the signing of the Religious Freedom Restoration Act (RFRA) by President Clinton, November 19, 1993.[7]

In 1978 FCNL supported passage of the American Indian Religious Freedom Act. But the Act had no effective way to ensure respect for Indian religious practices, as the Supreme Court's decision in *Lyng v. Northwest* demonstrated in 1988. FCNL continues to take the lead in urging passage of the Native American Free Exercise of Religion Act which would protect Indian religious practices not covered by the RFRA.[8]

The Death Penalty

For most Friends, the case against the death penalty is conclusive. It violates respect for the sacredness of human life. It forecloses forever the possibility of spiritual growth and redemption. It can never be called back if a mistake is discovered later. It enshrines revenge as public policy, because studies show it is not a deterrent to the crimes to which it is most often applied. It is applied unequally to poor and minority citizens. And it subtly approves the use of violence and undermines positive efforts to teach compassion and to build healthy communities.

Over the years, Friends at both the national and state level have helped lead opposition to capital punishment. Trevor Thomas and the Northern California Friends Committee on Legislation drafted and published, in 1955 and 1959, a highly effective and respected document against the death penalty, "This Life We Take."[9] FCNL worked closely with Senators Wayne Morse of Oregon in the mid 1950's and Philip Hart of Michigan in the mid 1960's in supplying material and drafting speeches, and with Senator Carl Levin of Michigan in the 1980's, in his "filibuster." Stuart Innerst in 1960, William Lunsford in 1972, Bernice Just in 1981, and Ruth Flower in 1982 opposed the death penalty before congressional committees. In 1967, FCNL took the lead in helping to organize the National Committee to Abolish the Federal Death Penalty. In the Reagan-Bush years, public opinion shifted toward support for the death penalty. In recent years, Ruth Flower and associates have worked to stave off legislative maneuvers to extend its reach and to broaden its application to more and more crimes. So far the efforts of those opposed to capital punishment have been amazingly successful given the public climate. But the many occasions on which legislation has almost passed make this story read like the heroine's narrow escapes in the early movie, "The Perils of Pauline."

Japanese American Redress

In the mid 1980s, FCNL committee member Tak Moriuchi's phone call alerted FCNL to the revived effort of the Japanese American Citizens' League to secure justice for those Japanese-Americans illegally interned by the United States during the second world war. This has been a longtime FCNL concern. Raymond Wilson has recounted FCNL lobbying and testimony by Homer Morris and Paul B. Johnson in 1947 and 1948 before House and Senate Judiciary subcommittees.[10]

From 1986 through 1988, Ruth Flower led FCNL's work to secure passage of legislation providing redress for Japanese American internees, through lobbying, testimony, rallying grass roots action, securing co-sponsors for legislation, and urging letters to the White House to assure President Bush's signature. Even after the bill was enacted in 1988, further efforts were necessary to secure adequate appropriations. At their celebration banquet the Japanese American Citizens' League honored the work that Ruth Flower and FCNL had done, noting especially FCNL's leadership role in the religious community.

African American Justice

It took 12 years for civil rights to become an FCNL priority. The December 1956 annual meeting identified the right to vote as one of three major priorities for the new Congress. Previously, FCNL had concentrated on postwar relief issues, antimilitarism, and support for international organizations and development. Work during the previous years on civil rights issues had been modest: opposition to the poll tax, support for the principle of a permanent Fair Employment Practices Commission, and joining several *amicus curiae* briefs filed with the Supreme Court on desegregation of District of Columbia schools and restaurants. In 1948, Byron Haworth, North Carolina FCNL committee member, filed a statement in support of federal anti-lynching legislation. In 1949, Frank Loescher supported fair employment practices. In 1956, Clarence H. "Mike" Yarrow urged Congress to confront the issue of segregated housing in the North. The power of Southern Senators during these years was so great that good bills were buried in committee or filibustered to death.

David Scull and Ralph Rose were partners at Turnpike Press in nearby Virginia. Each played key roles in FCNL history. Ralph, when working for AFSC in 1953, had urged President Eisenhower in several private interviews to support the process of desegregation in the District of Columbia. He later chaired FCNL's Executive Committee from 1978-1982. David chaired FCNL's newly formed Race Relations subcommittee in 1955 and provided leadership for

FCNL on civil rights and other issues for many years. David had been a plaintiff in the Supreme Court's *Thompson Restaurant* case that desegregated Washington restaurants in 1953. In 1959, the U.S. Supreme Court upheld his decision not to answer questions by a Virginia legislative committee about his activities on race relations. In May 1956, David testified for FCNL before the Senate Judiciary Committee. He urged creation of a civil rights commission and legislation to establish the right to vote. He ended by quoting John Woolman at some length, quaint language and all, to the Senators present.[11]

In 1957, Congress passed the first civil rights legislation in more than 80 years, a small first step toward safeguarding the right to vote. FCNL worked with a coalition of more than 20 organizations in lobbying and endorsing a joint statement to legislative committees. In 1958 and 1959, Robert L. Wixom, clerk of the Little Rock, Arkansas, Friends Meeting and B. Tartt Bell, AFSC Southern Regional Executive Secretary, testified regarding the large civil rights agenda still pending.

In June 1963, Richard W. Taylor, then of Coe College, Iowa, arrived in Washington to work as Friend-in-Washington on UN financing issues. But civil rights leader Medger Evers had been slain the day before, and by mutual decision he switched his assignment to civil rights. Dick's work for passage of the landmark 1964 Civil Rights Act won him the respect and appreciation of his colleagues on and off the Hill. He made FCNL a significant player in the ongoing struggle for civil rights. The FCNL conference room for a time in the early summer of 1964 became the command post for lobbyists working on the Senate bill.[12]

After passage of the 1964 act, described in the September 1964 FCNL *Newsletter* as "the most comprehensive civil rights legislation since enactment of the 13th, 14th and 15th Amendments," the struggle turned to economic and social legislation. And after Martin Luther King's assassination in 1968 and the burning in the cities, Friends' concerns translated into major FCNL priority action. Chuck Harker, then FCNL's acting Executive Secretary, played a significant role in supporting the Poor People's Campaign led by

117

Ralph Abernathy, in cooperation with AFSC and William Penn House personnel. And a third lobbyist, Ed Anderson, was added to FCNL's staff in 1968. His successor, Bill Lunsford, became FCNL's domestic issues lobbyist in 1971. Raymond Wilson asserts that Ed and Bill were only the second and third black persons to register as lobbyists–the first being Clarence Mitchell who led the civil rights struggle on the Hill for a generation.[13]

During the nearly five years that Ed Anderson and Bill Lunsford represented FCNL they opened many doors for FCNL on Capitol Hill and among nongovernmental organizations. They gave FCNL staff, committee members, and Friends across the country—for they also traveled widely–new perspectives and insights on what it was like to be black in America. Their task was not easy. Most Quakers in the United States are white and middle class, and this often makes it difficult to empathize fully with the black and poor, despite our best intentions. But the racial questions are insistent. Why should FCNL give a higher priority to manganese nodules at the bottom of the ocean than to the housing, hunger, and education of little black children in urban slums? Do Friends' concerns for the peace testimony override our concerns for justice? FCNL's January 1973 annual meeting confronted these issues. The minutes note: "Many Friends expressed themselves with varying degrees of support for domestic needs but with some feeling of inadequacy in the face of the immensity of both domestic and international problems. The interrelationship of domestic and international issues makes a choice of priorities far from simple." Bill Lunsford suggested to me when he left FCNL to become the Washington representative of the Child Welfare League, that it might be better for a white person to represent FCNL on domestic issues. This is one area where FCNL clearly may not be able to answer affirmatively the question posed at the beginning of this chapter.

On Capitol Hill, FCNL has found that members of the Congressional Black Caucus have been major allies especially on the alternative budget, human needs and conscience issues. Perhaps it is because we and the Black Caucus share the conventional criticism that we are "too far out to be effective."

I have been grateful to the black Friends who have associated themselves with FCNL–for their patient, persistent, and undoubtedly frustrated, willingness to share their insights with the rest of us. I think especially of the statements at FCNL business sessions and messages in meetings for worship from people like Barrington Dunbar, Jim Fletcher, Ted Robinson, and George Sawyer, and for the witnesses at Congressional hearings like Bernice Just and Jim Harvey. Fortunately, the domestic issues lobbyists who followed Ed and Bill–Harold Confer, Don Reeves and Ruth Flower–have carried forward FCNL's concerns for African American justice with sensitivity.

Native Americans

Quaker concern for American Indians is deeply rooted in American history. And since federal government officials have overwhelming power to influence the lives of Indians on and off the reservation, it has been natural for Friends to expect FCNL to play a significant role in supporting Native American goals.

FCNL's endeavors for Native Americans in its first 30 years included testimony in favor of vocational training and sanitary facilities, opposition to construction of the Kinzua dam in violation of Seneca Indian treaty rights, support for Alaska Native Land Claims, and a widely distributed "Report on Indian Legislation" prepared by Louise Farr and later by Richard Thompson.[14]

When the FCNL Policy Committee began the practice of soliciting Friends views on which issues should receive priority attention, Native American issues almost invariably fell on the line between priority and nonpriority issues. It may therefore be of some interest to trace the process by which, at the end of the first 50 years, these issues seem firmly embedded in FCNL's legislative priorities.

For many years, an ear of yellow seed corn sat on a shelf above my desk in FCNL's office. In the late summer of 1974 Warren Mesner had picked it out of a field surrounding the Central City, Nebraska, Friends Meetinghouse and handed it to me. Nebraska

119

Yearly Meeting had pledged $5000, including the proceeds from the sale of corn from this field, to employ a Friend-in-Washington on Native American affairs. This concern had arisen in Nebraska Yearly Meeting and found a positive response in the United Society of Friends Women and in Baltimore, Philadelphia, and New York Yearly Meetings.

Thus, on March 1, 1975, not one, but two, Friends-in-Washington began work–Diane Payne and Bryan Michener. Bryan left at the end of the one year program. Diane stayed on through the end of the congressional session. Before 1976 was over, the Indian Health Care Improvement Act had passed, the act on which she, Bryan and many others had worked so hard. During the next 17 years, FCNL lobbyists on Native American issues would struggle to obtain adequate funding for this important piece of legislation and to extend it when it was about to expire. The Friend-in-Washington program on Native American affairs clearly met a real need on health care–and other issues–and was widely appreciated. But FCNL's special funding had run out. We sought broad interreligious support, but that did not develop.

In 1977, Native American issues became an FCNL legislative priority for the new Congress, with Don Reeves as the FCNL lobbyist taking primary responsibility for the issue, supported by Phil Shenk. During the next several years, FCNL worked out a joint relationship with the Mennonite Central Committee (MCC) which supplied "volunteers," usually for two years, and with the Jesuit Social Ministries.(JSM) In 1987 and 1988, Indian work was carried on via FCNL's "Native American Advocacy Project" which was supported by four Friends Yearly Meetings and seven other denominations–Episcopal, Lutheran, Mennonite, Presbyterian, Reformed Church, United Methodist, and United Church of Christ.

The following people worked on FCNL's Native American priority during this period, and were fully integrated into FCNL's staff despite other organizational connections they may have had:

1975	Bryan Michener and Diane Payne, Friends-in-Washington;
1976	Diane Payne, FCNL Legislative Advocate;
1977	Don Reeves and Phil Shenk, then Jan Harmon, MCC;
1977-78	Jan Harmon, MCC;
1979-81	Steve Linsheid, MCC, and Ted Zuern, JSM;
1982	Steve Linsheid, then Cindy Darcy, MCC, and Ted Zuern, JSM;
1983-84	Cindy Darcy, MCC, and Ted Zuern, JSM;
1985-86	Cindy Darcy, MCC;
1987-88	Cindy Darcy, FCNL Native American Advocacy Project;
1989	Cindy Darcy, FCNL, and Steve Zehr, MCC;
1990	Jay Fikes, FCNL, and Steve Zehr, MCC;
1991	Steve Zehr, MCC, and Joanna McMann, MCC;
1992	Joanna McMann, MCC;
1993	Joanna McMann, MCC, and Melissa Shirk, MCC.

During the past 18 years, Native American issues have become an integral part of FCNL's legislative priorities. Friends feel a responsibility to continue their historic role, and some dedicated Friends feel this most intensely. But it has also become a priority because of the quality of the FCNL representatives who have listened sensitively to Native American priorities and have capably interpreted those views to senators, representatives and their staffs on Capitol Hill. Further, FCNL representatives have become nearly indispensable in providing legislative leadership on these issues in the interreligious and secular community in Washington.

But where should limited resources be applied? How to choose among the many crucial issues? FCNL representatives continually faced difficult dilemmas:

1. Should they give priority to overall issues which affect all Native Americans, for example, health care, which is abysmal; housing, which is completely inadequate; job creation, when reser-

vation unemployment was 48% in 1987? Or should they champion the cause of particular tribes and groups with very legitimate grievances about treaty violations, religious freedom, and water, fishing and mineral rights?

In a typical Quaker compromise, FCNL did both at the cost of an overworked, underpaid staff. For many years, Indian health was a top priority. FCNL Friends-in-Washington worked hard for enactment of the Indian Health Care Improvement Act in 1976. FCNL advocates worked for its four year extension in 1980; sought unsuccessfully to prevent a presidential veto in 1984; sought congressional passage in 1985 and 1986, again unsuccessfully because of congressional politics; finally, in 1988, after extensive congressional action and threats of another veto, President Reagan signed the Indian Health Care Amendments Act on November 23, 1988, the last bill passed by the 100th Congress to be signed into law.

FCNL has also supported other general legislation: for economic development, for additional housing, for better education, for expanded social services, for drug and alcohol treatment, for improved child welfare, and for prevention of toxic dumping in Indian country. FCNL played a key role in the creation of a permanent Senate Select Committee on Indian Affairs.

But FCNL has also taken up the cause of particular tribes, especially when the issue had wider implications. Among the many groups supported: Alaska Natives, Papago, Hopi, Navajo, Sioux, Texas Band of Kickapoo Indians, Cow Creek Band of Oregon, Lummi, Western Shoshone, Ft. McDowell Yavapai, Ojibway, and Mashantucket Pequot of Connecticut.

2. Support for treaty rights and self determination has been a major priority in Native American work. This involved questions of land claims, fishing and hunting rights, criminal jurisdiction, and particularly issues of religious freedom.

But on one issue, Indian rights conflicted directly with Quaker values. Some Native American leaders saw gambling casinos and other gaming establishments as one way to create jobs and bring additional resources to Indians. Friends have had a long history of opposing gambling. In the end, expressing the traditional Quaker position, FCNL supported the right of Indian groups to make their own decisions, even if they might be regarded as misguided.

3. FCNL representatives, who seek to take their lead from Native Americans themselves, whenever possible, are sometimes confronted with the question of who speaks for particular tribes when strong differences in policies and personalities exist. Often there may be a cleavage between traditional, sometimes older, leaders and more modern, "progressive," sometimes younger, leaders. Sensitivity is especially required in these situations.

While work on Native American legislation may seem quite specialized, there are numerous occasions where these issues intersect with other FCNL priorities. Some examples: opposition to placing MX missile sites on Indian land; support for a comprehensive test ban to end U.S. nuclear tests on Indian land; support for a comprehensive law to provide religious freedom for all; toxic waste dumping on reservations; U.S. racism as it affects Native Americans; and the fate of Miskito and other native people in Nicaragua during the U.S.-supported contra war there.

Women in the Life of FCNL

Friends often point to the traditional Quaker belief in the equality of the sexes, but we are also learning we have a long way to go. At FCNL's organizing conference in 1943 at Richmond IN, only 16 of the 52 Friends present were women. Though many able women served on FCNL committees over the years, it wasn't until 1973, 30 years after its founding, that a woman, Marian Fuson, served in one of the two FCNL leadership posts. Since then, Lilian Watford, Carolyn Rudd, Olive Wilson, and Jeanne Herrick-Stare have served as clerks of either the General or Executive Committees. FCNL adopted gender neutral language in 1974.

Frances Neely became FCNL's first registered woman lobbyist in 1967. In nine of the last ten years, all but one of FCNL's four or five person senior legislative team have been women. Over the years, more women than men have served as legislative interns and as non-legislative staff, though FCNL's executive secretaries, to date, have been men. Legislatively, FCNL supported inclusion of protection against sexual discrimination in the 1964 Civil Rights Act and passage of the Equal Rights Amendment to the Constitution. Today, FCNL sees empowerment of women as one of the crucial factors in limiting population growth and achieving economic and social development in the Third World.

Quakers, Force, Police, Sanctions

William Penn and most Friends are not anarchists. As Wilmer Cooper notes, Penn established his "Holy Experiment" in Pennsylvania "on the proposition that government was 'a part of religion itself, a thing sacred in its institution and end.'" But Quakers who participate in government or who urge policy makers to adopt certain policies eventually confront the ultimate dilemma: Behind the President, however benign, and the Congress, however enlightened, are the laws they have made containing sanctions for violations. And standing ready to enforce the laws are police, prosecutors, judges, and jailers.

Friends acknowledge Christ's commands of love and compassion. FCNL supporters also have the audacity to recommend policies to their *non*pacifist government consistent with these commands. In doing so we must approach these difficult questions with humility, "claiming neither completeness nor infallibility in a world of cruel dilemmas and difficult choices."[15]

Friends seeking to follow the leadings of the Spirit may, at times, experience a "love-hate" relationship toward government. Many Friends strongly oppose laws requiring military service, taxes for military purposes and restrictions on religious and other freedoms. But these same Friends may also endorse and encourage government action to extend civil rights and promote the general welfare, even though their ultimate enforcement is legal coercion enforced by police, tax collectors, judges and prison wardens. One FCNL role has been to seek a humane corrections system which emphasizes rehabilitation rather than punishment. Ultimately, however, "Law can and must increasingly provide the framework of justice, but law is harsh and sterile without the spirit of love and reconciliation."[16]

In attempting to insert a "spirit of love and reconciliation," Fay "Honey" Knopp gave effective congressional testimony in 1977 and 1978, based on her years of prison work. She opposed construction of new prisons and urged additional alternatives to incarceration instead. Bernice Just testified in 1977 and 1978, urging speedy trial legislation and opposing pre-trial detention. FCNL staff and committees have opposed various proposals to make the criminal code more punitive, and have urged basic solutions such as more jobs, better education and rehabilitation services, and supportive communities.

In international relations the "cruel dilemmas" are compounded a thousand-fold.[17] With no just and enforceable world law and no impartial courts with compulsory jurisdiction, nations whose vital interests are perceived to be at stake look to their own resources. Among nations, in the final analysis, anarchy reigns. Might makes right. How to oppose South African apartheid, ethnic cleansing in Bosnia, the conquest of Tibet, human rights violations and aggression around the world?

Recognizing that a just and peaceful international order is struggling to be born, FCNL, which rules out military force as a constructive part of that process, has supported efforts:

1. to reduce reliance on military options;
2. to make the UN and related agencies more effective in rule making, conflict resolution and economic justice; and
3. to confront the question of the appropriate use of *international policing* in trouble spots and *sanctions* against violators of international standards.

For years "policing" and "sanctions" have posed two of the most difficult questions facing FCNL. The following three sections indicate how these issues and the recent subject of "humanitarian military intervention" have been dealt with by FCNL.

UN Peacekeeping

Having identified "world law," "world federalism," or "world government" at various times as desirable goals, FCNL is forced to confront the issue of enforcement and policing. Even before the UN came into being, a January 13, 1945 FCNL statement on the Dumbarton Oaks proposals noted, "Even an international police system will not be truly a police system until nations are willing to relinquish national armies."

The UN Military Staff Committee and provisions for "combined international enforcement action" in Articles 45 and 47 of the UN Charter died a-borning as the cold war began. But two events prompted FCNL to face the issue of UN Police. One was the Korean War carried on under UN auspices, primarily with U.S. troops. The second was the formation of the UN Emergency Force to deal with the aftermath of the Israeli-Egyptian war of 1956.

In May 1957 an FCNL "Statement on United Nations Police Organization" was approved. This was well received at a House Foreign Affairs subcommittee hearing in my testimony of July 1958. A decade later, Dorothy Hutchinson, representing both FCNL and the Women's International League for Peace and Freedom, presented similar views to the Senate Foreign Relations May 2, 1968 in favor of a permanent UN peacekeeping force. The principles developed over the years:

- To be truly effective a UN Police Force must operate in a disarmed world under a system of world law. Until then,
- the concept of a UN Army is rejected, "No UN Force should be given great military power or engage in war as in Korea. The purpose of the UN is to prevent wars, not fight them."
- UN Police should be lightly armed if at all; preferably individually recruited and trained for this service, with limits on the number from any one country, especially the larger powers;
- They should be an integral part of a UN effort to stabilize an area of conflict and provide an opportunity for negotiation, arbitration or conciliation to take place. Simultaneous peacemaking efforts

are essential;
- Advance agreement by nations to permit such a force on their territory would be highly desirable; and
- The force must be adequately funded.

By 1993 more than 25 UN peacekeeping operations in various forms had been established.[18] Many were in the Middle East, often an FCNL priority area. John Volkmar testified for both FCNL and AFSC in 1975, presenting an FCNL policy statement opposing the proposal to send 200 armed U.S. technicians to the Sinai and expanding military aid to Israel. Don Peretz in 1981 opposed U.S. troops in an Israeli-Egyptian peacekeeping force outside the UN framework. After Israeli forces ran over UNIFIL forces in the invasion of Lebanon in June 1982, some drew the conclusion that UN peacekeeping forces were irrelevant. A major FCNL paper in February 1984 refuted the charge–see "The Scapegoating of UNIFIL."

Sanctions: Unacceptable Coercion?

The first "unresolved issue" listed under "Challenges to the Society of Friends" in the Statement of Legislative Policy approved November 1981 was this:

> Are economic sanctions an acceptable non-violent alternative to war or an adversarial first step *toward* war?

From the beginning, FCNL has opposed sending arms and other military equipment to any nation. FCNL has also opposed various economic sanctions and boycotts against countries when the policy represented one more way to fight a hot or cold war against communism, whether in the Soviet Union, the People's Republic of China, Cuba, Vietnam, North Korea, or elsewhere. FCNL has opposed efforts to use food or humanitarian supplies as a weapon against any nation, the most recent being the U.S.

boycott against Iraq.[19]

In one of FCNL's most effective lobbying efforts, we worked in 1974 with then-Rep. Tom Harkin of Iowa, to add Section 116 to the Foreign Assistance Act. That provision cut off U.S. economic aid to countries engaged in gross human rights violations *unless the aid directly benefits needy people.* (See discussion under "Human Rights" in Chapter 5 below.)

But the most difficult cases arise when a general international consensus identifies certain nations as engaging in such unacceptable conduct that concerted action is seen as necessary in hopes of remedying a grievous situation. Four examples: the refusal of the white minority government of Rhodesia to permit the process of independence to take place; the cruel reign of Idi Amin in Uganda in the mid 1970s; the Soviet invasion of Afghanistan in December 1979; and the existence of the system of apartheid in South Africa.

Each of these issues caused considerable discussion in FCNL's Policy Committee. The FCNL did support the boycott of Rhodesian chrome which was consistent with the 1966 UN sanctions against Rhodesia. The rationale was that the general international community, acting through the UN, had approved the resolution; it was not a cold war measure. Regarding Amin's Uganda, the FCNL did not support bills proposed by some of our friends in Congress because they called for mandatory, *unilateral* embargoes on exports and imports. On the issue of the Soviet invasion of Afghanistan, the Policy Committee in early 1980 "reluctantly accepted the Administration effort to move or cancel the summer Olympic games in Moscow as a non-violent response to the situation." But by mid-spring second thoughts had arisen because that move appeared to be merely one step in escalating hostilities with the Soviet Union.

South Africa was the chief topic of the Policy Committee on a warm evening in July 1986 at William Penn House. The House of Representatives, amazingly, had recently voted overwhelmingly for Ron Dellums' bill containing strong sanctions against South Africa. Should FCNL, which shared the general outrage at the destructive apartheid system, join the swelling chorus of support? The

Committee was deeply divided. "Friends ultimate yardstick of what's right in human relations is the teachings of Jesus...Against this yardstick international sanctions would seem clearly wrong...They are designed to hurt people..." Consistency calls us to oppose these sanctions as we have those against communist nations...It's fine for universities and churches to divest from investments there, but we're talking about government action, and that's different...BUT we need to listen to Bishop Tutu; sanctions are the last political tool we have–after that comes violence.... We need to support the Christian community in South Africa.... Economic pressure on business interests can help bring about change....

No agreement was reached that evening, but a small committee was formed to identify some creative ways FCNL could play a role in ending apartheid without joining the sanctions struggle. That was done. And in the ensuing several years Nancy Alexander and others worked to:

- support negotiations between the South African government and the African National Congress;
- help the frontline states–the nine black-ruled states surrounding South Africa–to gain economic and political independence from South Africa;
- end South Africa's illegal occupation of Namibia; and
- end U.S. covert funding of UNITA rebels attempting to overthrow the government of Angola.

A guarded sanctions statement became a part of the overall statement approved in November 1987. Since then, events in Iraq, China, and the former Yugoslavian area have demonstrated that the sanctions issue may become even more important in the post-cold war era. Here is the language approved November 1993 as part of the overall FCNL Statement of Legislative Policy:

Sanctions, whether economic, cultural, or political, are a problematic means of furthering negotiations and changing behavior. Yet sometimes sanctions may be the least offensive means available for ending injustice or aggression. Each proposed sanction must be carefully considered, and if used at all, must be focused to minimize damage to innocent people. Sanctions should be used only when there is a broad multilateral consensus. To the extent possible, there should be assurance that the basic needs of the people in the sanctioned nation will be met; that diplomatic and private channels are held open for further dialogue; that the objectives are clear and consistent with international law; and that the sanctions are proportional to their objective and likely to work.

"Humanitarian Military Intervention"

Instead of diminishing, pacifist dilemmas have escalated with the end of the cold war. What can or should be done regarding the tragedy following the breakup of Yugoslavia? Joe Volk describes, in his chapter, the heart-searching dilemma of the proper course of action in Somalia. Anarchy is spreading in parts of Africa and elsewhere. If bands of outlaws prevent UN and voluntary organization aid workers from reaching starving people, and lightly armed UN peacekeepers are ineffectual, why not use benignly motivated military units from the United States or elsewhere? Don't we believe in law and order?

These are the emerging issues with which FCNL must wrestle in the coming decades. Solutions must depend on the facts of each case and growing insights. The February 1993 *FCNL Washington Newsletter* article "Can Military Force Create Peaceful Solutions?" concluded with these words:

> As a society, we must reject violent force as an option, in order to release the energy and creativity we need to invent and implement realistic nonviolent alternatives.

FCNL's General Committee at the November 1993 annual meeting laid down general guidelines which will require much sensitive and creative application in the future:

> We believe that the lessons of Korea, Vietnam, Lebanon, Panama, Somalia, and other armed interventions serve as warnings against reliance on military force. In contrast, the birth of India, Scandinavian resistance to Nazism, and the civil rights movement in this country provide important lessons about the strength of nonviolent movements. These lessons need to be carefully studied and widely publicized. We also must be cautious about the harm which may accompany nonviolent actions.
>
> The United States, with its resources and expertise, is increasingly called to assist in humanitarian and emergency response efforts outside its boundaries. The military is not the appropriate mechanism for such assistance. The United States should develop and support nonmilitary assistance programs in partnership with appropriate international and nongovernmental organizations.

* * * * * *

FCNL, Friends, and pacifists in general have much homework to do. The first step is already well underway–to build an international consensus to stop the transfer of deadly arms throughout the world, which greatly exacerbates existing problems. Other steps are even more difficult but no less essential:

- to encourage military establishments to develop nonviolent methods to carry out international peacekeeping missions,

- to expand the effectiveness of UN peacekeeping operations,

- to find new and creative ways to channel efforts of nongovernmental organizations into international peacemaking and peacekeeping,

- to encourage and support nonviolent resistance to repressive governments and policies, and

- to apply internationally supported sanctions which focus directly on repressive elites who violate human rights, and enforce them effectively.

Notes

1. *Uphill for Peace,* pp. 53-55.
2. Many other Friends testified for other organizations, for example, Byron Haworth for Five Years Meeting, William Martin for Young Friends Committee of North America, Chester Graham for the Fellowship of Reconciliation, and Raoul Kulberg for Washington Friends Joint Peace Committee.
3. See FCNL Executive Committee minutes, June 15, 1951.
4. *Supra,* Chapter 2, note 5.
5. David's letter of May 2, 1992 describing his concern to the House Ways and Means Subcommittee is printed in the Hearing record at pp. 205-206. See next note for full citation.
6. Hearing, Subcommittee on Select Revenue Measures of the House Ways and Means Committee, May 21, 1992, on three bills, including H.R. 1870. Serial 102-98, pp.172-178.
7. See especially 1990 FCNL Annual Report, pp. 31-32 and 1993 FCNL Annual Report pp. 53-54.
8. See 1993 FCNL Annual Report, pp.54-55.
9. See *Uphill for Peace,* pp. 112-115.
10. Ibid. pp.140-142.
11. See also Charles E. Fager, *A Man Who Made a Difference: The Life of David H. Scull,* Langley Hill Friends Meeting (1985) and *Uphill for Peace,* pp. 147-148.

12. See also Raymond Wilson's account in *Uphill for Peace*, pp. 142-145.

13. *Uphill for Peace*, p. 150.

14. Ibid. pp. 128-140.

15. FCNL Statement of Legislative Policy, approved Feb. 1972, p.3.

16. FCNL Statement of Legislative Policy, Jan. 1967, under "Advancing Civil Rights," p. 7.

17. See Richard W. Taylor, "Friendly Persuasion and Power: Some Dilemmas of Pacifist Lobbying in Washington, D.C.," 10-page paper prepared for a conference on Current Trends in Peace Research, Wayne State University, October 18, 1985.

18. See Wolf Mendl, "United Nations Peacekeeping Operations and the Quaker Peace Testimony," p. 4, December 1993.

19. See, for example, *FCNL Washington Newsletter*, July 1980, "Economic Warfare and People..."; 1992 FCNL Annual Report,, pp. 20-21 regarding Iraq sanctions.

5. Has FCNL Put Too Much Faith in the United Nations and Other International Organizations to Achieve Peace?

Perhaps. But these institutions have been the only available alternative to war and anarchy. Nation-states have not been willing to relinquish enough sovereignty to bring an effective international organization into being. FCNL has recognized the UN's shortcomings and sought to strengthen the UN and related international organizations through adequate funding, universal membership, expanded jurisdiction in the fields of human rights, the law of the seas, peacekeeping and peacemaking.

From the beginning, FCNL saw the existing UN as inadequate to the tasks before it. In January 1945, FCNL issued a statement on the Dumbarton Oaks Proposals recommending changes. The April 2, 1945 *FCNL Washington Newsletter* carried 14 proposed amendments to the Charter which was about to be considered at the San Francisco conference.

> The parties to any dispute, the continuance of which is likely to endanger the maintenance of international peace and security, shall, first of all, seek a solution by negotiation, enquiry, mediation, conciliation, arbitration, judicial settlement, resort to regional agencies or arrangements, or other peaceful means of their own choice.
>
> *UN Charter, Chapter VI, Article 33, section 1.*

"Federal World Government"

FCNL's goal was "Federal World Government," as stated in the 1947 Statement of Legislative Policy. The 1948 Statement urged full U.S. support for the UN, but recognized "that it is not adequate, as now constituted, to build or maintain peace. We believe that the United Nations should be developed toward a genuine federal world government of limited powers, acting under law enforceable on individuals." Samuel Levering, who was also a very active member of the United World Federalists, testified for FCNL on May 12, 1948 at hearings on the structure of the UN before the House Foreign Affairs Committee. He called for fundamental changes in the Charter: to give it real authority to control armaments; to make laws enforceable upon individuals; and to provide dependable revenues. His message to a Senate Foreign Relations Subcommittee in 1950 in support of the "World Federation Resolution" and in 1955 in hearings reviewing the UN Charter was similar.

The temper of that time was different! The *FCNL Washington Newsletter* #64, June 13, 1949, reported that on June 7, 91 Representatives from 34 states joined in cosponsoring resolutions stating "that it should be a fundamental objective of the foreign policy of the United States to support and strengthen the United Nations and to seek its development into a world federation, open to all nations, with defined and limited powers adequate to preserve peace and prevent aggression through enactment and interpretation and enforcement of world law."

An effective World Court is also essential in a world of law, as Esther Holmes Jones testified on July 12, 1946 before the Senate Foreign Relations Committee, chaired by Senator Tom Connally of Texas. She urged the United States to accept the compulsory jurisdiction of the International Court of Justice. When the resolution reached the Senate floor, Senator Connally led a successful effort to amend the resolution so that the United States could decide for itself which cases it would allow the Court to hear against it. Nine years later on January 27, 1960, FCNL witness Harold Evans urged the same committee to repeal the "Connally Reservation." U.S. participation in the Court was further restricted in the 1984 to 1986 period. The U.S., reacting to Nicaragua's suit protesting U.S. mining of its harbors, destruction of oil installations, and arming of contras, withdrew from the jurisdiction of the World Court.[1] The U.S. "self-judging" reservation remains in effect today. Its repeal would still be a major step toward a more effective international order.

The First 30 Years

FCNL's 1972 Legislative Statement of Policy looked back in sorrow:

> The United Nations has brought no basic change in the international war system. As presently operating, it is unlikely to do so. But to place blame on the United Nations is unjust and inaccurate. The real problem lies with the world's peoples and nations.
>
> The world's peoples in 1945 lacked an adequate recognized sense of a world community of common interests, and also lacked adequate knowledge of the requirements for world peace. Reflecting this, national governments of powerful nations refused to give the United Nations any real authority, or to relinquish any significant aspects of national sovereignty to the United Nations, or to give the United Nations an effective structure.
>
> Many nation-states, especially large ones, have violated the spirit or the letter of the United Nations Charter, and have failed to support and use the United Nations. Flagrant examples are the United States in Indochina, Britain and France at Suez, and the Soviet Union in Czechoslovakia. Failure of nations to use UN facilities and good offices or to give adequate financial support have been equally damaging.

In 1964, as a member of the Quaker UN Team, I commuted weekly by train between Washington and the UN in New York. I was frequently overcome by the sense that I was shuttling between the past and the future: Washington, the resistant status quo, self-absorbed in power, fear, and protection of territory and acquired wealth; the United Nations, carrying the hopes of present and future generations, optimistic, with a global perspective. President Lyndon B. Johnson, pleading for public support as the Vietnam war escalated, reminded the citizenry: "I'm the only president you've got." I felt that way about the UN. With all its shortcomings it was, and is, the world's best hope for peace and justice.

As a public interest lobby in Washington, the capital of the UN's most powerful member, FCNL has been in a place to help to make that vision a reality. Indeed, the FCNL in terms of longevity and constancy of support has, over the UN's first half century, been one of–if not the–prime advocates for the UN in the nongovernmental community in Washington.

During FCNL's first 30 years major priority was given: to work for adequate UN funding, to support the seating of the People's Republic of China at a time when this was an extremely controversial issue in the U.S., and to support human rights conventions. FCNL's support of the Law of the Seas Treaty and the work of Sam and Miriam Levering was a major thrust. The treaty is a major extension of international law with worldwide application. It enhances the UN's relevance and credibility and makes progress on two long term FCNL goals–dependable revenues and dispute resolution mechanisms.

> **We hope and believe that the oceans, at least the deep seabeds, offer the next great opportunity for extending the area of peace--through law, through just treaties and effective international organization.** *Sam Levering in testimony to the House Oceanography Subcommittee, May 25, 1972.*

The Next 20 Years Were Harder

Hindsight shows the first 30 years were the easy ones. As more and more former colonies became independent, the Afro-Asian bloc developed a working majority in the General Assembly. The United States, which formerly could use the UN for its own foreign policy objectives, found itself outvoted on key issues in the General Assembly. Yet it was still paying about 30% of all UN costs. Furthermore, the new third world majority sided with the Arab states against Israel, a major U.S. client state.

1975 was a crucial turning point. Several UN bodies granted observer status to the Palestine Liberation Organization, and Israel was excluded from a UNESCO grouping. A move to expel Israel from the UN was expected in the fall. Congressional committees responded by deleting funds for UNESCO and the International Labor Organization. The Senate resolved to review all aid to states voting for such expulsion and to examine whether the U.S. should remain in the UN. FCNL's Policy Committee met in the midst of this furor and approved a statement which said in part:

> For Israel to be denied effective participation in the United Nations would be contrary to this spirit [of magnanimity and empathy] and the necessity for international cooperation. Yet, if it occurred, we would still oppose any effort to have the United States withdraw its presence or financial support from the United Nations.[2]

In October a General Assembly committee adopted a resolution equating Zionism with racism and racial discrimination. In ensuing years FCNL's efforts to assure adequate funding for UN programs were much more difficult. The United States fell far in arrears in its UN dues. The task was further complicated by the loss of support from major segments of the U.S. Jewish community, which had been among the UN's most active and effective proponents since the

UN's founding. Fortunately, the personal friendships with Jewish colleagues on civil rights, civil liberties, peace and justice issues were invaluable as we discussed UN and Mid-East issues.

From 1980 to 1983 Frances Neely chaired the Council of Washington Representatives on the United Nations. She and Robert Cory played important roles in that group for years. In 1986 and following years, FCNL lobbyist Nancy Alexander organized a crucial set of conferences on Capitol Hill to support the UN. She convened a new coalition called the "UN Education and Advocacy Group" which played a key role in changing congressional perceptions and attitudes in the late 1980s. During this period the United Nations Association identified FCNL as the most active advocate for the UN in Washington. By the end of the decade as the cold war ended, more people on Capitol Hill and in the executive branch recognized the UN's importance. Undoubtedly the forums which Nancy Alexander took the lead in sponsoring on Capitol Hill, attended by up to 350 people, helped to create a better climate for the UN.[3] FCNL had been there through the dark times.

The Middle East–A Continuing Concern

Israel was created by the United Nations, and both the UN and the U.S. have focused attention on that region during FCNL's first 50 years. FCNL's priority work on the Middle East has included:

- opposition to the Eisenhower Doctrine in 1957. Paul Johnson before the House Foreign Affairs Committee and Elmore Jackson before the Senate Foreign Relations Committee gave effective testimony. The *Washington Star* report of the House hearing said: "The most detailed analysis of the Middle East situation and criticism of the resolution were presented late in the afternoon by Paul B. Johnson, speaking for the Society of Friends Committee on National Legislation."
- consistent opposition to the huge international arms shipments to the region;

- support for adequate funding for Palestine refugees, for UN resolutions and negotiations, and peacekeeping programs;
- support for Landrum Bolling's work as Friend-in-Washington in 1969 as he interviewed officials and prepared for the AFSC's working party that produced "Search for Peace in the Middle East;"and
- opposition to U.S. military action in the area–in Lebanon, Iran, Iraq.

Both Frances Neely and Nancy Alexander gave impressive leadership in organizing "Middle East Forums" during the 1980s. International and national speakers in and out of government from across the political spectrum helped the many participants to understand the underlying causes of conflict in the region.

Nancy Nye gave an immediacy and credibility to FCNL's Mid-East priority when she joined the staff in 1992. As former head of the Ramallah Girls School and wife of a Palestinian human rights activist, Nancy's quiet, persuasive manner won additional respect on the Hill for FCNL.

Human Rights

Surprisingly, most of what we now think of as international human rights law has emerged since 1945. [4] In the early postwar years the subject was a peripheral factor in foreign policy considerations, a matter for Eleanor Roosevelt and like-minded "do-gooders" to talk about. It was not something those dealing with national security matters took very seriously. Military and hard-nosed political and economic factors were what counted.

"Human rights" entered the mainstream thinking of the foreign policy establishment only gradually. The Universal Declaration on Human Rights was proclaimed in 1948 (and endorsed in FCNL's January 1949 Policy Statement,) but it had no binding force. The Genocide Convention was adopted in 1948; U.S. presidents sought Senate approval beginning the next year, but not until 1986 did the

Senate approve it, and even then with crippling reservations. Many people have viewed the Genocide Convention as a symbolic and rhetorical gesture. In 1970, FCNL tried to give "genocide" a meaning beyond the holocaust of the past. Our analysis suggested that it also applied to the launching of a nuclear attack. That interpretation never gained wide currency, but our statement setting forth this view is a part of the hearing record of the Senate Foreign Relations Committee. Further, the Treaty's conspiracy provisions would seem to apply to the preparation to wage nuclear war, which the United States and the USSR were clearly doing.

The human rights and other provisions of the Final Act of the Conference on Security and Cooperation in Europe, Helsinki, 1975, have been of great importance in ending the Cold War.

Two very important Covenants implementing the Human Rights Declaration were adopted in 1966–one on "Civil and Political Rights," the other on "Economic, Social and Cultural Rights." The United States and many western countries emphasized the former; the USSR and many socialist states emphasized the latter. I believe the UN's wholistic approach to human rights is immensely helpful in understanding this issue and making it relevant worldwide. My statement to the Senate Foreign Relations Committee, December 19, 1979, argued for speedy Senate approval of both these treaties, plus the American Convention on Human Rights and the Convention to Eliminate Racial Discrimination. In 1992, the "Covenant on Civil and Political Rights" was approved, but the "Covenant on Economic, Social, and Cultural Rights" and a number of other international human rights treaties and conventions are still awaiting Senate action.

In the mid-1970s the human rights movement suddenly gathered momentum. Representative Don Fraser, aided by his human rights staff member, John Salzberg, drafted and secured passage of legislation preventing U.S. *military* aid to governments which engage in gross violations of internationally recognized human rights. FCNL took the lead with Joe Eldridge of the Washington Office on Latin America and then-Rep. Tom Harkin of Iowa in restricting *economic* aid to governments engaged in gross violations of internationally recognized human rights–unless the aid would directly benefit needy people. Similar amendments were added to U.S. food aid legislation and to U.S. contributions to various international lending institutions.[5] Congress drastically restricted U.S. aid to Chile and Uruguay, and cuts were threatened for South Korea, Indonesia, and the Philippines.[6]

What put human rights on the map for policy makers? The Indochina anti-war movement, well organized and recently victorious, took up the cause.[7] Activists were worried that the United States would again be drawn into foreign quagmires through aid to repressive regimes. The "Human Rights Working Group" of the Coalition for a New Foreign and Military Policy, became the focus of action for nearly 50 national organizations. From the mid-1970s through most of the 1980s, this was the coordinating group for most of the legislative action undertaken by nongovernmental human rights organizations. FCNL played a key role in the Coalition and the Working Group. I was co-chair of the Coalition for a New Foreign and Military Policy from 1975-81 and 1985-87. Alison Oldham and FCNL interns played important roles in the Human Rights Working Group and the Central America Working Group. Another indication of the relevance of the anti-war movement to the human rights movement: key Congressional leadership on human rights came from anti-war members: Fraser and Harkin in the House; McGovern, Kennedy and Abourezk in the Senate.

The major player on human rights in the 1970's was, of course, Jimmy Carter. His decision to make human rights one of his major priorities echoed around the world. And still does. After Carter's nomination, I helped organize and lead a delegation to Atlanta on October 2, 1976, to talk with his deputy director of issues about human rights and foreign policy. A detailed six page analysis and series of proposals formed the basis of our discussion. The delegation represented people with various roles in the National Council of Churches, Church Women United, Jesuit Social Ministries, United Methodist Church, Church of the Brethren, Clergy and Laity Concerned, and FCNL. We also submitted our recommendations to President Ford's representative, the Director of the Office of Humanitarian Affairs in the State Department and his aides on October 17. The first two years of the Carter presidency were very active years for FCNL and for progress on human rights.

The issue has domestic aspects, too. In 1989 and 1990, FCNL worked for rights of Americans with disabilities. Ruth Flower played a key role in reminding church groups they should not seek exemptions from the bill's requirements because of the church-state issue.

We rejoice when human rights criteria are applied to restrict shipment of military and non-essential economic aid to repressive regimes. But the question is not as easy if human rights criteria are used to slow down negotiations for arms reductions, or to inhibit trade in peaceful goods, or to restrict human contacts. The "sanctions" discussion in Chapter 4 indicates this can be a difficult question. In the March 1982 *FCNL Washington Newsletter,* concerning relations with the Soviet Union, the crucial question was raised: "To Link or Not to Link?" There the avoidance of nuclear war was felt to have a higher priority than human rights. What about serious human rights violations by China and others? There are no easy answers.

FCNL began its first 50 years calling for fundamental reforms in the UN's structure to move in the direction of world federal government. Time and experience have taught many lessons. At the end of FCNL's first 50 years that vision has faded. Now the task is to support all organic growth in positive directions. The relevant section of the Statement of Legislative Policy principles approved in November 1993 states:

> World peace depends on increasing cooperative ties among nations and peoples, forged within a global framework of law, justice, and orderly social change. International cooperation requires greatly strengthened world and regional institutions, with fuller representation of all relevant parties. The security of all will be enhanced only as states and parties accept the decisions reached cooperatively.

At FCNL we live in hope. At times there seems little else. One of the sustaining thoughts that I have often shared with others, especially in those dark times when a nuclear catastrophe seemed a real possibility, comes from Eric Fromm:

> To hope means to be ready at every moment for that which is not yet born, and yet not become desperate if there is no birth in our lifetime. There is no sense in hoping for that which already exists or for that which cannot be. Those whose hope is weak settle down for comfort or for violence; those whose hope is strong see and cherish all signs of new life and are ready every moment to help the birth of that which is ready to be born.
> *The Revolution of Hope,* p. 9, Bantam Books (1968.)

Notes

1. See FCNL Doc. G-931, July 27, 1989.
2. See Aug. Sept. 1975 *FCNL Washington Newsletter* for full statement and brief background.
3. See 1986 FCNL Annual Report, p. 20-21; 1987 FCNL Annual Report, pp. 15-16.
4. R. B. Bilder, "The Status of International Human Rights Law: An Overview," p. 1, in *International Human Rights Law and Practice,* J.C. Tuttle, ed., American Bar Association, March 1978.
5. For a description of this period and FCNL's role, see Lars Schoultz, *Human Rights and United States Policy toward Latin America,* pp. 80-82, 195-198, Princeton University Press (1981).
6. See *FCNL Washington Newsletter* Dec. 1976; 1976 FCNL Annual Report, pp.4-5.
7. See Schoultz, *op. cit.*, p. 75. See also my paper for the Conference on the Military Budget, May 20, 1974, "Military Aid: More Vietnams?"

6. Has FCNL Had the Right Approach to Helping People in the Developing World Help Themselves?

We are learning. We are clear that more arms and military training don't help; and that respect for human rights does. We have accepted the goal of economic and social development as desirable, though difficult to define. From the beginning we have supported aid based on sound motivation, primarily through international or nongovernmental channels, on terms which avoid massive debt. We now give very high priority to participatory and sustainable development programs. Equitable trade policies are also essential for sound development.

NO to Military Aid, Training, and Sales

FCNL has yet to win a significant battle to reduce military aid. The national security establishment, the U.S. arms industry, and the lobbyists for foreign countries and their U.S. supporters are powerful. But that has not stopped FCNL from marshaling the

> We have to meet these frustrations. It is not pleasant, but I like your tone, I like your heart, I like your sympathy, I like your sincerity, and I compliment you for coming. I think we need people like you to shake us up every once in a while....You are a breath of fresh air.
>
> Senator John Pastore (RI) to FCNL lobbyist Frances Neely at the conclusion of a spirited exchange between two senators and Frances concerning the foreign aid program before a Senate Appropriations Subcommittee, September 24, 1968.

various cogent arguments against military aid, training, and sales.

FCNL's 1957-1958 Statement of Legislative Policy noted:

> Foreign military assistance programs should be discontinued. These programs conflict with such fundamental United States policies as opposition to colonialism and to totalitarian forms of government and hamper constructive economic and technical assistance given by the government and by private organizations.

Official support for FCNL's questions about foreign military aid came in the report and studies of the 1957 Special Senate Committee to Study the Foreign Aid Program. FCNL staff reviewed the Committee's work and quoted its findings under five headings:

1. Military assistance as aiding totalitarianism;
2. Military assistance as slowing down economic development,
3. Possibility of diverting military aid to uses other than contemplated;
4. Adverse psychological impact of military aid; and
5. Military aid as benefiting the ruling class as against the people.

FCNL's summary was appended to three of the testimonies given to congressional committees that year. Senator Wayne Morse of Oregon quoted and discussed the excerpts during debate on the Senate floor on the foreign aid program.

FCNL's opposition was not new. Ten years earlier, Henry Cadbury, as chairman of the American Friends Service Committee, had testified against U.S. aid to Greece and Turkey as the cold war heated up. That same year, 1947, Ernest Galarza testified for FCNL against military aid to Latin American countries.

At FCNL's annual meeting in January 1978, my heart sank as I listened to the discussion of FCNL legislative priorities for the coming year. The priority list was already much too long for our small staff to handle adequately. But one Friend had arisen in the final session, after agreement seemed to have been reached, to reiterate his insistence that we should do more to oppose arms to the Middle East. And there was considerable support for his plea. I was thinking of our various efforts within the preceding two years—all overwhelmingly unsuccessful: to stop $6 billion in arms sales to the Mideast, proposed in September 1976 by President Ford; to end one of the Pentagon's favorites, the International Military Education and Training program, IMET, which trains future military leaders in the developing nations; to cut military aid to South Korea, Iran, Indonesia, or the Philippines.

Less than four weeks later, President Carter proposed a $4.8 billion package of arms sales to Israel, Egypt, and Saudi Arabia. The inclusion of aid to Israel with aid to Arab states made it possible to frame the issue as one of opposition to arms sales in general, rather than opposing aid to one particular nation. I marveled once more at the relevance of FCNL's decision making process which flows from Friends' concerns.

Before the May deadline for Congressional rejection of the package sale, my intern, Catherine Shaw, and I drafted a 12-page legislative memorandum entitled "Symbols of Friendship Which Kill." We arranged for John Sullivan of the AFSC to testify against the sales before the Senate Foreign Relations Committee, and sent out action calls around the country via the May *FCNL Washington Newsletter*. We drafted a letter signed by 14 representatives of religious organizations which was taken to the offices of almost all senators and a number of representatives. Appreciation was expressed several times for FCNL's approach, which emphasized the danger to peace in the region rather than a partisan perspective. Regrettably, the sales were approved 54-44, thereby permitting them to go ahead without a House vote. Our apprehension about the consequences of massive arms transfers to the volatile Middle East has come true–in the carnage in Lebanon in the early 1980s and the Iran-Iraq and Persian Gulf wars. Yet arms transfers to Israel and Egypt continue to dominate the entire foreign aid program, ironically to compensate them for entering into the 1979 Camp David agreement.

FCNL's 1985 analysis, "U.S.-Soviet Conflicts in the Developing World: The Search for Ground Rules," discussed U.S. and Soviet arms transfers to the Third World and the 1978 Conventional Arms Transfer (CAT) talks between the U.S. and the USSR in Mexico City. The talks broke down when the U.S. delegation wanted to talk about Soviet arms shipments to Latin America, but refused to listen to Soviet concerns about U.S. arms transfers to states on Soviet borders![1]

As FCNL's first half century ends, a major new effort is underway to reduce arms transfers. Joe Volk is chair of the Arms Transfer Working Group representing some 40 arms control, religious, peace, development, human rights, women's, scientific and international organizations. This group has fashioned a "Code of Conduct on Arms Sales" which opposes arms sales or gifts to any government that:

1. Abuses the human rights of its people;
2. Denies its people democratic rights, including the right to choose their government via free and fair elections;
3. Attacks its neighbor or wages war against its own people; and
4. Undermines international efforts to control arms.

Congressional leadership is being taken by Senator Mark Hatfield of Oregon, who has given leadership on many other FCNL priorities as well–against the Vietnam war, against the draft, and for the peace tax fund and human rights. In the House, Representative Cynthia McKinney of Georgia is the lead sponsor.

Opposing the massive international arms trade is an uphill battle, but the rewards can be enormous: lessened violence, resources used for constructive purposes, and major reductions in casualties in local, ethnic, religious, and national strife. But major public education is essential. The task is at least as daunting as the decades-long struggle against nuclear weapons testing and production.

YES to Economic and Social Development

The task of achieving worldwide economic and social development is proving to be nearly as intractable as abolishing the institution of war. But this has been a major FCNL priority for two basic reasons: First, there is a moral imperative to meet human needs, to prevent poverty, hunger, ignorance, and disease, and to promote a decent life for all God's children. Second, it is impossible to have a peaceful world with nonviolent social and political change while a huge and growing gap exists between the haves and the have-nots.

More FCNL witnesses have testified before Congressional committees on this subject than on any other. One reason: there have been more opportunities to testify. Foreign aid programs, being unpopular with many members of Congress, are usually subject to annual renewal. This requires at least four hearings–before both the authorizing and the appropriating committees in the House and the Senate. And there are often additional hearings for separate international banking and food for peace bills. Usually the "foreign aid" bill contains both military and nonmilitary aid, despite the earnest efforts of groups like FCNL to separate them. This creates much soul-searching at FCNL when the question is whether we should support or oppose the bill on final passage, a bill which authorizes huge military transfers as well as funds for UNICEF and other worthy UN and U.S. development programs.

Postwar Years and Point IV

While the second world war raged, FCNL supported legislation for food for starving people in occupied Europe. In the immediate post war years, FCNL urged food for the defeated German people, and the use of U.S. grain for relief and not for liquor. A major effort in 1947, which was repeated in 1956, increased shipments of relief supplies through voluntary agencies by providing government payment of ocean freight.[2]

The concept of "economic development" received its major impetus in President Harry Truman's Inaugural Address of January 20, 1949. In "Point Four" the President called for "a bold new program for making the benefits of our scientific advances and industrial progress available for the improvement and growth of underdeveloped areas." Legislation specifying details was submitted to Congress June 24.

In January 1950, Delbert Replogle, New Jersey businessman and later Chairman of FCNL's General Committee from 1955 to 1958, testified for FCNL before the House Foreign Affairs Committee. He had recently returned from six months service as the first field director for the AFSC under the auspices of the UN Relief for Palestine Refugees program in the Gaza area. Delbert's testimony gives the flavor of the times:

> My first acquaintance with Point IV was in Cairo, after returning from a visit among these [Palestinian] people who had lost everything and whose very life depended upon the little relief which came in through the United Nations. They were destitute, without clothing, without adequate housing and without means of employment....
>
> There seemed to be no hope of getting them back in their homes and because of the political entanglements, no hope for getting them into any place they might call a home. George McGhee [U.S. State Department official] came out and met some of us in Cairo and explained to us for the first time the big, bold, new program which had been suggested by President Truman a little earlier in his inaugural address. It was the first ray of hope we had....
>
> When we heard of Point IV, therefore, you can imagine what it meant to us. Our country, of which we were mighty proud (I can tell you–you feel that way when you get away from it) was taking the lead in proposing to

the world an investment in humanity that was far reaching, farsighted, and that would implement some of the heritage that Americans have always had for the dignity of the human being. This could also break the circle of fear which has caused us to be so worried about containment, and could make a climate in which the isms that are so antagonistic to us, would not grow.

It was a bold, new program and we began to look around immediately to determine how, in that area, it could be implemented.[3]

Some Constant FCNL Themes

Across the years, FCNL lobbyists, FCNL witnesses at congressional hearings, and FCNL *Newsletter* articles have consistently stressed certain themes:

1. Channel most U.S. aid through UN and other international programs. "There is deep suspicion now in the world that Americans are primarily interested in using their power for the purpose of buying the support of allies," Clarence Pickett told the Senate Foreign Relations Committee on April 3, 1950, in commenting on the Point IV program.

FCNL's 1967 Statement of Legislative Policy summarized the issue as follows: "UN programs are less likely to be suspected of seeking to control or dominate the policies of the recipient countries. UN recommendations for reform in the recipient countries can often be accepted with less embarrassment than similar suggestions from any national government. The UN can also draw upon a wider range of personnel and technical experience. Moreover, personnel from other less highly mechanized countries may well be able to make more practical suggestions for the solution of some kinds of problems."

2. Focus first of all on basic human needs–especially food and hunger. Not surprisingly, the two FCNL lobbyists who were farmers–Raymond Wilson and Don Reeves–used their expertise and concern to concentrate on food, hunger, U.S. surpluses, and rural development at home and abroad. Raymond's story is told in Chapter 5, "The Battle to Feed the Hungry," in *Uphill for Peace*. Don's is still being written, but part of it can be found in FCNL Annual Reports for the four years he was on FCNL's staff, 1977 through 1980. More recent chapters involve his role as Clerk of FCNL's General Committee and his work in our colleague organization, Bread for the World.

3. Stress the importance of sound motivation for aid workers. "A willingness to live simply and with a reasonable degree of humility is of extraordinary importance," Clarence Pickett told the Senate Foreign Relations Committee regarding Point IV.

The U.S. Peace Corps is an example of a program which taps into the idealism, goodwill, and readiness to sacrifice which is well received by people in developing countries. When I walked with Representative Walter Judd to the committee meeting where he would consider Rep. Henry Reuss' proposal for a Point Four Youth Corps (the forerunner of the Peace Corps), he told me he had just received a letter from a friend in Korea working in a U.S. aid program. The friend told him of the "golden ghettos" in which U.S. aid workers lived, isolated from the people they were supposed to be helping. Needless to say, he was receptive to my plea that he support the Reuss proposal. FCNL witness Ruth Replogle, speaking also for the Board on Peace and Social Concerns of the Five Years Meeting, was the first nongovernmental representative to endorse the peace corps idea in Congress in her testimony of March 14, 1960:[4]

> We hope this committee will amend the mutual security bill to include Representative Henry Reuss' proposal to study the establishment of a point 4 youth corps.... The field of world economic development offers a great new frontier in our generation. It calls young people to adventure and to serve their fellow men around the world. It provides a constructive outlet for young people's energy, enthusiasm, and idealism....It would give them a sense of purpose and challenge them to sacrificial service, as William James puts it, 'the moral equivalent of

war,' and would surely help to build a firm foundation for world peace.

4. Stress the need for adequate capital as well as technical assistance in the development process. Again, Clarence Pickett in his 1950 testimony, noted that in addition to technically competent personnel contemplated by the Point IV proposal, experience had demonstrated to the AFSC that "it has been necessary for at least a modest amount of outside capital to be brought in to stimulate local investment." Whether the maze of agencies which have sprung up to dispense capital is what Clarence Pickett had in mind is doubtful. But the "alphabet soup" list of such agencies–many of which have been supported by FCNL witnesses–is impressive: DLF, IDA, IDB, ADB, IFAD, UNDP, among others.

In 1958, Elton Atwater, on leave from Pennsylvania State University at the Quaker UN Program, and I worked successfully to prevent the U.S. contribution to UN technical assistance programs from being reduced from 40% to 33 1/3%. Our second effort, to expand the base on which the U.S. percentage was computed, failed in 1958, but passed the next year. That amendment included "assessed and audited local costs" in the figure on which the U.S. contribution was based; it increased the U.S. contribution by more than one million dollars a year.

From 1967 through the 1970s, FCNL Policy Statements called for the United States to contribute 2% of its gross national product to transnational economic aid. This would have been a substantial increase since in 1972 all U.S. economic aid was less than one-half of one percent. This did not happen, in fact the trend has been toward even less U.S. true economic assistance.

Instead, an economic monster has been let loose in the world. Most aid has been transferred in the form of loans rather than grants–a policy FCNL has long questioned, fearing that the debt burden for developing countries would become too great. That, indeed, proved to be one of the major development problems in the 1980s. In 1988, FCNL lobbyist Nancy Alexander reported that $1.3 *trillion* in debt had been piled up by Third World countries, requiring massive annual payments of interest and principal which greatly exceed their aid receipts. "Currently, there is a 'trickle up program,' or *a net transfer of some $30 billion from poor to rich countries.* U.S. and international lending agencies were not inclined to forgive such debt, as FCNL and others recommended and as hundreds of activists from the Third World demanded at the 1989 meetings of the World Bank and International Monetary Fund. But a 1989 effort to have the U.S. forgive debts of the poorest countries, primarily in sub-Saharan Africa, was successful.[5]

In order to obtain necessary capital, the banks generally require the developing country applicant to adopt certain "structural adjustments," which are stringent economic measures tending to fall most heavily on the poor. Nancy Alexander argued that, "The U.S. must address the ethical implications of its practice of working to impose economic austerity programs in developing countries while being unwilling to practice such discipline at home." As one way to counter the emphasis on structural adjustment, Nancy Alexander worked with John Mitchell, head of the World Development Movement in London, to develop the "poverty effort" proposal. This proposal revises the formula which the World Bank and the International Development Association use to allocate aid. Formerly, the formula rewarded countries primarily based upon the extent to which they implemented economic reforms leading to a liberalized, free market economy. The "poverty effort" proposal took a different approach. It sought to ensure that countries which demonstrate effort or commitment to eradicate poverty should receive higher levels of aid. In a major achievement, the proposal was adopted in 1989.[6]

Increasing Insight

The goal of "economic and social development" is relatively new in human experience. We are still very much in the learning stages and constantly gaining new insights.

Population growth was identified as a concern fairly early. Better food, medicine, and health care caused, and still cause, explosive growth. The 1970 statement on "Encouraging International Development" stated provocatively:

> All public and private efforts to institute sound programs of family planning and population control should be supported. But it should be recognized that there is often only a limited role that 'outsiders' can play without generating adverse reactions. As a part of our individual responsibility to stop population growth, we should limit the size of our own families to two children, adopting others if a larger family is desired.

The 1993 Policy Statement carried a dire warning:

> Recognizing our responsibilities to our earth and its inhabitants, we are concerned that one source of environmental pressure is the rapid growth of population and consumerism. At current growth rates, the human population on our already crowded earth will double to around eleven billion in two generations. Globally, population growth spreads and deepens human suffering. It increases deforestation and desertification, spreading starvation, homelessness, and disease. High rates of consumption and pollution in our own country magnify this problem and result in huge inequities in the distribution of the world's resources.

To meet this overwhelming challenge, the Statement set forth this principle:

> Women and children carry an undue share of the burdens imposed by population growth. Increased respect for and attention to the human rights of women and children–including education and economic security–are crucial to relieving the threat posed by excessive population growth. Although our approach to the problem of

providing every human being with enough resources to support a secure, healthy, and fulfilling life must be multifaceted, the availability of family planning must be part of the solution. We endorse education, services, and the availability of family planning.

"**Rural development**" has been seen by FCNL as one relevant way to deal with world–and U.S.–development issues. Its importance is suggested by the massive migration from rural to urban areas worldwide and the huge social problems created by slum areas in the world's major cities. Its difficulty is suggested by the post World War I song: "How're you going to keep them down on the farm after they've seen Paree?"

In 1979, FCNL lobbyist Don Reeves and FCNL research intern Chris Miller presented testimony to a House Agriculture subcommittee on effective land reform programs. Don also took an active part in the Coalition to Support WCARRD (World Conference on Agrarian Reform and Rural Development.) The group urged the U.S. delegation attending the world conference held in Rome to support land reform and other peasant-oriented participatory development programs. The *FCNL Washington Newsletter* for October 1979 noted that one of the conference findings was that women constitute the majority of the rural poor. Over two thirds of the rural farmers in developing nations are women. They must be recognized and involved in the development process.

Environmental issues have emerged as a major factor in the international development equation, as noted in the statement on Population, above. As early as 1970, FCNL Policy Statements had noted that modernization and its injurious by-products raise "fundamental questions regarding the nature and extent of desirable economic development."

As the impact of development projects on the environment grew and the damage was recognized by the increasingly active environmental movement, tensions escalated between those concerned for environmental protection and those concerned to relieve poverty in the Third World. World Bank officials found themselves targeted by critics from both sides. In 1987, FCNL lobbyist Nancy Alexander was asked to undertake a seven-month contract with the World Bank to see if any common ground existed between the two groups. After a carefully prepared process, representatives of environmental, anti-hunger, and provider groups attended a consultation with officials of the Bank. The conclusions reached were directly in line with FCNL policy: the best way to achieve sustainable development is to increase the participation and access to the decision making processes of the poor. And nongovernmental organizations should play a greater role in World Bank projects.[7]

The UN Conference on Environment and Development (UNCED) in Brazil in 1992 brought these two issues together. Building on her previous experience, Nancy Alexander played a key role in 1990 and 1991 in organizing meetings with administration officials and working with congressional staff and nongovernmental organizations as the U.S. prepared its position to be presented at the Conference.[8]

> To be sure, we cannot meet all problems of the world, or those at home, with money or material grants. But our great material strength entails great responsibility....Technical know-how is not the only thing that has helped to make America great, although it certainly has helped to make us rich and powerful. Greatness is rather a matter of heart and spirit which we have in combination with technical skill and political and economic freedom. Response to the needs of others is but a natural reaction from a country that is rich in heart as well as in things.
>
> *Warren Griffiths, FCNL lobbyist on leave from Wilmington College, in testimony before a House Appropriations subcommittee, July 9, 1957.*

Fundamental questions continue to be raised about "development." What is "progress?" Are there limits to growth? Is it possible to make a transition from "growth" to "equilibrium?" What about

E. F. Schumacher's thesis that *"Small Is Beautiful?"* After an intensive discussion of international economic issues, FCNL's Policy Committee, July 15, 1989, affirmed the importance of "development" as a goal, but opposed the kinds of changes now required of developing countries by international lending institutions. One Friend summarized his doubts: "It is almost impossible for the rich to give up their privileges to 'help' the poor." In Chapter 7, FCNL's struggle to deal with the process of economic and social development globally and within the United States is described.

1972: Moment of Truth?

Every once in a while it is useful to look up from the immediate task, to see the forest as well as the trees, to try to gauge how serious the situation really is. Such a moment seems to have occurred in FCNL's life in 1972, just two years after the rather upbeat statement "Encouraging International Development" was approved. The 1972 Statement is even more relevant today than it was then in many respects. It is cited here, not to discourage action, but to concentrate the mind on the magnitude of the task, if we wish to be relevant and obedient to our best leadings:

> The old rosy dream of international economics–*more* production, *more* consumption for everyone almost without limits; faith in science and technology to solve all problems; self-limitation of population resulting from economic development, all moving forward and upward almost automatically under the guidance of an invisible hand–has run into harsh realities, contradictions, and troubling issues:

- The earth's thin envelope of air and limited supply of pure water are becoming dangerously polluted. The thin mantle of soil is becoming eroded and depleted. Some mineral resources are being exhausted, sources of energy consumed.
- When will world food production be unable to meet the needs of expanded population? How can pesticides needed for

food production and health be balanced against damage to the environment?
- Could even the present world population be long sustained at the present level of U.S. consumption?
- Is the widening gap between rich and poor people consistent with morality and durable peace? (One-third of the world's population enjoys seven-eighths of the world's product.)
- Is the affluence of the United States to a considerable degree based on exploitation of poorer peoples?
- Can Americans really love their fellowmen and continue to waste more resources than the total resources which deprived people have available to sustain life?

Surely new goals are needed:

1. A durable balance between population and consumption and resources and environment, which will best serve the well-being of present and future generations and preserve the beauty and utility of planet earth.
2. Growing equality for all people, and respect for cultural diversity and freedom of expression for individuals and groups.

We suggest that achievement of these goals will require:

- A drastic change in personal and national values, from seeking increased *quantity* of material things and gross national product, to joy in *quality* of life and the well being of others.
- Seeing that the raw materials and other products of poor peoples make a maximum contribution to their own welfare, instead of to the affluence of rich peoples.
- A leveling process, with consumption by rich people going down and consumption by poor people coming up.
- Worldwide action to protect the environment from pollution and destruction of beauty, limit certain types of consumption,

stabilize population and conserve natural resources.

TRADE, An Essential Ingredient

The 1970 Policy Statement "Encouraging International Development," under the heading "International Trade and Investment" states:

> While economic assistance can be a catalyst, nations achieve development primarily through the use of domestic savings and foreign exchange earnings. Increased international and interregional trade, therefore, is essential to sustain long-term development and sound relationships among the nations in our increasingly interdependent world. It is crucial also in the short run to complement development assistance, create jobs and generate foreign exchange. The developed countries must reduce their trade barriers and open channels of trade for products of the developing nations, along the lines recommended by the 77 "have-not" nations at the UN Conference on Trade and Development. International price stabilization for basic commodities is imperative.
>
> Skills, technology and capital are also transferred to developing nations to a substantial degree through the activities of international business corporations. Some of these enterprises have been charged with "economic imperialism" and resistance to land tax and other reforms. One way to help avoid such abuses would be to develop and achieve acceptance of an international code of corporate practices, which an appropriate UN agency or the World Bank might take the lead in formulating. The U.S. government should discourage those practices by U.S. corporations abroad which are exploitative in nature, and should encourage fair wages and a fair return to the people of the country involved through taxation, co-ownership

and expansion of indigenous control.

"Free" or "freer" trade has been a cardinal principle during most of FCNL's history. The rationale: it breaks down economic nationalism and helps build interdependence and peaceful relations, it helps raise living standards in developing countries, and it brings mutual economic advantage by encouraging efficient production.

FCNL witnesses presented statements to congressional committees ten times between 1947 and 1962 against trade barriers and in favor of extension of the Reciprocal Trade Program. Witnesses included Caleb Smith of Swarthmore College, Peter Franck of Haverford and American University, Delbert Replogle, New Jersey businessman, Joseph Coppock of Earlham College, and Emile Benoit, faculty member of the Columbia University Graduate School of Business.

Emile Benoit in his March 7, 1958 testimony before the House Ways and Means Committee made the political and economic arguments in support of trade liberalization, and then said:

> It seems to me that government policies can in the last analysis be satisfactory only if they coincide with our fundamental moral and spiritual convictions. Most of us subscribe to one or another religion which emphasizes the doctrine of human brotherhood as a central truth by which our daily lives should be inspired and directed. I do not, therefore, think it unbecoming or in any way far-fetched to examine even as practical a problem as the tariff in the light of this teaching.
>
> So viewed, it seems to me, trade liberalization gains a new meaning and a new value. Protective tariffs seem, from this point of view, inherently repugnant in that they set up artificial barriers between man and man, and interfere with that free commerce in commodities which is after all a partial expression of human cooperation and mutual assistance.

Protective tariffs do violence to this principle. Their essential purpose is discriminatory. They make it difficult or impossible for foreigners to sell to us, just because they are foreigners....

FCNL has also supported the Trade Adjustment Assistance program which helps workers, companies and communities adversely affected by U.S. liberal trade policy.

But support for freer trade can conflict with other FCNL priorities, for example:
- maintaining and creating jobs in the U.S., especially lower paying jobs;
- maintaining stable communities and preventing the flight of factories abroad;
- ensuring markets for U.S. family farmers;
- opposing the export of tobacco, various hazardous substances, and military products.

In the late 1970's and early 1980's, Frances Neely implemented FCNL's concern for international trade. She was elected chair of the Consumer Education Council on World Trade, a loose coalition of public interest groups in 1978.

The next year she joined delegations meeting with members of Congress on the Geneva Codes of Trading Conduct and in support of the omnibus implementing legislation; she also arranged Hill visits for Sylvain Minault, the Friends World Committee representative at the Fifth UN Conference on Trade and Development on his return from Manila.

In 1980, she recommended to a House subcommittee chaired by Jonathan Bingham of New York that it draft comprehensive legislation prohibiting the export of hazardous substances whose use is banned in the U.S. and the export of hazardous waste. Those products which are "significantly restricted" in the U.S. should not be exported unless three UN agencies approved. At a 1981 State Department meeting on hazardous shipments, Frances circulated her letter to Representative Bingham. She ruefully reported that

FCNL recommendations were "greeted with indulgent chuckles."

In 1986 the issue of a UN Code of Conduct was again alive. Nancy Alexander arranged for an FCNL-sponsored forum on the Code of Conduct for Transnational Corporations then being negotiated. Representatives from the UN, the State Department and a multinational corporation presented their views to about 100 attenders. The *Washington Post* reported the meeting at length.

FCNL's ambivalence on the trade issue came to a head in the 1993 debate on NAFTA, the North American Free Trade Agreement. The value of freer trade in breaking down economic nationalism and trade barriers was still there. But the main beneficiaries seemed to be huge corporations, free to roam the world looking for cheap labor, low taxes, and few safety and pollution restrictions. Some modest Clinton administration side agreements on labor and environmental safeguards were insufficient to garner FCNL support for the Treaty. Friend-in-Washington Jean Rosenberg analyzed NAFTA from FCNL's perspective, aided by FCNL General Committee clerk Don Reeves whose article on NAFTA appeared in the *Christian Century*.[9] In conversations on the Hill, FCNL's in-depth approach was appreciated. In the end, FCNL and most religious organization colleagues took no position on final passage of NAFTA.

FCNL continues to stress the importance in the developing world of labor's right to organize, safe working conditions, and sound environmental practices. At the same time, FCNL must be sensitive to the concerns of colleagues from developing nations that such trade conditions have been used unfairly against their products.

The triple explosions of population, weapons, and AIDS in the developing world, exacerbated by the breakdown of restraints in traditional societies, the lack of jobs and increasing pressure on resources and the environment all come together in dire predictions for the future. As has happened during other times of crisis, FCNL must very carefully choose priorities so that our necessarily modest efforts will achieve constructive results.

Notes

1. See FCNL Doc. G-517, p. 19, citing Andrew J. Pierre, *The Global Politics of Arms Sales*, Princeton University Press (1982), pp. 286, 288-289.
2. See *Uphill for Peace*, pp. 57-69.
3. Hearings, House Foreign Affairs Committee, Jan. 1950, "Act for International Development," p. 405.
4. See *Uphill for Peace*, pp. 175-180 for more details.
5. See FCNL 1989 Annual Report, pp. 27-28.
6. See FCNL 1989 Annual Report, pp. 23-29; *FCNL Washington Newsletter*, Jan. 1990, p. 5.
7. See 1987 FCNL Annual Report, pp. 10-12.
8. See 1990 FCNL Annual Report, pp. 19-20; 1991 FCNL Annual Report, p. 32.
9. See FCNL Docs. G-3105-FOR, G-3127-FOR, and R-3106-FOR.

7. Is FCNL Pursuing Effective Policies to End Poverty and Build Livable Communities in the United States?

We are clear on our goals but less clear on how to reach them. We support the right of all to minimum basic human needs. But many difficult questions remain about the best methods to create jobs, to manage the economy, to determine appropriate federal and state roles. We have spent considerable time and effort seeking a generally acceptable "Quaker" position on some of these issues with only modest success.

Crisis in Human Rights at Home

Not until the cities began burning in the 1960s–Watts in 1965, Detroit and Newark in 1967, and nationwide after Martin Luther King's assassination in 1968–did FCNL seriously undertake a domestic legislative agenda beyond issues traditionally associated with Friends' testimonies for peace, civil liberties, civil rights and American Indians. The impact of urban and racial turmoil and its close relation to the Vietnam war virtually mandated a significant FCNL response.[1]

On July 8, 1968, Edward T. Anderson became FCNL's "Human Rights Secretary" and lobbyist. Within the month he was testifying before Republican Convention Platform subcommittees on "Meeting the Crisis in the Cities," "Peace Planks," and "Meeting Rural Poverty." Before Ed left for Common Cause at the end of 1970, he had traveled among Friends, forged new contacts for FCNL with black members of Congress and their staffs, and testified for FCNL on expansion of the food stamp program, broadened powers for the Equal Employment Opportunity Commission, welfare reform, voting rights, and the "safe streets act."

During the two years William G. Lunsford was with FCNL,

March 1971 to March 1973, he earned the respect of his colleagues on the Hill, among Friends, and in the nongovernmental community. His chief priorities were programs for the poor–welfare reform, legal services, child care, and extension of the poverty program. He also testified against the death penalty and discrimination in employment; he lobbied against proposals which would have ended the school desegregation process, and he urged strengthening of equal employment opportunities.

FCNL's "Human Rights" program continued through 1976 with Harold Confer covering many issues, but concentrating on health and full employment lobbying from mid 1973 to mid 1976. Ed Honnold provided able support on prison construction and myriad other issues. Stephen W. Angell ("Steve the Younger") after his intern year was a legislative assistant in 1976 working especially on full employment and criminal justice. Tim Atwater in 1976 specialized on food and hunger. Don Reeves, 1977 through 1980, and Ruth Flower, 1981 to the present, have covered domestic issues but within a much broader context, as FCNL has increasingly made connections between domestic and international priorities.

A Difficult Context

While FCNL was seeking to play a constructive role in domestic economic and social matters, deep forces were at work in the nation, negating positive efforts by many people. Families, the foundation of a society, were undergoing radical change. Divorce, single parent families, and growing awareness of spouse and child abuse impacted children. Pervasive violence in the home, in communities and in the mass media created nearly unmanageable stress for the educational system. Mobility and mass communication splintered the restraints of traditional communities. People were often more familiar with fictitious TV characters than they were with their neighbors next door. Pervasive racism identified by the Kerner Commission report in 1968 became worse as time passed. The impact of the drug culture affected all classes, but the chief victims were in urban ghettos where firearms were ever present.

Politically, the Reagan-Bush agenda prevailed. Military spending went up, domestic programs were cut, taxes were reduced dramatically, especially for the upper income brackets. The public was persuaded that "government" was bad, taxes were anathema, and a balanced budget was essential. Thus when huge deficits inevitably resulted from the Reagan policy, neither taxes nor additional borrowing were readily available. A major share of revenues, more than a quarter of all federal income taxes, had been dedicated to domestic and foreign creditors in interest payments. Since continued high military spending was a given, there was very little money left to expand programs for the poor.

Beyond Policy Generalities

From 1968 to 1974, FCNL's Policy Committee under the leadership of Mary Cushing Niles developed a set of wide ranging policy statements to guide the new domestic agenda. Annual meetings during those years were consumed with issues like jobs, welfare, farm labor, population, health care, and taxation.

- "Population and Family Planning" was approved by the General Committee at the January 1971 meeting. The portion of the statement on abortion was modified at the 1975 meeting. The new position limited FCNL to opposing efforts to amend the U.S. Constitution to say that abortion shall be illegal. Basically, this supported the Supreme Court's decision in *Roe v. Wade*. At the November 1981 Annual Meeting, agreement could not be reached on this proposition either. The whole question of abortion, so far as FCNL's Policy Statement was concerned, was placed in the section on "Challenges to the Society of Friends." The relevant section said: "Boundaries of life. What is the proper role of government with regard to critical issues or life, such as 'right to die' laws, euthanasia, abortion, genetic engineering and medical intervention? Should the U.S. Constitution or federal laws be used as a final response to abortion." The "Challenge" in the 1993 approved Policy Statement simply asks: "What is the proper role of government with regard to abortion."

- "Taxation and the Distribution of Wealth and Income in the U.S.A." was approved January 27, 1974. This Statement contains 13 basic principles, plus explanatory background material prepared by the Policy Committee. George Bliss, when traveling for FCNL, reported that this document was picked up more often than any other on FCNL's literature table. The Statement reaffirms a number of the position in the 1969 Statement on "Jobs and Assured Income."

- An "Energy and Nuclear Policy Statement" was approved at the Annual Meeting, January 25, 1976, well before the issue claimed the headlines in President Jimmy Carter's administration. The Statement emphasized conservation, renewable

> **President [Carter] and his staff have made an unprecedented effort to develop the principles and the strategy of a national energy policy. In doing so they have taken political risks. On issues of conservation, non-proliferation, and environmental protection, the President will need public support in battles against vested interests. On issues such as appropriate technology, protection of the poor, and protection of the rights of American Indians, there is a need for citizen pressures to assure that Carter's broad promises are actually implemented."
> *Energy Policy 1977: An FCNL Perspective, FCNL Doc. G-26 p.8, May 25, 1977.*

energy resources and decentralized energy systems. It called for a moratorium on construction of new nuclear powerplants.

Reconnoitering the Policy Frontiers

The complex issues raised by FCNL's various policy statements in this period created a policy buff's paradise. Over the next several years the Policy Committee set up "task forces" and "dialogues" to seek further light and specificity. The process proved exceedingly stimulating for the participants. But the process also disclosed considerable disagreement among Friends on global and domestic economic issues.

The "Task Force on a New Global Economic and Political Order" was created at the 1976 annual meeting. It came into being because a survey of General Committee members had disclosed that their second highest priority was an "attempt to define in some detail and suggest specific next steps toward a new global economic and political order to replace the present war system." The ten member Task Force sought to develop "a legislative focus on next-steps in globalism which puts human needs at home within the global context." The hope was that fresh perspectives would lead to new policy positions and legislative priorities.

Frances Neely's seven-page "grab bag of ideas" was circulated widely among knowledgeable Friends and drew many responses. Kenneth Boulding responded helpfully on a number of the proposals, but ended by suggesting "The genius of the FCNL is in promoting small marginal changes for the good. It has no genius whatever in promoting a new global, political, and economic order. My own view frankly is that the task force should be disbanded." His handwritten "P.S." said "I'm afraid this sounds a bit sharp, but you know I love the FCNL. I just don't want it to get into business beyond its ability to manage."

Emile Benoit, another economist who had testified for FCNL, wrote Frances about the various responses:

> I hope you won't be discouraged by the diversity of criticisms....The crucial question is raised by Kenneth in asking whether this is the sort of thing the FCNL should be doing. I don't think that the FCNL is trying to 'set out a new global political and economic order,' but to stimulate discussion about the political and economic and social changes required to cope with the awful dangers we confront. 'Small marginal changes for the good' will no longer suffice. We will not have the time for them to bear fruit, unless we also make progress on solving some of the fundamental problems, too. It seems to me that the FCNL is trying to move with the times and to supply a testimony that is relevant to the large emerging problems as well as the small, conventional, incremental ones.

After two years work by an able Task Force supported by a prodigious amount of research and consultation by Frances Neely,[2] the Policy Committee noted at its November 19, 1977 meeting that "many of the Task Force's conclusions confirm existing policy, hopefully giving a deeper and wider perspective".

In 1977 with the prospect of a Carter administration tax package in the offing, Frances sent FCNL's 1974 statement on "Taxation and the Distribution of Wealth and Income" to 95 Quaker economists and sociologists with a series of questions about what might be included in an "FCNL Tax Package." Again, replies indicated the wide diversity among Friends beyond the 1974 policy guidelines.

In 1980, three "Quaker Dialogues" were held on "What Changes are Needed in the U.S. Economy." Social scientists, corporate executives, small independent entrepreneurs, and professors brought differing insights and experiences to the discussions held at Richmond, Indiana in April, at Pendle Hill, Wallingford, Pennsylvania in June, and at Guilford College, North Carolina October 31-November 2. Hugh Barbour and Kenneth Boulding were among the resource leaders. Frances Neely's 12-page summary, "Gleanings from Quaker Dialogues" is a fascinating compendium of conflicting ideas about what changes are needed in the U.S. economy.[3]

Exploring these frontiers makes one marvel at the level of agreement which has actually been reached over the years on these complex economic and social issues.

From Beliefs to Action

How are the FCNL legislative priorities which are selected by the General Committee at the annual meeting translated into specific legislative programs? Soon after each annual meeting the legislative staff meets to review the legislative priorities, to recall the surrounding context of the decisions and the nuances of Committee members' comments which may be relevant, to analyze the upcoming Congressional agenda, and to try to anticipate national and international events.

Another key factor is staff experience and expertise–which many Committee members have already factored into their priority recommendations. The presence of Don Reeves, a live dirt farmer from Nebraska, gave FCNL a unique resource in the Washington religious community. For the four years, beginning in 1977, he was an FCNL lobbyist, Don provided leadership in the Interreligious Task Force on U.S. Food Policy and chaired its Agricultural Policy Work Group. He helped fashion proposals to protect family farms, to provide grain stocks and reserves for world food security, and to support agrarian reform and rural development in the U.S. and abroad.

Robert Cory, formerly with the Quaker UN office and William Penn House, acted as consultant to FCNL throughout the 1970s on issues involving the UN, disarmament, and international development. On domestic issues, Bob was convenor of FCNL's Policy subcommittee on Energy Policy, which developed the Statement adopted at the 1976 annual meeting. When President Jimmy Carter made major energy proposals in 1977, Bob took the lead in analyzing the plan in light of FCNL policy.[4]

Ralph Kerman brought his expertise in physics and his concern for energy, the environment and nuclear policy to FCNL as a nearly full time volunteer in 1988 and 1989 and as Friend-in-Washington in 1991 and 1992. He lobbied, testified on renewable energy, and worked on comprehensive energy policy legislation. He made FCNL a knowledgeable participant in various Washington coalitions on energy, plutonium, and transportation fuel efficiency.

FCNL lobbyists and interns also pool their efforts when a national or international issue involves several different priorities. In addition to the annual Budget analysis *Newsletter*, special "integrated" *Newsletters* have been written, for example, on the Drug Crisis, February 1990, Homelessness, July 1988, Terrorism, May 1986, and Advancing Economic and Social Development in the Third World, August/September 1985.

Putting It All Together

Ruth Flower went to work in Washington less than three weeks before Ronald Reagan did. She was still there when FCNL's 50th anniversary occurred, and when Ronald Reagan and his protege, George Bush, had left town. But Ronald Reagan probably has had more impact on Ruth Flower's working life than any other single person. His philosophy, his budgets, his priorities set the agenda for the domestic work of FCNL and the religious community for a decade. His deficits, his military priority, and his no-new-taxes philosophy still determine whether human needs programs will survive or wither.

In a time of severe reductions in domestic programs, advocates for the poor found triage necessary. Like battlefield surgeons, they were forced to separate programs into three categories: those that were expected to survive without great attention, those that probably wouldn't survive even with great effort, and those that might make it if enough attention and effort were expended. Gone were the days when the prospect of sufficient resources made it possible to experiment creatively with innovative ideas. The bottom line was: how much will it cost, or is it revenue neutral?

In this environment, representatives of religious organizations forged new common bonds. Churches were deeply involved in soup kitchens, homeless shelters, clothing distribution, and counseling. Washington representatives knew first hand of the needs, and they knew that the Reagan administration's hope that private organizations could substitute for government programs just would not work. Only government had access to sufficient resources to meet the need.

> All personal income taxes should be progressively graduated. Income for tax purposes should be defined comprehensively and treated uniformly. The deductions and special forms of treatment contained in the present tax system are really subsidies and almost all should be eliminated. However, the tax system should encourage contributions in support of voluntary non-profit organizations and modest individual contributions to the political party or candidate of one's choice.
> *Excerpt from 1974 FCNL Statement on Taxation and the Distribution of Wealth and Income in the U.S., p. 7.*

Identification with the cause of poor people separated church representatives from other groups and from some "liberal" Democrats. Ruth Flower in 1983 was chosen to chair the Domestic Human Needs Work Group of Interfaith Action for Economic Justice. Over the years this group had worked intensively to develop creative approaches to the broad issue of "welfare reform." In 1988, she reported, their efforts affected the shape of the House bill "substantially." "Ultimately, nearly every point we raised was corrected in the House bills." The Senate was a different story; the Senate bill was both inadequate and punitive. Church representatives analyzed the bill and proposed amendments to Senator Moynihan's legislative aide who was shepherding the bill. Ruth's report suggests the tribulations of a domestic issues lobbyist:

Her reaction was very different from the response we had received in the House. She rejected *all* the proposals, even those that were later added as simple technical corrections. She lectured our group on our responsibility to support the liberal program, and told us pointedly that she and not we would define what was liberal and therefore acceptable. It was a classic confrontation between a conscientious effort to represent the poor and a tenacious adherence to a "Hill-centered" definition of political reality.

Among our lobbying colleagues, related confrontations occurred. The religious-based lobbies were firm in their opposition to the Moynihan bill, and sought vigorously to amend it, slow it down, or scuttle it completely. Among our "secular" colleagues, however, in a group called the Coalition on Human Needs, there was not such unity. Nearly all agreed that the Moynihan bill would be damaging to the welfare program. Yet several organizations chose, for political or strategic reasons, not to oppose the bill. This disunity caused much anguish and flaring of tempers among colleagues that normally consult peacefully with one another. This lack of unity in opposition to the bill was at least in part responsible for the bill's final passage.

The bill as finally passed did include many of the improvements urged early in the process, but job training funds and some procedures were seriously inadequate. Ruth concluded, "We are disappointed in the outcome, but respectful of the work that the religious lobby community was able to commit to the effort."[5]

Getting Specific About Ending Poverty

Given the difficulties several of the FCNL policy groups had in deciding how to implement FCNL's domestic priorities, what actions have FCNL lobbyists actually taken?

1) Setting the goal: In 1985, Ruth Flower led an effort to make *elimination of poverty* the national goal, rather than seeking ways to *alleviate* the problems of the poor. A statement setting forth the long term goal of eliminating poverty was drafted, signed by 36 national leaders of religious organizations, and released to the press and the public. The "Call to End Poverty" was used as a basis for discussion in visits to about 150 offices on Capitol Hill.

What basic steps are needed to end poverty? The August/September 1985 *FCNL Washington Newsletter* analyzed the concept of economic and social development both in the United States and in the developing countries. Three "cornerstones of development" were identified: (a) democratic participation by those immediately affected in planning and execution in order to give them a sense of control over their own lives; (b) assistance for the most vulnerable while addressing the patterns which perpetuate their poverty; and (c) self-reliance and sustainability, using local resources and existing institutions, if appropriate.

2) Assuring the safety net: To make sure minimum human needs were met, FCNL lobbied, testified, wrote and spoke out to assure adequate funding for the food stamp program, WIC (Special Nutrition Program for Women, Infants and Children,) AFDC (Aid to Families with Dependent Children,) school lunches, rent subsidies, and aid to the homeless.

3) Creating jobs at adequate pay: Among the proposals supported have been:
- Various job training programs. But these can lead to heightened frustration unless jobs are available when training is completed.
- Job creation programs in the private sector if possible, plus public employment. Strong support was given in 1984, for example, to the "Youth Incentive Employment Act" which aimed to help 16 to 19 year olds from low income families who remained in or returned to school or vocational training. Part time work during the school year and full time in summer with either private or public employers would be subsidized

100% in the first 6 months, 75% thereafter. Congress never found funds to start this project.
- Programs to enable low-income women and unemployed people in general to start new small businesses. This is in preference to "enterprise zones" which often create or increase employment opportunities by allowing companies to violate minimum wage, safety and health requirements.
- Policies which ensure adequate compensation, for example, by increasing the minimum wage, by supporting equal pay for equal work, and by increasing the Earned Income Tax Credit which increases the income of families with children via the income tax and the Internal Revenue Service. (In the early 1970s FCNL supported a similar minimum income proposal which was not limited to wages or families with children.)
- Provisions for child care and family and medical leave to help families make the transition to the job market.

> The definition of work should be expanded and the system of compensation rethought. We call for *a new work ethic*–an expansive view which emphasizes the right and need for each individual to be able to do things that are creative, productive, useful, and meaningful for society or for the individual's own personal life. This view includes under the rubric `work' a multitude of activities, paid or unpaid, including the work done by children as they learn, housework, community work, care of children or old people, artistic activity, thinking...
>
> In contrast, the traditional work ethic describes `work' as something for which one is compensated financially, even though such `work' might require little physical or mental effort, or might, in fact, be socially harmful."
>
> *Excerpt from FCNL response to an invitation from Secretary of Health, Education, and Welfare, Joseph A. Califano, Jr. to comment on welfare reform and related matters, February 24, 1977. FCNL Doc. T-1.*

- Encouraging people to move from welfare to work with policies that are *enabling rather than punitive*, thus encouraging individuals to live up to their full potential.
- Examining all health care proposals to ensure that the poor and near-poor are adequately protected. As FCNL's first half century ended, FCNL was devoting major efforts to the health care issue.

The next frontier, which has been advocated by FCNL for two decades, is to examine seriously the concept of "work" and compensation in our economy. Legislation introduced in FCNL's 50th Anniversary year to calculate the amount of "unremunerated work" in our society is already providing a powerful tool to educate members of Congress and the general public.

Where Your Treasure Is ...

"There will your heart be also." The annual Budget of the U.S. Government" is Exhibit #1 demonstrating our nation's true values. That is why the FCNL staff annually engage in the frustrating, time consuming, but very enlightening, weeks-long task of analyzing the federal budget. From that process, staff learn the nuances and the sometimes hidden meaning behind the numbers. And, at times, after many phone calls to officials in various departments of the executive branch, have found the official figures needed revision.

> We are continuing to buy a lot of weapons we don't need, with money we don't have, to fight an enemy we can't even identify.
> *Admiral Gene R. LaRoque, 1993.*
> *Center for Defense Information.*

The annual "budget pie" requires repeated explanations of "federal funds," "trust funds," the "unified" budget and related esoteric items. For a small but select group of readers and tax filers, however, the figures giving the percentages of the income tax attributable to military and military-related spending were eagerly awaited.

Early in the Reagan years the Congressional Black Caucus took the lead in fashioning an alternative budget, at one time called the "Quality of Life" budget. FCNL strongly supported this alternative and worked closely with members of the Black caucus and their staffs on the details. The project was satisfying because, under the budget process adopted in 1976, it was possible to engage the full range of budget issues: cuts in the military establishment, increases in specific domestic programs, and possible increases or decreases on the revenue side. Frustration was rampant, however, because the Black Caucus was never given budget figures soon enough to fashion their alternative budget. This meant outside organizations never had enough time to mount a concerted public campaign to support it. It was also disappointing because, over the course of a decade from 1984 to 1993, the number of Representatives voting for this alternative never reached 100 members, out of 435. In 1989, FCNL and other groups formed the Citizens' Budget Campaign to support the Black Caucus alternative budget and use it as a vehicle to engage local activists in budget priorities issues. In 1991 the Campaign developed "Reinvest in our Communities," a project Friends and others around the country found helpful in engaging local officials and activists in the priorities debate.

* * * * *

It is a fact that Friends have not reached the clarity on economic issues that we have on questions of peace, overt violence, religious freedom, and racial justice. Why do we have such difficulty? Without basic Quaker testimonies as a guide, we are caught up in secular debates on capitalism vs socialism, competition vs cooperation, private enterprise vs government organization. Thus we tend to forget that any long term solutions undoubtedly will require elements of all these alternatives. We should concentrate on specifics.

Moreover, we come to these questions from many different personal and occupational perspectives. We probably also differ on some fundamental assumptions about human nature and society. Is narrow self interest the dominant human motivation? What are the necessary ingredients to build a society in which altruism plays a major role in personal and community life? Do individuals and organizations thrive best in a climate of competition or cooperation? What does Love require? Can John Woolman challenge us today as he did our predecessors?

Friends are challenged, intellectually and spiritually, to fashion an approach to economic and social policy which places "quality of life," in all its dimensions, at its core. Hopefully, the references in these two chapters to FCNL soul searching to date will encourage even more intensive exploration of public policy alternatives infused with Quaker insights.

Notes

1. See "The Crisis in Human Rights at Home: Some Guidelines for the FCNL," approved at the January 1968 FCNL annual meeting.
2. See 1976 FCNL Annual Report, pp. 7-12
3. Available at FCNL in folder, "1980 Quaker Dialogues."
4. See *FCNL Washington Newsletter*, "Oil, Wind, and Sun," July 1977.
5. See 1988 FCNL Annual Report, pp. 8-10.

8. Has FCNL Been Effective on Public Policy Issues?

What is "effective"? It is impossible to claim a causal connection on major public policy issues. FCNL is listened to respectfully on Capitol Hill for its facts, and usually for its views, even when Members of Congress are not in agreement with our moral perspectives. Whether or not FCNL has been "effective," it is clear that progress has been made on a number of issues on which the Committee has worked over the years. One FCNL role has been to help frame the issues. Another has been to support and encourage those Members of Congress, their staffs, and people in other organizations who share our values and perspectives.

FCNL is a small organization without the two most important attributes of power in Washington—money and votes. It is also a religiously based, pacifist organization—two more strikes against it.

> Senator Byrd: "Thank you, Mr. Tatum. I know how conscientious the Friends are, and I know also the accuracy of your statement. The Quakers often take a lonely position; they take a position against war and conscription as violations of the Christian faith. I am impressed, too, with the statement you make on your last page: 'The challenge of our age is to build the institutions of peace to meet the needs of mankind."
>
> *Response of Senator Harry F. Byrd, Jr. (VA) to Lyle Tatum testifying for FCNL, AFSC, and the Friends Coordinating Committee on Peace before the Senate Armed Services Committee on Feb. 9, 1971 against extension of the military draft.*

FCNL's very existence is testimony to its faith in the democratic system, and an audacious belief that someone will listen and perhaps respond. "Effective?" Compared to what? Historians try to examine cause and effect, later historians often reexamine, revise and dispute earlier conclusions. In the grand scheme of things FCNL may be only a footnote in the conventional wisdom of historians. But a small organization with a realistic outlook—that also believes that small is beautiful—should not expect grandiose results.

The temper of the times is the crucial factor in determining a place in the history books for individuals and organizations, large and small. Is it a time of peace or war? Prosperity or depression? Hope or fear? Outward looking or inward turning? Altruism or egotism? Forgiveness or vengeance? Who will be remembered, George McGovern or Richard Nixon? Walter Mondale or Ronald Reagan? Bill Clinton or George Bush or Ross Perot? Most historians cite the majority mood, the apparent winner.

Michael J. Nugent, for his 1969 masters thesis at the University of Maryland, analyzed FCNL's first ten years: the years of the anti-UMT effort, pro-world federation, foreign relief, and disarmament. He concluded:

> Its record on working for increased appropriations for foreign aid and relief was a mixed one. On the outcome of a few minor bills, the Friends Committee made a genuine difference. In the major foreign aid battles of the Truman years, on such programs as the Marshall Plan and the Point Four Program, the Friends Committee played a small part in a large cooperative effort. (p.64)
>
> With the notable exception of its work against universal military training, the Friends Committee enjoyed little success in translating its goals into realities. Its program for international economic development was economically farsighted, but politically unfeasible. Practically no chance existed that Congress would push for the F.C.N.L.'s dream of world federation

181

since the performance of the United Nations proved to be mediocre at best. There was little room for the total disarmament that the Friends Committee espoused in the official American policy of containment. During the Truman years, pacifism remained, as it had been through three centuries of the American debate on war and peace, mere chips and foam on the stream of American politics.

Given the ideological position of the Friends Committee on National Legislation, a position that most Americans of the postwar decade considered "extreme," the surprising fact of the F.C.N.L.'s record was not that it achieved so few of its legislative goals, but that it achieved anything at all. (p. 148)

"What If..."

Without attempting to quantify FCNL's role, it can be said that a number of FCNL's distinctly minority positions during its 50-year history became generally acceptable:

- opposition to UMT, the draft and compulsory service;
- normalization of relations with the People's Republic of China;
- U.S. detente with the Soviet Union;
- raising awareness of the nuclear danger;
- acceptance of the concept of human rights;
- support for the Law of the Seas treaty;
- establishment of the goal of general and complete disarmament;
- growing sense of public responsibility, nationally and internationally, to help others help themselves.

What if the FCNL hadn't existed? Would all of this have happened anyway? This, according to one analyst of lobbying,[1] is a central question: would the policy process be the same if groups disappeared? David Forsythe, who analyzed the work of various interest groups on human rights issues, including FCNL, noted, "This is a 'what if' question and therefore unsatisfactory for social science analysis, but for reasons explained in the text it seems to me that the American process would not have been the same 1973-1979 if the human rights non-profits had not existed." [2] Where would the world be today if there had not been groups like FCNL opposing militarism and nuclear weapons, and urging far reaching goals like general and complete disarmament and better relations with the Soviet Union and the People's Republic of China?

Regarding China, Karen Shaw Kerpen wrote a 1981 Ph.D dissertation for New York University on "Voices in a Silence: American Organizations That Worked for Diplomatic Recognition of the People's Republic of China by the United States, 1945-1979." During the period 1954 to 1968, groups in favor of recognition "faced tremendous obstacles." She identified four groups as the leaders: FCNL, AFSC, the National Council of Churches, and the organization these and other groups helped create–the National Committee on U.S.-China Relations. Regarding FCNL, she identified Raymond Wilson's longtime concern and the work of Eugene Boardman, FCNL's Friend-in-Washington, 1965-1966, who, she reported, conducted 185 interviews in his year in Washington–157 with senators and representatives, nine with Congressional staff members, and 19 with administration officials and embassy personnel. Kerpen credits Gene Boardman with persuading the Chairman of the House Foreign Affairs Committee, Clement Zablocki, to hold hearings on China policy. "The Zablocki hearings inspired Senator William Fulbright, Chairman of the Senate's Committee on Foreign Relations, to schedule similar discussions in the spring of 1966." The Fulbright hearings were "a pivotal point" in changing U.S. China policy. (pp. 113-123)

Kerpen also identified the work that FCNL Friend-in-Washington Cecil Thomas did representing AFSC in organizing conferences on China policy. Cecil worked out of FCNL's office in arranging for the "first significant national conference on American-Chinese relations since the Communists came to the mainland." The June

183

1965 conference was attended by more than 800 people from 40 states, 30 universities and 50 organizations. (pp.125-128) The "most active early staffers" of the National Committee on U.S.-China Relations, according to Kerpen, were "all Quakers." Cecil Thomas, Bob Mang, formerly director of Northern California FCL, Pamela Mang, and Eleanor Bacon. (p. 152) Not mentioned in this study, but known to those at FCNL was the indefatigable Stuart Innerst, whose China experience and wisdom made him an impressive writer and interviewer on Capitol Hill.

The history of the work of Sam and Miriam Levering on the **Law of the Seas** is still being written. It will demonstrate that the Leverings played a significant role in their work as FCNL Friends-in-Washington in 1972 and 1973 and throughout the remainder of the decade in the follow-on organizations they created.

U.S. Ambassador Eliot Richardson, who played a leading role in negotiating this treaty, views it as the most far-reaching body of law ever negotiated in a multilateral forum. At FCNL's annual meeting in 1980 Ambassador Richardson thanked Sam and Miriam Levering for their "dedicated, constructive, resourceful, patient, persistent and cheerful" contributions to an extraordinarily complex and difficult effort.

Naming the Problem

One important role for any public policy organization is to identify issues, to bring them to public attention, and to suggest constructive ways to deal with them. My experience is that the problems no one knows about or no one talks about are the ones that blow up in your face. The problems that are identified and anticipated, that people worry about, argue about, propose and reject solutions for, are the ones that are much more likely to be resolved peacefully. Naming the problem is the first step to finding a solution. The FCNL is very good at naming problems, as one can easily see by reading the Statement of Legislative Policy.

Advocating solutions, and gathering public support for them is one very good way to provide political space for politicians to move ahead constructively. Supporting officials who take creative and courageous stands is another.

Phyllis Piotrow, then Legislative Assistant to Senator George McGovern, told Washington Semester researcher Mark E. Bell in 1965: "The Friends Committee gains influence by the constant posing of their side of issues, so that a Congressman keeps hearing such talk as aid to Red China over and over again till it doesn't sound so radical."

Some Specific Issues

Peace Corps: Representative Henry Reuss of Wisconsin who introduced legislation to establish a "Point Four Youth Corps," which Ruth Replogle endorsed in FCNL testimony before the House Foreign Affairs Committee in 1960, told Earl L. Conn, then editor of *Quaker Life* about "the absolutely pivotal role which the FCNL played in the creation of the Peace Corps."

ACDA: In 1961 the work of FCNL and a small group of other organizations surprised the Kennedy White House and Congress by gathering sufficient public and Congressional support to enact the law creating the U.S. Arms Control and Disarmament Agency. Representative Bob Kastenmeier, one of the chief congressional sponsors, gave FCNL much of the credit for final enactment: "The Committee did an exceptional job." [3]

Food for Peace: Senator George McGovern of South Dakota was asked if the FCNL had supplied useful information to him. (The time was the early 1960s, before the Vietnam War, the McGovern-Hatfield amendment and other events.) His reply:

> I've felt for a long time that the United States has a tremendous opportunity to contribute to the cause of peace and freedom all over the world by using our agricultural abundance to feed the hungry. There isn't any organization in Washington that has spoken out so

decisively and so consistently in support of that point of view as the Friends Committee.

Some of the amendments that have improved our basic Food for Peace Law were made possible because of the activities of the Committee on Capitol Hill. During the time I served as Director of the Food For Peace Program, representatives of the Committee worked closely with me. Both as a legislator and as an administrator, I've come to a special appreciation of the work of the Committee.[4]

Some Quakers in Congress

The number of Quakers in Congress over the past 50 years has not been large, perhaps commensurate with the proportion in the general population. But they have been markedly Republican: Richard Nixon, California; William Bray and David Dennis, Indiana; Edward Miller, Maryland; Edwin Forsythe, New Jersey. Senator Paul Douglas of Illinois was the only Democrat. Others have been "friends of the Friends" like George E. Brown, Jr. of California who helped found the FCL in Southern California. Interestingly, Quakers in Congress have often had major policy differences with FCNL, while many non-Quakers have been very comfortable with FCNL positions.

Lockhart Kiermaier of Earlham College conducted an Independent Study in 1974 on "The Effectiveness of Friends Committee on National Legislation." He had a number of interviews with members of Congress and their aides. Kiermaier reported, p. 4:

> In interviews with two Quaker Congressmen from Indiana, William G. Bray and David W. Dennis, the view was expressed that FCNL does not accurately reflect the predominant views of the Society of Friends. Their main reason for this alleged alienation is in fact rooted in a criticism of the priorities that FCNL has espoused for the

past several years, specifically their anti-military stands. Stemming from this basic disagreement, Bray made the following points:
- because of their alienation from the mainstream of current thought in the Society of Friends, they have lost their effectiveness. The radical views put forth by FCNL today are counterproductive.
- they [FCNL] forget their responsibility to examine the two sides that exist for every story.

In much the same vein, Dennis made these points:
- he did recognize FCNL as representing a certain, but not large, Quaker constituency.
- he feels that many Friends in his district disagree with FCNL.

Based on my experiences and observations at FCNL I would interpret these conclusions by Congressmen Bray and Dennis as confirming the acknowledgement made by FCNL that in no way do they represent the views of all Friends.

Kiermaier also interviewed the legislative assistants to the two Pennsylvania Senators, Hugh Scott and Richard Schweiker, who also have a number of Quaker constituents. Like Bray and Dennis, they are also Republicans. But Scott's aide "feels that FCNL speaks for most Quakers and many others," and though Scott disagrees with FCNL on the Vietnam war issue, "compared to other antiwar groups they were quite effective because they were calm and reasonable." They have a "factual presentation which is based on first hand information; credible."

Senator Schweiker's aide "spoke at length on the sizable Quaker constituency in Pennsylvania, thus FCNL represents them and Schweiker is aware of them." He commented favorably on FCNL's restrained lobbying technique: "even on very emotional issues they are still easy to talk to."

This issue cannot be satisfactorily resolved. There are major political differences among Friends in the United States and they will remain. FCNL's task is to be very careful in acknowledging those differences and attempting to incorporate them if possible. The fact that FCNL's policies and priorities are decided by Friends appointed from 26 Yearly Meetings and Conferences and some eight other Friends organizations provides evidence of its representative nature. There are many channels open to concerned Friends who wish to participate in the searching policy discussions that take place in FCNL. FCNL must also raise an annual budget, now more than one million dollars, and this provides an annual referendum on FCNL's acceptability and responsiveness to Friends.

This section cannot be complete without acknowledging the humble leadership that Paul Douglas gave on civil rights legislation in the Senate during the crucial battles in the 1960s. I have been in strategy sessions in his office where Douglas sat quietly listening while lobbyists debated and analyzed strategies and tactics and finally turned to him with a proposal. His response: "I'm a soldier in the rear ranks. Let me know what I can do."

In 1957, FCNL ran a series in the FCNL *Memo* on Quaker members of Congress. Paul Douglas, an economist by training, had joined the Society of Friends but during the second world war he enlisted in the Marine Corps and was wounded twice in the South Pacific. In reply to an FCNL query, Paul Douglas sent the following statement which appeared in FCNL *Memo* No. 53, November 15, 1957:

> I joined the Society of Friends in Seattle, Washington, in 1920 after having been impressed for years with the integrity of Quakers and their courage and imagination in trying to apply the leaven of active good will into the life about them. Most of all I was influenced by John Woolman's *Journal*, which in Quaker parlance "spoke to my condition."... I have tried to study Quaker history and to acquaint myself with the activities of Friends here and abroad. The principles and example of Friends have been a source of internal guidance and strength.
>
> Close observation of Hitler, Mussolini and Stalin and the movements they headed, convinces me, however, that

no democracy could properly adopt pacifism in dealing with such police states since to do so would mean the triumph for long centuries of time of total tyranny—which to me is the worst fate which can befall mankind. I cannot, therefore, accept the doctrines of our more articulate Friends as an infallible guide to national policy, even though I respect their motives and principles. I hope, however, that in other ways I may be able, in some small degree, to advance the principle that goodwill can triumph over hate, if given a chance.

Richard Milhous Nixon

Nixon's public career spanned most of FCNL's first 50 years, but close contact with him by FCNL representatives was minimal. Raymond Wilson regularly included Rose Mary Woods, Nixon's personal secretary, among the recipients of his summer bouquets distributed on Capitol Hill. But he was seldom successful in making appointments to see Representative, then Senator, then Vice-President Nixon. There was a wide policy gulf between Nixon and FCNL on civil liberties, military, and national security issues.

Nixon was brought up in the pastoral East Whittier Friends Church in then-California Yearly Meeting. His relatives on his mother's side were devout Quaker leaders. When Nixon came to Washington as a young member of the House of Representatives, he was uncomfortable in the unprogrammed Friends Meeting of Washington on Florida Avenue, so he and his family attended the Westmoreland Congregational Church. He maintained his membership in East Whittier Friends Church, however.

During the years of his presidency, when antiwar tensions were high, Nixon invited various ministers to conduct Sunday morning services in the White House rather than venturing out to Washington churches. This created an interesting connection. One of the invited ministers was T. Eugene Coffin, pastor of the East Whittier Friends Church, who was also an at-large appointee to FCNL's

General Committee during the early 1970s. Gene would visit FCNL's office on Monday to catch up on FCNL activities after leading the White House services on Sunday.

FCNL strenuously opposed President Nixon's continued bombing of Vietnam, the invasion of Cambodia, Vietnamization and other military policies. We supported his efforts for detente and arms control with the Soviet Union. We applauded his normalization of relations with the People's Republic of China and his proposal for a Law of the Seas Treaty. I believe Nixon's finest hour was in November 1960 when he did not contest the highly questionable vote count for Kennedy in Illinois, Texas and elsewhere. His decision may have cost him the presidency, but avoided what would surely have been a major constitutional crisis.

The Watergate scandal and possible impeachment of Nixon deeply concerned Friends across the country and created a difficult situation for FCNL. A vocal stand could have brought intense media coverage. An analysis of Friends Meetings' views indicated considerable difference of opinion.[5] The judicious decision at the January 1974 annual meeting to await Congressional recommendations and to encourage local Friends to conduct their own decision making process enabled FCNL to continue to focus on our chosen priorities.[6]

FCNL's Executive Committee on August 2, 1974, following out the process authorized in January, reviewed and supported the House Judiciary Committee's recommendation of impeachment, but urged individual Friends and Friends Meetings to study the issue and communicate their views to their own Representatives. The Executive Committee said in part:

> With other American citizens we approach in sorrow and anguish this present crisis of confidence in our government and its leaders. We express our compassion for Richard Nixon, his family and his colleagues, and join in prayer for him and for our nation.

FCNL as Catalyst

As a small lobbying organization, FCNL needs all the help it can get. We learn from others, they learn from us; together we count for more than each of us singly. Some coalitions are made up exclusively of groups with a religious base; others are predominantly secular. The impetus to congregate and coalesce runs deep. Those who work on unpopular or minority issues appreciate, indeed need, the sense of community and fellowship which joint action fosters. In addition, FCNL's longevity, experience and "respectability" may be useful in launching new enterprises. And FCNL's prime lobbying location on Capitol Hill, directly across the street from the Hart Senate Office Building makes it an attractive place for meetings. One role for FCNL lobbyists in coalitions may be as "glue" to hold together their colleagues.[7]

FCNL staff members, at times, devote what often seems like an inordinate amount of effort to coalitions in which FCNL participates. This is especially true when the coalition has paid staff, budgets to raise, and personnel and administrative problems. FCNL staff have been deeply engaged as directors of organizations with budgets in the tens and hundreds of thousands of dollars, groups like the Coalition on National Priorities and Military Policy, the Coalition to Stop Funding the War, the National Council to Repeal the Draft, the Coalition for a New Foreign and Military Policy and its Human Rights and Central America Working Groups, and the Interreligious Task Force on U.S. Food Policy and its follow-on groups. Other coalitions are primarily involved in information sharing, which often leads to legislative action. These have included groups like the Washington Interreligious Staff Council and its various subgroups, the Monday Arms Control Lobby and its Task Forces, and the Citizens Budget Campaign.

FCNL's Policy and Personnel Committees constantly need to ask FCNL lobbyists to justify their coalitional efforts when they involve major time commitments.

A list of coalitions, clearing houses, campaigns, task forces, and

191

working groups in which FCNL staff took significant leadership roles at one time or another during its first 50 years looks something like this:

- National Civil Liberties Clearing House;
- Point Four Information Service;
- International Development Conference;
- Disarmament Information Service;
- Washington Interreligious Staff Council (WISC) with its subgroups on foreign policy, Native Americans, human needs, civil liberties, environment, energy and agriculture;
- Vietnam war: Wednesdays in Washington;
- Vietnam: Challenge to the Conscience of America;
- Set the Date Now;
- Coalition to Stop Funding the War;
- National Council to Repeal the Draft;
- Committee Against Registration and the Draft;
- Coalition on National Priorities and Military Policy;
- Coalition for a New Foreign and Military Policy;
- Human Rights Working Group;
- Central America Working Group;
- Interreligious Task Force on U.S. Food Policy with its Farm Policy and Domestic Human Needs Working Groups;
- Interfaith Action for Economic Justice with its Domestic Human Needs and Economic Policy, and International Development Policy Work Groups;
- Middle East Forums;
- International Development Forums;
- Foreign Assistance Working Group;
- UN Education and Advocacy Group;
- Development Bank Assessment Network;
- Churches for Middle East Peace;
- Monday Arms Control Lobby with its subgroups the U.S.-Soviet Working Group and the Arms Transfer Working Group; and
- Citizens Budget Campaign.

Three organizations which I like to believe FCNL had some small part in launching are:

- the Washington Office on Latin America (WOLA). Diane Edwards LaVoy helped initiate this group in 1973 and 1974 after leaving her work as one of FCNL's first two interns. The highly effective Joe Eldridge, Methodist missionary, made WOLA a major player in human rights in Washington in the 1970s and 1980s.
- the National Campaign for a Peace Tax Fund. This grew out of the Historic Peace Churches concern for an alternative C.O. provision in the income tax laws. Marian Franz, Mennonite, is currently the able and articulate leader of this organization.
- NETWORK, a Catholic nuns lobby on peace and social justice issues. NETWORK organizers used FCNL as one model for its work which began in 1970. It tapped into the deep vein of peace and social activism in the Catholic Church and has provided impressive leadership among religious organizations on these issues on Capitol Hill. NETWORK and FCNL share many of the same policies and priorities and comprise a Mutual Admiration Society (MAS.)

> We know there are no utopias, no pure visions. We know we are part of the problem, that evil is not totally out there. Living with that kind of tension makes us more tolerant. We don't expect instant results. We realize we are always in transition, that making a difference is complicated....Our activity may be absurd, but...we look at Jesus, somewhat the fool in His historical context. Yet He started something. We don't measure success by whether we achieve a lot. We are getting somewhere if the process continues. Eventually things will be different. God promised.
>
> *Excerpt from NETWORK statement reviewing their history, quoted in FCNL MEMO No. 251, Sept. 1979, p.6.*

Should We Have Done More?

Of course. Could we? This attempt to summarize some of the activities of FCNL on Capitol Hill during 50 years leaves me doubtful we could have done much more. My impression now is the same as when I came to FCNL in 1955 from a large private law firm: FCNL efficiently produces a remarkable amount of relevant work, given its small staff and limited resources. Contributors get their money's worth.

Have we missed the boat by working too much or not enough on some issues? One hesitates to second guess a process in which a great deal of trust is placed in the leadings of the Spirit and sensitive Friends. Two questions which we must continue to ask are:

1) When should we stand firm on principle and when should we compromise to be relevant to the legislative process?

2) Is there a major campaign FCNL should undertake now in an attempt to establish some basic principles in national policy–similar to the 1950s campaign for general and complete disarmament? Is there some way, legislatively, to encapsulate our basic belief in nonviolence and justice? Should more be done to support nonviolent resistance as a national security policy? Should we try even harder to refine proposals for global and domestic economic and social policy?

On several celebratory occasions involving coalitions, I have shared a message which is especially appropriate to FCNL:

> A Friend in a Meeting for Worship once told about an incident in Saudi Arabia where he was working at the time. His family was enjoying a picnic in the cool of the evening, overcome by the beauty of the brilliant colors of the desert sunset. Across the scene came a jet so distant they could see nothing but the

plume of the contrail against the magnificent sky. He thought about the passengers on the plane–eating, sleeping, reading, absorbed in their own private thoughts or conversations. Probably almost all were completely oblivious to what was happening just outside the cabin window.

"They were passing through Glory, and they didn't even know it." May we be given the sensitivity to know when we are passing through Glory—even in Washington, D.C., even on Capitol Hill.

Notes

1. Harmon Ziegler, "The Effects of Lobbying: A Comparative Assessment," in Norman R. Luttberg, ed. *Public Opinion and Public Policy*, Homewood, Ill.: The Dorsey Press, 1968.

2. D.P. Forsythe, "Humanizing American Foreign Policy: Non-Profit Lobbying and Human Rights," Institution for Social and Policy Studies, Yale University, 1980, n.50, p.F9

3. Buell Trowbridge, "To Win the Assent of Reasonable Minds," FCNL Publ. (1965)

4. A Conversation with Senator George McGovern," FCNL Publ. undated (1963?)

5. See FCNL Doc. G-56, July 23, 1974.

6. FCNL "Statement on the Issue of Presidential Impeachment," Jan. 27, 1974.

7. L. Schoultz, *op. cit.*, p. 81.

Ed and Bonnie Snyder at FCNL's 1989 Annual Meeting.

General Committee member, Jim Bristol, helps Ed Snyder celebrate his 35 years at FCNL during FCNL's 1989 Annual Meeting.

In 1992, the Arms Transfers Working Group presents a plaque to Senator Patrick Leahy (D-VT) commending him for passage of the anti-personnel land-mine moratorium prohibiting sales and export of U.S. land-mines to foreign countries. Left to right: Darryl Fagin, Americans for Democratic Action; Amy Wilson, FCNL Legislative Intern; Joe Volk, FCNL Executive Secretary; Sima Osdoby, Women's Action for New Directions; Senator Patrick Leahy; Thomas Cardamone, Council for a Livable World, Education Fund; Bob Alpern, Unitarian Universalist Association; Caleb Rossiter, Project on Demilitarization and Democracy; Tim Rieser, Senate Foreign Operations.

FCNL: In the Moment Or of the Moment?

by Joe Volk

Every day we on the FCNL staff handle demands of the moment, matters of real importance and of genuine concern to Friends. From administrative duties, to fundraising activities, to hearing concerns of visitors or reading heartfelt correspondence, the staff and committee members respond adequately as they can to many calls of the moment: What is FCNL doing about Rwanda? How can I best advocate for true health care reform? What is FCNL's position on the status of Jerusalem? Why does FCNL advocate arms control over abolition? Should we support gambling on Indian reservations? If FCNL were to respond to each call of the moment, we would soon be making empty gestures. True lobbying requires more than policy stands or statements. It requires work to determine facts, recruiting people with firsthand experience, knowledge of whom to approach with what might be accomplished, and time for prayer and worship in which to seek guidance. Fortunately, FCNL has set some outside parameters to the scope of its work through the biennial legislative priorities selection process. Yet, in my short tenure, there have been two principal challenges to our calling as proponents of Quaker vision and values: an internal questioning of the Peace Testimony and an external question of what does FCNL stand *for?*

The following reflections come from two papers presented by a call to address Philadelphia Yearly Meeting in 1993 and by a June, 1994 demand from Representative Ron Dellums (D-CA) for the peace movement to present policies, not protests. Outside of weekly worship, in my day-to-day duties I have little time for reflection. And, although we must always be ready to respond to openings of the moment, we must also be ready to act in the moment — the moment of truth, the moment of way opening, and in the moment grounded in God's grace.

Quaker Peace Testimony: Past or Future?

As a spokesperson for FCNL, an organization which wants and needs all the Quaker support it can get, I am in no position to offend anyone. And yet, I now address what has become in Philadelphia Yearly Meeting and in other yearly meetings a controversial topic: the Quaker Peace Testimony.

"The Quaker Peace Testimony, controversial?" Yes, but then it always has been controversial. The Peace Testimony has been tested through a series of wars which include the 17th century civil wars in England, the Indian Wars in Pennsylvania, the colonies' revolution, the Mexican War, the Civil War, the Spanish-American War, the war against the Indian Nations in the West, the War to End All Wars, the War Against Hitler's Nazis, Mussolini's and Hirohito's Fascists, the Korean War, the Bay of Pigs, the Dominican Republic Invasion, the Vietnam War, the U.S.—supported military coup against the elected Allende government in Chile, the UNITA war with the Angolan government, the Central American wars of the late '70s and the '80s, the covert war in Afghanistan, the '48, '56, '67, '72, '82 Arab-Israeli wars, the invasion of Grenada, the invasion of Panama, the Gulf War of 1990-91, and the big one, the 50 years' war which we called the Cold War. Indeed, much of our public life is shaped by war.

In each of these wars, and others, Friends have disagreed about the meaning and demands of the Peace Testimony. Yet, for more than three hundred years, the Quaker Peace Testimony has held an important place at the center of our society, the Religious Society of Friends.

Friends of whom? Early on it was the Religious Society of

Friends of Jesus, the Prince of Peace. The one who told Peter to put away his sword in the Garden of Gesthemene; the one who said, "Love your enemy as yourself"; the one who reminded his disciples that "... in as much as you do it unto the least of these my brethren, you have done it unto me."

Philadelphia Yearly Meeting's *Faith and Practice*, adopted in 1955 and revised in 1972, says this:

> "...We want security for ourselves and for our neighbors. There is no security except in creating situations in which people do not want to harm you. This is a difficult truth for most people to face, but the difficulty is more emotional than rational or scientific. If thine enemy hunger, feed him,' is not only Christian teaching, but it is profound wisdom, for the best way of getting rid of an enemy is to convert him into a friend..."[1]

During our own bloody civil war, a woman chided Lincoln, saying he should *destroy* the rebels. He answered, "What, madam, do I not destroy my enemies when I make them my friends?" Clearly, one does not have to be a pacifist or a Quaker to understand the basis of peace making.

Another selection about the Peace Testimony is especially pertinent as we face the problem of evil in Somalia, Cambodia, Bosnia-Herzegovina, and other hot spots:

> "We feel bound explicitly to avow our continued unshaken persuasion that all war is utterly incompatible with the plain precepts of our Living Lord and Law-giver, and with the whole spirits and tenor of His Gospel; and that no plea of necessity or of policy, however urgent or peculiar, can avail to release either individuals or nations from the paramount allegiance which they owe unto Him who has said, 'Love your enemies.' To carry out such a profession consistently is indeed a life attainment, but it should be the aim of every Christian. It is a solemn thing

to stand forth to the nation as the advocates of inviolable peace; and our testimony loses its efficacy in proportion to the want of consistency in any amongst us."[2]

John Woolman, too, is cited in *Faith and Practice:*

"Oh, that we who declare against wars, and acknowledge our trust to be in God only, may walk in the light, and therein examine our foundation and motives in holding great estates: May we look upon our treasurers, the furniture of our houses, and our garments, and try whether the seeds of war have nourishment in these our possessions."[3]

These examples of the Quaker Peace Testimony from the past are familiar. What about our present? The problem of evil and how to respond to it exists at home and abroad. Some manifestations of the problem of evil are armed violence in the streets; so-called ethnic cleansing (which is genocide) in the former Yugoslavia and in parts of Africa; systematic rape of women and children; ecocide, the purposeful destruction of the environment; the targeting of civilians by combatants, and the use of food as a weapon.

As always, trust is the first casualty of war. But, make no mistake, these evils are being done to real and innocent people. We cannot close our eyes to evil. But, seeing it, what will we do?

Somalia posed this question, and President Bush sent 28,000 combat troops to make that country safe for humanitarian aid delivery. In his December, 1990 public send off of the Marines, President Bush said, "You are doing God's work." A different Quaker response to his remark demonstrates that our Peace Testimony is not a formula which is easily applied to every situation. We need and must ask for the leading of divine guidance. Let me give you a personal example of what I mean.

On the evening of December 23rd, the MacNeil-Lehrer News Hour opened with a thirty minute, heart-rending report by Charlene Hunter Gault, who was in Somalia. The human tragedy shown on the TV was irrefutable. It demanded an urgent human response. It was two days before Christmas. The U.S. military families had sacrificed much so that these, mostly young, Marines could serve and protect in Somalia. The humanitarian intervention, the report said, would save lives and do good.

Next came a panel of six religious leaders — a rabbi, a nun, an Islamic leader, a Southern Baptist minister, an Episcopal priest, and a Quaker. We panelists had no rehearsal, and we had no script. It would be a round table discussion.

Robin MacNeil turned first to the rabbi. Was the U.S. humanitarian military intervention God's work? Rabbi Alexander Schindler said yes. He explained that some wars are justified and some are not. He served in World War II but would have refused to serve in Vietnam. This U.S. mission to Somalia was not even a war, it was humanitarian service. Of course, this was God's work.

MacNeil then turned to me and asked, "Mr. Volk, can the military do God's work?" It was a sudden, and for me, unexpected, transition. I had to represent Friends appropriately and tell the truth. But what was the truth? I said, "No, you cannot do God's work with a sword or a gun . . . "

Whether my answer was divinely led or only my opinion, is for others and for time to judge. Our FCNL Policy and Executive Committees have carefully considered how FCNL policy was applied by staff in the Somalia situation, and they have affirmed this approach.

My answer was informed by consultations with Quaker and Mennonite aid workers in Somalia and their direct experience. I had also been in an off-the-record consultation with heads of very large aid agencies, a consultation convened by AFSC (American Friends Service Committee) and MCC (Mennonite Central Committee).

When the program was over, Richard Land, the director of the Christian Life Commission of the Southern Baptist Church, and I rode together to LaGuardia Airport. We had disagreed about the humanitarian intervention policy. On the way back we spoke mostly about family and our experiences in rural and urban living. However, just in case it had not sunk in, he did remind me that war can be, and often has been, justified by the Bible and that Christians have been able to justify wars for centuries using just war principles. In fact, he had helped President Bush to see that the just war theory could undergird the U.S. military intervention in Somalia.

Some concerned Friends have agreed with the just war approach. Take, for example, this letter from a thoughtful and concerned member of Philadelphia Yearly Meeting:

> "...(I am) stimulated to register my strong disapproval of your position on the MacNeil-Lehrer program re: Somalia relief aid by the U.N. peacekeeping force (mostly U.S.A.). I heard it and was saddened and humiliated ...I assume that you must have conferred with your executive committee in advance of this appearance. I presume you obtained a majority approval from them. I hope that you will register my disapproval to them...I thought the Protestant (Baptist minister, I believe) expressed the logical view, and your view made Quakers appear to offer nothing....I think that the FCNL position on pacifism should be that we respect each individual's right to refuse to bear arms. This, however, does not translate into a recommendation of national policy by the Society of Friends. This Somalia action seems so clearly a humanitarian use of police force that I think others will think we are stubborn fools in refusing to support it..."

This Friend's letter goes on to make additional thoughtful points. It illustrates that some thoughtful Friends not only found the FCNL position uncomfortable, but they found it downright wrong and pigheaded. No one likes to hear such tough criticism, but we will do more than hear it. We will give it thoughtful review and consideration as we evaluate our work and direction. Indeed, in January 1994, FCNL convened Quaker workers from Europe, Canada, and the U.S to reexamine our position on peacekeeping and peace making forces.

In contrast, I welcomed news of a syndicated column by the

author Howard Fast. He said that he watches the News Hour regularly and had seen the segment on Somalia. Howard Fast wrote this in his Christmas column:

> ...in the course of watching and listening to this debate (on the MacNeil-Lehrer News Hour) I had witnessed the most gently and valid expression of this Christmas Season. It came from the Quaker, Joseph Volk, and from the nun, Sister Camille.
> ...Volk listened to this discussion and when it came his turn to speak, he shook his head and said, "No, no good can come from violence" and that, in his faith, there was a long tradition of healing the sick, and feeding the hungry, that it had always been done without guns or violence, and that it still could be done that way....He was not hooted down; the four men who backed the Somalia move were too polite for that, but they put aside his words as if they were meaningless dreams of a slender, gentle person who was not of the world of practical man, although the Quakers have managed to work and live by those words for a long time.
> Volk was firm but neither argumentative or loud. Unquestionably, he had heard the arguments of the others many times. He was not shaken. This was the world he lived in.[4]

Indeed, I have heard the arguments of the others many times before. Almost always, they say, "We tried all the alternatives. Using the military was only a last resort. What else could we do?"

First, I argue that even if one has arrived at the option of last resort, even if taking that option is legal and constitutional, you may not want to take it. Why? Because it may fail to keep its promises. Remember, just because it is the last resort does not mean it will work.

Second, even if the military option will work, I have to ask two questions: (1) how can you answer to that of God in every person with the barrel of a gun or a rocket launcher?, and (2) can you train a person to use weapons on order against other human beings and still answer to that of God in the trainee? I have gone through basic combat training, advanced individual training in the infantry, and mechanized cavalry combat training in Vietnam. I have lived in an Army stockade with fellow human beings who used that kind of training in Vietnam. My brother is also such a veteran. On the basis of that personal experience and on the basis of my experience of God in worshipping community, I do not see how Friends could endorse or advocate military intervention, even for purposes of humanitarian intervention.

Third, I want to offer a reply to the question, "Well, but what else could we have done in Somalia?" Some humanitarian aid workers in Somalia, many Somalis included, strongly disagree with the decision for "humanitarian military intervention." As I have listened to their stories, here is what I have heard: They think the United States and the international community should have:

Formed better options for Somalia: For example, U.S. and Soviet Cold War policies for the Horn of Africa narrowed options to the militarization of the region. Inappropriate development boondoggles by the Italian government in the '70s and '80s corrupted the Somali culture and government. U.S. policies of support to the dictator, Siad Barre, in the '80s formed options for dictatorship and decline. The Soviets bear similar responsibility. The superpowers and Italy could have shaped options for democracy and development. Their money could have been channeled through multilateral—perhaps the U.N.—development agencies to support indigenous Somali non-governmental organizations to strengthen Somalia's self-reliance.

But that is history. The relevant question is whether practical alternatives to military intervention exist now. **Yes. The United States and the international community could still:**

Use Economic Incentives to Disarm the Warlords' Gangs: Somalia is poor in food and medicine and rich in weapons and ammunition. Think about that. How is that possible?

Economic incentives for giving up weapons will be more effective—even more cost-effective—than militarily coerced disarmament. U.N. purchasing of weapons and munitions would start the flow of weapons out of Somalia. Food, medical care, supplies of seeds for planting, sets of agricultural tools, and vocational training vouchers would all serve as the currency for these transactions. This kind of currency would foster appropriate economic development and reduce the levels of armaments

Send Emergency Food and Medical Aid in a more appropriate way: Food and medicine need to be delivered to Somalia through many, diverse, unarmed, and small projects, each entering the country from numerous points and focussing on different regions of the country that need help. Most important though, whatever aid is provided should be in answer to needs defined by civilian Somali leaders and organizations, and the aid should (must!) be directed and implemented by them, not by outsiders. The AFSC has been able to do this by sustaining an indigenous staffed program over a period of years, since 1982. Quakers *have* been actively involved; we are not offering nothing. The MCC and some NGOs have done without armed security, too.

Somalia needs the humanitarian aid equivalent of a fleet of bicycles; instead, it got a few behemoth Edsels. The warlord's violence has followed the "aid streams" of the big, centralized aid projects, from cities out to villages. Good intentions were thwarted by an aid design and a scale that fed the warlords' greed. Compounding this well-meant but inept aid delivery system, some humanitarian agencies called for "U.S. humanitarian military intervention" to protect themselves, so that they could serve starving Somalia.

Empower movements for reconciliation, peace and civilian government: A stable and enduring peace will be built from the bottom up, not from the warlords down. The warlords are just what the term says, the leaders of wars. They are not the leaders of the teachers, the women's organizations, the farmers, the religious communities, or of the professionals. International peacekeeping efforts can direct scarce resources, such as radio broadcasting facilities, to the real, civilian Somali leaders. Somalis across several clans and regions want to educate and communicate for a culture of peace. Peace negotiations should start with these teachers, professionals, poets, musicians, and public servants—not with the warlords. A reconciliation and peace process which begins with the warlords at the national level will end with a transfer of power to armed thugs.

The options in Somalia and elsewhere are not limited to either doing nothing or taking military action. In the long run, those two choices have the same result: violence and injustice.

God's work cannot be done with a sword or a gun. We reap what we sow. Now that our world has leapt "from Cold War to Hot Peace," we must not repeat the Somalia model. We need new, mature thinking that is based on the fact that means and ends are related. Nonviolence—submitting to the power of truth and acting as if every person is a holy place—it is still our best hope.

I offer these observations—some might say declarations—not in the belief that these remarks settle the matter, but as an invitation to our continued dialogue. By the grace of God we may be given new light and a renewed center.

Notes

1. *Faith and Practice,* p. 91, quoting James Vail's Pendle Hill Pamphlet No. 70, pp. 12-15.

2. Ibid. pp. 90-91, quoting London Yearly Meeting, Epistle, 1854.

3. Ibid. p. 90, quoting John Woolman, *Journal*, New Century ed.: 1900, p. 279.

4. Howard Fast, "Is U.S. Doing God's Work in Somalia? Opinions Differ," quoted from *Lincoln Journal-Star*, 1/1/93, syndicated through *Greenwich Times*.

Envisioning the Next *Fifty Years:* Six *Revolutionary Trends*

by Stephen L. Klineberg

During the past fifty years, Friends' witness in Washington was sorely needed and clearly made a difference. The Friends Committee on National Legislation was intimately involved in mitigating the intimidation and chauvinism in the years after World War II, when human rights and freedoms were threatened both at home and abroad. Its staff and volunteers worked to defuse the increasingly dangerous Cold War and to reverse the accelerating arms race that was fueling many smaller and hotter wars throughout the world. When too few in Congress were listening, FCNL pressed for programs to improve the prospects of America's hungry and homeless, to stand with Native Americans in their struggle to preserve their heritage and treaty rights, to enhance worldwide economic and social development, and to halt the destruction of the earth's environment.

Through it all, this small organization has brought sophistication and consistency to a spirit-led voice in the halls of Washington. For fifty years, with gentle persuasion it has urged government officials to transcend the immediate pressures of money and votes and to work instead for a world in which justice, peace and hope might reign.

An anniversary of this importance is an appropriate time to reflect not only on the achievements, struggles and disappointments of the past, but also on the work that lies ahead. As part of the Fiftieth Anniversary Jubilee, a small working committee of FCNL, known as the Futures Committee, identified six revolutionary trends that have clearly been reshaping our world and that seem likely to grow ever more compelling in the decades ahead. They were offered then, and are presented below, as a way to stimulate reflection and discussion. They may help to clarify the dominating challenges that lie ahead, and enable us to envision some of the ways in which Friends may be called to respond.

1. Demographic Revolutions

The earth's population now exceeds 5.6 billion, and it is growing by more than 95 million additional human beings every year. In Jesus' time, just 2000 years ago, the entire human population of the earth was less than the current U.S. population of 250 million. Not until the year 1800 did the earth's population reach one billion human beings. Just one hundred years later, there were 2 billion. In only 60 years, 3 billion. Fifteen years later, 4 billion. Eleven years after that, 5 billion. Almost all analysts predict at least another doubling to 10 billion people by the middle of the next century, absent catastrophe.

More than 95 percent of that growth will occur in nations that can least afford it. As the population of the world's poorest countries continues to expand, it will greatly complicate efforts to mitigate the continuing high levels of hunger, poverty and despair, of unemployment and social unrest, of environmental and migration pressures. By almost any measure, world population growth in a context of global industrial expansion is the most critical challenge we will face as a human family during the next fifty years. Somehow we must find a way, with strengthened regard for the human rights, dignity and freedom of each individual, to bring the earth's human numbers and appetites rapidly into sustainable relationship with the life-support systems of the planet.

Two other unfolding demographic revolutions are happening in American society itself. We are witnessing both the "aging" of America and the rapid growth of its Hispanic and Asian populations. Despite mounting disparities in income and life circumstances, the American people generally are living longer, healthier, richer and more varied lives than human beings ever have before. There are no precedents for the mass of a population living into old age. In 1850, only 2 percent of Americans survived to age 65. Today, more than 75 percent do so, and the fastest growing age segment of all is comprised of Americans over the age of 85. Old age itself is a new life stage in human experience. Its boundaries are fluid and unclear, its nature and meaning as yet undefined.

The "gift of mass longevity" has been so recent, dramatic and rapid that it still takes us by surprise, and in many respects it is still profoundly unsettling. For all of us eventually, the gift of long life will come at the cost of chronic disease and disability. The medical expenses incurred in the last few months of a person's life typically exceed those in all the preceding years. In previous eras, most Americans died "before their time." Today, increasing numbers of us are living "past our time."

At the end of its 1987 Statement of Legislative Policy, the General Committee of FCNL listed several unresolved issues as "Challenges to the Society of Friends." The first such challenge spoke to the "Boundaries of life. What is the proper role of government with regard to critical issues of life, such as euthanasia, medical intervention, and abortion?" The demographic revolutions are bringing these terribly difficult issues to the forefront of public debate. Increasingly, we are challenged to re-examine traditional assumptions as we seek to understand what these times demand of us, to consider what we are called to do in a world that is, in this as in so many other respects, unprecedented in human history.

A third demographic transformation is occurring in the ethnic composition of the American population. Between 1492 and 1965, more than 80 percent of all persons who came to these shores came from Europe. The United States of America was deliberately an amalgam almost exclusively of European nationalities. Until 1965, immigration was governed by the notorious National Origins Quota Act of 1921. One of the most viciously racist laws in American history, the act established a preference system designed to freeze the ethnic mix of the American population. Permission to immigrate into the country would henceforth be determined by an applicant's ethnicity and national origin. In addition, the act explicitly identified Slavs, Jews and Italians as racially and culturally inferior, to be limited to tiny quotas. "Mongols" were believed to be especially dangerous, and Asians were banned entirely.

After 1965, when Congress finally revised the immigration laws, the numbers of newcomers into America began to grow rapidly, and the proportions among them who were Europeans fell precipitously. In the decade of the 1960s, 3.2 million immigrants arrived, of whom only 34 percent were Europeans. There were 5 million immigrants in the 1970s, with only 18 percent from Europe. In the most recent decade, almost 10 million immigrated to America, and only 11 percent of them were Europeans. Immigrants from Asia, Latin America and the Caribbean accounted for more than 83 percent of all the new entrants during the 1980s.

The current wave of immigration, like those before it, enriches and renews the older American community, but it also subjects it to social tension. This is especially true in bad economic times, when jobs are scarce and even native-born citizens are unsure of their place in society. Little wonder that today, as in previous eras of large-scale immigration, ugly expressions of anti-immigrant sentiment are sweeping over the U.S. and many other countries.

Resentment is taking the form of legislation that would seal the borders, close down economic opportunities, and diminish the freedoms that newcomers might otherwise find in the U.S. As the new immigration continues, there will surely be additional proposals to deny education, health care and other benefits to undocumented immigrants, and require schools to report to the federal government on the legal status of their students. Friends' voices will be needed to remind this nation of its fundamental commitment to human rights. The overheated rhetoric that paints all newcomers as threatening terrorists or burdens on society will need to be countered vigorously by the charge to treat all persons—particularly the most vulnerable—with dignity, fairness and decency. There are legitimate concerns about the new immigration, but they need to be tempered by a clear understanding that immigrants are not the cause of the nation's problems and that closing American borders will do little to solve them.

Inevitably and irreversibly, the U.S. is in rapid transition from having been basically a biracial society dominated by white males into becoming a truly multi-cultural and multi-ethnic community. In the new America, no one ethnic group or gender will ever again automatically predominate. Once an amalgam primarily of European nationalities, the U.S. is rapidly becoming the first nation ever in human history to be a microcosm of all the world's people, the first truly "universal nation." The evolution into a conspicuously multiethnic society will be marked by conflict and controversy, but it is irreversibly the America to come. In the course of navigating that remarkable transition, Americans will need frequently to be reminded that the diversity of its people strengthens and enriches society as a whole and enhances its ability to meet the challenges that lie ahead.

As a result of these demographic revolutions, the "aging" of America is turning out to be a division along ethnic lines as well as generational ones. It is primarily the European population that is aging rapidly, while younger generations are likely to be African-Americans, Hispanics and Asians. According to the Bureau of Labor Statistics, in the year 1990 non-Hispanic white males comprised 43 percent of all full-time American workers. During the next fifteen years, the Bureau projects a net increase of 26 million American workers. Fewer than 4 million of them (less than 15 percent) will be native-born white males. Women will comprise 57 percent of the expected growth in the labor force; Blacks, Hispanics and Asians will account for 54 percent. America's future now depends, in a way that has never been as true before, on the education and opportunities it provides to its "minority" children.

Far from recognizing the importance of investing in that future, the nation has instead instituted a remarkable transfer of wealth and influence from younger to older Americans. Thirty years ago, before the great expansion of social security and the abandonment of the "great society" programs, there was an equal probability that a child under six and a person over 65 would be living in poverty. Today a child under six is four times more likely to be poor than is a senior citizen. Since 1970, welfare payments to parents of young children have been cut in real terms by 42 percent. And by 1990, more than 60 percent of all federal outlays to individuals were going to the 12 percent of Americans who were 65 and older.

Issues of generational and interethnic equity, along with society's moral obligation to care for its children, thus combine to call for sweeping transformations in the priorities that govern public expenditures. But poor parents are far less likely to vote or to contribute to political campaigns than are the affluent elderly, and the A.A.R.P. has become one of the most powerful lobbies in Washington. Achieving greater justice in the allocation of government resources will require strong countervailing efforts to strengthen the voices of those whose needs are too easily ignored in the halls of Congress.

2. The Transformation of the American Family

Americans generally continue to think of the "traditional" (and the only "correct") family as the one that consists of a breadwinner-father and a homemaker-mother with two or more biological children. Historians tell us that that particular kind of family generally predominates in the early stages of the industrialization process. Indeed, the rise of the "breadwinner" family reached its peak in the U.S. in the year 1890, when the fewest number of married women were employed outside the home; then it began to evolve toward the "two-paycheck" family. But during the extraordinary period of affluence after World War II, the "traditional" family experienced a remarkable resurgence.

The postwar years, from 1945 to 1973, were a time of unparalleled economic expansion. Through the application of wondrous technological inventions combined with ever cheaper energy, the national GNP per capita literally doubled between 1950 and 1970. Median family incomes were growing by 2.5 to 3.5 percent per year, inflation was virtually non-existent, and unemployment kept moving steadily downward. Those were the years when the "marital and procreative imperative" dominated the national psyche and Americans celebrated the stay-at-home housewife-mother in suburbia, when families had an average of 3.6 children and the Baby Boom was launched upon the land.

After 1973, most of the economic indicators suddenly changed direction. The annual growth in output per worker dropped from an average of 2.5 percent per year over the 1948-1973 period to 0.8 percent between 1973 and 1979, and to 0.4 percent in the 1980s. Between 1973 and 1990, the real wages earned by the average American worker actually declined by 7 percent. Family incomes could keep pace with inflation only by putting more people to work.

The effort to maintain high living standards despite declining wages was the primary reason for the most profound social revolution of the 20th century—the great trek of married women into the labor force that brought an end to the family patterns and rigid sex-role distinctions that had dominated the industrial era. In 1947, only 20 percent of married women living with their husbands worked outside the home. That figure rose slowly to 25 percent in 1950 and to 29 percent in 1960. The percentage of wives in the work force accelerated to 45 percent by 1970, and to 58 percent in 1980. By 1990, more than two-thirds of all married women were working outside the home. In 1970, less than ten percent of infants under one year of age had mothers in the work force. In 1990, well over half of all mothers of children younger than one were working outside the home to support their families.

Thus the central realities of family life in America have changed profoundly over the past 30 years. The traditional breadwinner family has been largely replaced by single-parent and two-paycheck families. Yet the nation's school schedules, work roles, public policies and role expectations continue in ways that were appropriate to the 1950s, impeding effective responses to the real needs of families and children today.

American schools continue to dismiss the children at 3:00 p.m., as if there were still a full-time mother at home, ready to drive them to enriching after-school activities and to supervise their homework. American pupils continue to be given the longest summer vacations of any children in the Western world, as if they were still needed to help with the harvests on the family farm. European children generally go to school for 220 days a year, and Japanese children are in school for 240 days. But the average American child receives less than 180 days of schooling per year. It should come as no surprise that American high-school students consistently rank below their European and Japanese counterparts in international comparisons of scholastic achievement. They spend on average 25 percent less time in school, and parents in the full-time labor force are no longer able to supplement their children's learning as they once could.

Not only the schools, but America's employers as well appear to be stuck in a 1950s time warp, rooted in the assumption that their employees must surely have someone else at home to attend to the responsibilities of house and children. Most, of course, do not. Of all parents of young children in the American work force in 1990, fewer than 20 percent were married men with non-working wives; 80 percent had to make non-traditional arrangements to care for their children. Despite the urgent and obvious need, only 10 percent of the nation's employers offered *any* help with child care to employees with young children.

The singular notion that there is only one "correct" family pattern is necessarily giving way to a richer image of a wide variety of alternative arrangements. Yet deep-seated prejudices remain that continue to cause unwarranted pain and to obscure a clearer vision of what a true "pro-family" policy would be in our time. In the years immediately ahead, American legislators need to be encouraged to develop public policies that can offer meaningful assistance to parents as they seek to balance simultaneous responsibilities to jobs and to children in increasingly difficult times. And all citizens need to acknowledge that there are no magical solutions that might somehow reconstruct nostalgic images of the family and economy of the 1950s, that American families are struggling and they need the support and assistance of the wider community.

3. The Shift from Resources to Knowledge

In another truly historical transformation, the "resource economy" of the Industrial Age, in place for the past 250 years, is suddenly and definitively over. In that economy, the dominant occupation was the semiskilled production worker, and wealth came primarily from control over natural resources. Today, the good jobs that semiskilled workers used to take for granted have largely disappeared, and a nation's most crucial economic resources no longer derive from the raw materials of nature, but are to be found instead in the creativity and skills of its people.

In the global "knowledge economy" of the 1990s and beyond, all adults now find themselves swimming in a single worldwide labor pool. The global labor force is adding 45 million additional workers every year, many well educated and highly motivated, prepared to start work immediately for a fraction of the U.S. wage. The only way to make a good salary in this new world is to have well-developed skills and to be able to do things that people in other countries cannot do. Failing that, the only alternative way to compete is to be willing to work for low wages. As a result of these new realities, the income gap between rich and poor in America is widening rapidly.

According to the latest census, men in the full-time workforce who had college degrees in 1990 were earning on average 9 percent more, controlling for inflation, than college-educated men earned in 1980. But men with just a high-school diploma were earning 7 percent less compared with high-school graduates ten years earlier, and those who had not graduated from high school in 1990 were making 14 percent *less* than did men of comparable education in 1980.

Low-skilled jobs in the U.S. are paying less than ever before. Among all Americans today who are working at full-time jobs (40 hours a week, 50 weeks a year), 18 percent are unable to earn enough to lift their families out of poverty.

As the ethnic transformation of America continues in an economy in which education is the central determinant of life chances, it is more important than ever to reverse the educational inequalities that continue to separate Americans of European background from others. Only if the nation can find a way to ensure that Black, Hispanic and Asian children receive the same opportunities as those of European descent to learn in school and throughout their lives, will there be a chance to build a country and a people that can redeem the promise of the new millennium.

The critical challenge will be to develop the political will and commitment to initiate and sustain new investments in infrastructure and "human capital." The nation will need to provide more and better education to the less favored 60 percent of its children. It will need to institute family-support systems that make learning possible for poor children and provide additional training after high school to all noncollege-going students.

Any meaningful program of this sort would fly in the face of prevailing political sentiment in America. The current conventional wisdom continues to be based on the belief that taxes on the wealthy should be lowered, public spending cut, and government deficits reduced, while total military-related spending, including the military share of interest on the national debt, claims 45 percent of the federal budget.

Those with the greatest power and wealth in America, whose incomes derive from their favored positions in the transnational economy, are able to provide their children with private schools, private recreation, private child-support systems and private security. They are unlikely to believe that they stand to benefit personally and directly from major increases in public investments. Enlightened self-interest is no longer a sufficient motivator, and there are few signs that a new social vision is emerging to inspire sacrifice for the common good.

The economic reforms most needed by the majority of Americans are unlikely to be initiated and will not be sustained unless they are rooted in a broadly shared moral vision of human interdependence. More than ever, this nation will need to hear Friends' witness to the truth about human persons and communities and to the imperatives and responsibilities that derive therefrom.

4. The Rise of the Global Economy

The nations of the world are now linked into a single worldwide economic system, spearheaded by a few hundred corporate giants, supported by government policies and trade agreements among the leading states. With products that can be produced anywhere and sold everywhere, the new economic system is spreading credit and consumerism around the world through interconnecting global channels of communication that can penetrate any village or neighborhood. National boundaries are eroding, along with the authority and power of national governments, as corporations search worldwide for the lowest possible wage scales, the fewest governmental regulations, the highest profits and the lowest taxes. People everywhere are becoming entangled in global webs that are transforming their lives, severing family ties, undermining established authority and straining the bonds of local communities.

Many millions in North America, Europe and Asia are benefiting handsomely from the new globalization, but there is a huge and growing gulf between the beneficiaries and the excluded, between those who have access to modern knowledge, technologies and jobs, and those who do not. As subsistence agriculture declines everywhere, hundreds of millions are drawn into the money economy and need jobs in order to survive, but for vast numbers of them there are not enough opportunities to earn a living wage.

The fatal flaws in the emerging global economic system are increasingly evident. The new order founders on the inadequacy of the work-roles it provides, and on the environmental consequences of industrial production. As world population grows and new technologies continue to destroy more jobs than they create, huge and increasing numbers of gifted and undervalued human beings are simply not needed to provide goods or services, because too many people in the world are too poor to buy them. And when they do find jobs in the global workforce, many in poor nations are subject to indignities and abuse that violate the most elementary standards of human decency. Either nations will find a way to raise global standards to some basic minimum, or workers everywhere will be dragged down together by the forces of international competition.

Moreover, the frail hope that enough new jobs might yet be created through an heroic expansion of global production and consumption is contradicted by the limitations inherent in the earth's capacity to withstand massive increases in industrial activity. How much more environmental destruction can be tolerated as the price of such expansion? And who will bear the economic and human costs associated with the enormous increases in pollution that would be generated by the spread of Western-style mass production and consumption on a global scale?

All around the world, local citizens' movements and nongovernmental organizations are resisting this narrow version of the global order. They are developing alternative strategies to meet basic human needs in a way that can preserve local traditions, religious and cultural life, biological species and other treasures of the natural world. Some of the new movements are animated primarily by environmental concerns; others by human rights, by concern for the dispossessed, or by hostility to patriarchy and racism. Together, they are developing visions of human community that are based on the coming together of cultural diversity with a common commitment to ending poverty, oppression and violence. Increasingly, Friends' concerns are part of a worldwide struggle for human dignity, premised on a belief in the capacity of human beings everywhere to organize their collective lives on the basis of nonviolence, equity and sustainability.

An alternative form of global civilization may thus be emerging, spinning different webs of transnational solidarity. There is new hope that a more humane and participatory civil society on a truly global level may yet be possible, that the earth might be sustained by respect for human diversity and by an overarching frame of community sentiment that embraces all of creation. Government policy in Washington will play an important role in determining the way these differing versions of globalization will interact to shape the coming century.

5. Identity and Governance in a More Unstable World

The end of the Cold War was a blessing for humanity, but it has resulted in the often violent severing of established nations and institutions along ethnic or religious fault lines, as ancient animosities, submerged for generations, suddenly explode. Individuals and communities increasingly lay claim to exclusivist nationalisms, profoundly challenging the world's hope for greater universality, tolerance and democracy.

More than ever, it will be critical to make progress in demilitarizing the international system and in developing strong and effective multilateral peacekeeping institutions. World military expenditures in 1991 were conservatively estimated at $655 billion, while world expenditures on all UN peacekeeping efforts amounted to just $4.2 billion. In the words of FCNL's Newsletter of April 1994: "It is time for national and world leaders to promote non-military, nonviolent means of preventing and resolving conflicts. It is time to fully fund the United Nations."

The ending of the Cold War offers a realistic hope that American public policy might finally begin to address real national and global priorities. But the terrible waste and economic distortion of the Cold War era continues. The Pentagon still engages more than one-third of the nation's scientists and engineers and still demands a staggering $270 billion annually (amounting to more than $30 million every hour). The promised "peace dividend" is being diverted by vested interests that are seeking to protect their shares of the military pie and by the invention of new enemies around the world. Above all, it is threatened by the absence (so far) of widespread public demand for a significant shift in these spending priorities.

America's excessive military spending necessarily saps the nation's present and future economic strength. More broadly, human civilization as a whole will need to marshall hundreds of billions of additional dollars every year to cope successfully with hunger and poverty while healing the damage to the earth's environment. The only possible source for such funds lies in recycling the world's military budgets into peaceful purposes.

6. The Environmental Challenge

In the light of mounting evidence that is increasingly impossible to dismiss, it is clear that we humans are in the process of destroying the genetic diversity of the world's tropical forests, the purity of lakes, streams, inland seas, underground aquifers and oceans, the quality of the air we breathe, even the balance of atmospheric gasses that keeps our planet habitable. The dangers are coming both from the profligate use of resources by the rich and from the destruction of forests, soils and grasslands as the poor struggle for subsistence. Human numbers and appetites increasingly press up against intractable limits to the life-support systems and cleansing capacities of nature, forcing upon all human beings a genuine awareness of our shared fate on a finite and vulnerable planet.

It is now clear that nature's most potent threats to human welfare lie not so much in her age-old destructive powers, such as earthquakes, floods, hurricanes and tornadoes—devastating though these may sometimes be. The greatest dangers are to be found instead in the fragility of the web of life, in the limits to the earth's waste-absorptive and cleansing capacities, in the delicate interdependencies that support the processes of life itself on this planet. As noted management consultant Peter Drucker has observed, "Until the 19th century, the never-ending challenge was the protection of mankind and its habitat against the forces of nature. But in this century a new need has arisen: to protect nature against man." The survival of humanity itself depends on finding effective ways to reconcile human fulfillment with environmental protection and sustainable development.

There can be little doubt that industrial growth will soon have to slow down and change direction. The global civilization of the 21st century will necessarily rest on an economy that makes it more profitable to protect than to destroy the environment. It will be based on sustainable yields and renewable energies, on the recognition that serious environmental damage anywhere threatens everybody everywhere. It will be characterized by much slower growth in human populations and by the valuing of lives based more on being and becoming than on having.

As the late John McHale once put it, "It is not a question of alternatives to growth, but of alternative ways of growing." And a political party in New Zealand gave profound expression to the requirements of stewardship with these words: "We have not inherited the earth from our parents; we are borrowing it from our children." Friends' historic testimonies regarding simple living and the obligations for right sharing of nature's gifts are becoming urgent practical responsibilities.

On the Hinge of the Twenty-First Century

These are six of the converging revolutions that will surely inform the early decades of the new millennium. They call upon us to consider carefully the decisions we make in our personal lives, in our communities, in our lifestyles and our occupations, in the way we spend our money, time, talents and energies. Above all, they challenge us to strengthen our commitment to join with FCNL in collective efforts to influence the policy decisions that will be made in Washington and will affect the prospects of every person on earth.

Two insights from ancient China offer an appropriate way to end these reflections. First, that famous curse: In the old days of ancient China, when you were really angry with somebody, you might grab him or her by the lapel and say, "May you live in interesting times!" The Chinese knew that interesting times are extraordinarily difficult ones in which to live. They are the times when we experience the greatest discrepancy between the traditional assumptions with which we have long approached the world and the new realities that are suddenly upon us.

A second insight derives from the way in which the Chinese render the word for "crisis." It consists of two characters, one signifying *danger*, and the other, *opportunity*.

In this period of extraordinary transition, we are called to join in a committed effort to seize the opportunities and to derail the dangers that are inherent in the revolutionary trends that are changing the world. We are charged to undertake together the kinds of collective actions and sustained commitments that will build a global civilization that is imbued with justice and freedom for all persons, at peace with one another and the earth.

We do not yet know with what degree of understanding and foresight, compassion and faithfulness, we human beings will rise to the challenges of our time. What we do know is that the voice and wisdom that Friends will bring to these issues, important as they were in the first half-century of FCNL's work in Washington, will be even more critical in the years to come.

Some Suggested Readings.

Barnet, Richard J. and John Cavanagh. *Global Dreams: Imperial Corporations and the New World Order.* New York: Simon & Schuster, 1994.

Brecher, Jeremy, John Brown Childs, and Jill Cutler (Eds.) *Global Visions: Beyond the New World Order.* Boston: South End Press, 1993.

Cleveland, Harlan. *Birth of a New World: An Open Moment for International Leadership.* San Francisco: Jossey-Bass Publishers, 1993.

Drucker, Peter F. *The New Realities: In Government and Politics/In Economics and Business/In Society and World View.* New York: Harper & Row, 1989.

Gore, Al. *Earth in the Balance: Ecology and the Human Spirit.* New York: Houghton Mifflin, 1992.

Hawken, Paul. *The Ecology of Commerce: A Declaration of Sustainability.* New York: Harper, 1993.

Kennedy, Paul. *Preparing for the Twenty-First Century.* New York: Random House, 1993.

Reich, Robert B. *The Work of Nations: Preparing Ourselves for 21st-Century Capitalism.* New York: Knopf, 1991.

Skolnick, Arlene. *Embattled Paradise: The American Family in an Age of Uncertainty.* New York: Basic Books, 1991.

Thurow, Lester. *Head to Head: The Coming Economic Battle Among Japan, Europe, and America.* New York: Morrow, 1992

APPENDIXES

FCNL Officers

General Committee Chairs/Clerks

Murray S. Kenworthy	1943-1946
Sumner A. Mills	1947-1948
David E. Henley	1949-1953
Samuel R. Levering	1954
Delbert E. Replogle	1955-1958
Charles L. Darlington	1959-1965
Stephen L. Angell	1966-1975
Ralph Rudd	1976-1981*
Robert Fetter	1981-1984
Walter Schutt	1984-1987
Mark Hulbert	1987-1988
Olive Wilson	1988-1991
Don Reeves	1991 -

Executive Committee Chairs/Clerks

Thomas A. Foulke	1943-1947
Willis H. Satterthwaite	1948-1950
Richard H. Rhoads	1951-1954
Samuel R. Levering	1955-1972
Marian D. Fuson	1973-1978*
Ralph Rose	1978-1983
Lilian Watford	1983-1986

Carolyn Rudd   1986-1988
Mark Hulbert   1988-1992
Jeanne Herrick-Stare   1992-

* The month of appointment changed in 1978 from January to November.

FCNL Employees

January 1, 1975 - December 31, 1993

(For Employees, November 1, 1943 - December 31, 1974, see *Uphill for Peace*, E. Raymond Wilson, FUP, 1975)

Adams, Abigail, Intern, 9.1.88 - 7.31.89
Alexander, Nancy, Legislative Secretary 4.23.84 - 8.18.91
Amarantides, Eunice, Intern, 9.6.77 - 2.1.78
Ancypa, Donna, Intern, 9.1.91 - 8.31.92
Anderson, Ruth Ann, Intern, 9.1.76 - 9.1.77
Angell, Stephen, Jr., Field Secretary, 9.1.84 - 7.31.87
Angell, Stephen W., Intern, 9.1.75 - 6.76; Leg. Ass't. 6.76 - 1.77
Armstrong, John, Accounts Manager, 11.30.92 - 7.15.93
Atkinson, Michael, Support staff, 4.27.87 - 7.1.88
Atwater, Thomas (Tim), Intern, 9.1.74 - 8.31.75; Leg. Ass't. 3.1.76 - 10.31.76
Autenrieth, Aline, Assoc. Sec'y, Development, 3.89 - 12.90

Bach, Karl, Support Staff, 1.9.74 - 8.22.75
Bennett, Alyssa, Intern, 9.1.91 - 8.31.92
Blankfield, Ralph, Field Secretary, 2.1.86 - 11.1.89
Bliss, George, Field Secretary, 8.7.67 - 8.31.80
Bliss, Helen, Support Staff, 9.11.67 - 8.31.71; 9.77 - 8.31.80

Appendixes

Block, Nick, Administrative Secretary, 7.3.72 - 10.15.82
Booth, Kathy, Intern, 9.1.93 -
Bowman, Julianne, Intern, 8.27.79 - 7.31.80
Boynton, David, Associate Secretary, Adm., 3.4.85 - 1.31.93
Bradshaw, Evelyn, Support Staff, 6.1.72 - 1.23.81
Bronner, Sylvia, Intern, 9.1.75 - 8.31.76
Brown, Doris E., Support Staff, 1.1.63 - 6.75
Brown, Jonathan W., Intern, 1988-89, 1989 - 90
Brown, Michael, Intern, 9.1.91 - 8.31.92
Bruce, Barbara, Support Staff, 6.75 - 10.75
Bullard, Kate, Support Staff, 3.17.88 - 4.14.89

Call, Ruth, Support Staff, 6.8.81 - 11.30.92
Clark, Franklin, Field Secretary, 11.8.82 - 11.84
Clark, Mary, Field Secretary, 11.8.82 - 11.84
Clifford, Melissa, Support Staff, 2.21.93 - 3.11.93
Cobin, Martin, Field Secretary, 3.1.88 - 2.28.89
Coffin, Linda, Support Staff, 6.2.80 - 5.15.85
Coles, Tara, Intern, 9.1.92 - 8.31.93
Confer, Harold, Legislative Secretary, 5.21.73 - 6.76
Conway, Jean, Support Staff 1.15.76 - 8.31.76
Cory, Robert, Legislative Secretary (p.t.) 2.1.67 - 10.1.79
Countryman, Matthew, Intern, 9.1.83 - 7.31.84
Cullinan, Michael, Accounts Manager, 7.5.93 -
Curtin, Elizabeth, Support Staff, 9.17.84 - 5.30.86

Darcy, Cindy, Legis. Assistant, (Jt. MCC app't.) 9.1.82 - 12.31.89
Day, Sylvia, Intern, 9.1.85 - 7.31.86
Dempsey, Catherine (Kate), Intern, 9.1.90 - 8.31.91
Dickerson, Laverne, Support Staff, 5.19.86 -
Doty, John, Intern, 9/1/93 -
Dougherty, Carolyn, Intern, 9.2.80 - 7.31.81
Downey, Shawn, Support Staff, 4.13.93 -

Erskine, Lynn, Intern, 9.1.90 - 8.31.91
Evans, Jonathan, Intern, 9.6.77 - 8.4.78

Ferm, Carol, Intern, 9.1.83 - 7.31.84
Fetter, Elizabeth, Intern, 9.1.90 - 8.31.91
Fikes, Jay, Legis. Ass't., Indian Affairs, 1.16.90 - 1.1.91
Flower, Ruth, Legislative Secretary, 1.1.81 -
Forbes, Stephanie, Support Staff, 8.7.86 - 5.13.88

Foreman, Catherine, Support Staff, 6.3.74 - 7.30.75; p.t. 10.75
Foster, Herbert, Field Secretary, 11.1.84 - 11.11.85
Franz, Gail, Support Staff, 6.30.78 - 8.18.78
Franz, Marian, Support Staff, 4.15.82 - 8.15.82
Fullerton, Florence, Staff Support, 7.22.90 - 7.23.92
Fuson, Helen, Field Secretary, 1.1.85 - 11.7.85
Fuson, William, Field Secretary, 1.1.85 - 11.7.85

Gey, Sandra, Field Secretary, 3.1.86 - 2.29.88
Ginsburg, Barbara, 12.8.90 -
Gish, Carol, Support Staff, 5.11.88 - 12.31.90
Goodman, Selig (Sig), Associate Secretary, Development, 1.1.83 - 3.31.89
Goulding, Paul, Field Secretary, 6.2.80 - 4.23.81
Griffin, Julia, Research Intern, 9.1.79 - 5.31.80
Guthe, William, Intern 9.1.76 - 8.4.77
Guthrie, Kathleen, Field Program Coord. 9.1.92 -

Hall, Gretchen, Coordinator, 50th Anniversary Campaign, 3.23.92 -
Hammond, David, Intern, 9.1.86 - 7.31.87
Hannah, John, Intern, 2.1.78 - 8.4.78
Harmon, Jan, Legis. Assistant, (Jt. MCC app't.) 9.6.77 - 8.15.78
Harrington, Marcia, Intern, 6.15.80 - 7.331.81
Hart, Tricia, Support Staff, 6.3.86 - 7.16.86
Hartzler, Wilton, Associate Secretary, Adm., 9.15.80 - 3.30.85
Hasset, Seth, Intern, 9.1.89 - 8.31.90
Henry, Seth, Intern, 8.27.79 - 7.31.80
Hill, Renee, Intern, 9.1.85 - 7.31.86
Hinshaw, Martha, Support Staff, 8.11.80 - 7.31.81
Hinshaw, Robert, Field Secretary, 3.15.89 - 1990
Holzinger, Ann, Intern, 9.3.74 - 8.31.75
Honnald, Edward, Intern, 9.3.74 - 8.31.75
Houghton, Jeanne, Support Staff, 3.3.86 - 5.13.87

Isaacs, Julie, Intern, 9.1.83 - 7.31.84

Jackson, Amy, Support Staff, 11.1.91 -
Jeffreys, Neda, Support Staff, 5.27.85 - 5.30.86
Johnson, Jim, Field Secretary, 10.1.87 - 8.31.88
Jones, Ellen, Support Staff, 8.29.78 - 8.3.79
Jones, Gloria, Support Staff, 2.1.80 - 9.18.81
Jones, N. Lynne, Intern, 9.1.84 - 7.31.85

Kalkstein, Hannah, Support Staff, 8.1.75 - 9.77
Kelley, Alexia, Intern, 9.1.89 - 8.31.90, Support Staff, 9.1.90 - 12.31.90
Kulberg, Eve Anne, Support Staff, 10.73 - 4.74; 8.15.84 - 5.3.85

Lafferty, John, Support Staff, 1.18.80 - 5.30.80
LeVee, Scott, Support Staff, 5.7.85 - 5.24.85
Lewis, Leslie, Custodian, 8.18.88 -
Linscheid, Steve, Legis. Assistant (Jt. MCC app't.) 9.23.79 - 9.23.82

McMann, Joanna, Leg. Advocate, (Jt. MCC app't.) 6.1.91 - 8.93
McNeil, Stephen, Intern, 9.1.76 - 8.31.77
Markowitz, Amy, Intern, 9.1.87 - 8.31.88
Marsden, William, Intern, 9.5.78 - 8.3.79
Martin, Sharon, Support Staff, 9.2.76 - 1.15.80
Mast, Amy, 50th Anniversary Support Staff, 7.6.92 - 12.16.92
Miller, Christina, Intern, 9.5.78 - 8.3.79
Mills, Lena, Field Secretary, 11.1.85 - 1.31.87
Mills, Lowell, Field Secretary, 11.1.85 - 1.31,87
Morris, Laura Nell, Support Staff, 3.21.83 - 6.30.83

Neely, Frances, Legislative Secretary, 1.1.57 - 2.29.84
Neff, Ted, Field Secretary, 6.2.80 - 12.31.81
Newlin, Lawrence, Intern, 9.1.75 - 8.31.76
Newman, Nancy, Intern, 9.1.81 - 7.31.82
Nicholson, Chris, Intern, 9.1.85 - 7.31.86
Nissenbaum, Ellen, Intern, 9.1.81 - 7.31.82
Nunez, Christina, Intern, 9.1.83 - 7.31.84
Nye, Nancy, Field Sec'y. Coordinator, 11.6.89 - 2.28.92; Legislative Sec'y, 3.1.92 -

O'Brien, Dennis, Assoc. Secy., Finance, 6.6.88 - 8.90
Oldham, Alison, Field Secretary, 7.1.81 - 8.31.84, Legislative Assistant and Action Coordinator, 3.6.84 -

Packard, Caroline, Intern, 9.1.81 - 7.31.82
Parnell, Vereene, Support Staff, 9.8.81 - 7.24.84
Payne, Diane, Friend in Wash., Indian Affairs, 3.1.75 - 9.76
Perugino, Roxanne, Leg. Consultant, 11.4.91 - 2.28.92
Petroff, Laura, Support Staff, 2.1.83 -
Pierson, Louise, Intern, 9.1.84 - 7.31.85
Press, Betty, Support Staff, 2.2.87 - 4.1.87

Pruett, Petra G., Intern, 9.1.87- 8.31.88

Reeves, Don, Legislative Secretary, 1.1.77 - 12.31.80
Revier, Paul, Support Staff, 7.7.86 - 3.9.88
Rodin, Joshua, Intern, 9.1.92 - 8.31.93
Rutenberg, Taly, Intern, 9.1.84 - 7.31.85

Satterthwaite, Cameron, Field Sec'y., 9.1.88 - 12.31.90
Schlitt, Marge, Field Secretary, 11.15.92 -
Schultz, Robert J., Intern, 9.1.87 - 8.31.88
Schutt, Elizabeth, Intern, 9.5.78 - 8.3.79
Segal, Barbara, Intern, 9.1.86 - 7.31.86
Semmler, Carl, Intern, 9.2.80 - 7.31.81
Shaw, Catherine, Intern, 9.1.77 - 8.4.78
Shea, Meredith, Intern, 9.1.93 -
Shirk, Melissa, Legislative Advocate, (Jt. MCC app't.) 8.15.93 -
Smucker, Deb, Staff Ass't., 4.1.89 - 7.30.90, Admin. Ass't., 12.1.92 - 6.15.94
Snope, Robert, Intern, 9.1.82 - 7.31.83
Snyder, Edith, Intern, 9.1.79 - 7.31.80
Snyder, Edward, Legislative Sec'y., 4.1.55 - 1.31.62; Executive Secretary, 2.1.62 - 2.28.90, Emeritus, 3.1..90 -
Snyder, William, Support Staff, 1.19.78 - 4.29.78
Sparger, Celia, Support Staff, 1.25.81 - 7.31.81
Stanhope, Victoria, 50th Anniversary, 1.5.93 - 3.31.94
Stickel, Ruby, Support Staff, 9.17.81 - 12.20.85
Stout, Alice, Support Staff, '45, '46, '48 - '51, '52 - '53, 10.15.55 - 11.76

Tannenwald, Nina, Intern, 9.1.82 - 7.31.83
Tirk, Marguerite, Field Secretary, 6.1.80 - 11.15.82
Tirk, Richard, Field Secretary, 6.1.80 - 11.15.82
Tischbein, Harry, Field Secretary, 11.1.89 - 2.1.90
Tjossem, Ardith, Field Secretary, 3.15.89 - 7.30.92

Ufford-Chase, Catherine, Intern, 9.1.88 - 8.31.89

Van Hoy, Michael, Intern, 9.1.86 - 7.31.87
Volk, Joe, Executive Secretary, 3.1.90 -

Wahrmund, Catherine, Field Secretary, 11.8.82 - 11.84
Wahrmund, Robert, Field Secretary, 11.8.82 - 12.31.83
Walker, Della, Field Secretary, 7.15.82 - 11.84
Watford, Clyde, Field Secretary, 6.2.80 - 11.15.82

Watford, Lilian, Field Secretary, 6.2.80 -11.15.82
Wilkinson, Margaret, Support Staff, 1.19.76 - 6.30.78
Wilson, Amy, Intern, 9.1.92 - 8.31.93
Winder, Ann Harker, Support Staff, 7.1.79 - 5.22.81
Wise, Clarence, Custodian, 5.6.60 - 8.88

Zehr, Stephen, Leg. Advocate, (Jt. MCC app't.), 2.27.89 - 6.30.91
Zuern, Ted, Legis. Assistant, (Jt. App't., Jesuit Office of Social Ministries), 10.1.79 - 85

Appendixes

FCNL Witnesses Before Congressional Committees 1944-1993

The following individuals presented testimony for FCNL, occasionally without a personal appearance, and at times on behalf of others as well, on the subjects and dates indicated. The text of their statements appear in FCNL Bound Volumes. Usually, their statements also appear in the Congressional hearing record. Most of the Congressional hearings in which FCNL witnesses appeared can be found at the FCNL office. Many testimonies cover more than one subject, especially on foreign aid. Space limitations prevent listing statements more than once. Please check related subjects. Space limitations also prevent listing the many statements and letters to individuals in the executive branch and Congress, especially in recent years, and to party platform committees. For these, see FCNL Bound Volumes, Annual Reports, and hearings and documents on file at FCNL and the Swarthmore Peace Collection.

AMNESTY
Harrop Freeman 3.11.74.

ARMS CONTROL AND DISARMAMENT AGENCY
Sam Levering 8.16.61, 8.29.61; **Raymond Wilson** 3.30.62, 5.2.63, 11.12.63; **Ben Seaver** 4.10.63; **Elton Atwater** 9.11.63; **Ed Snyder** 3.12.64, 7.8.64, 1.29.65, 2.26.65, 6.24.65.

ARMS CONTROL TREATIES, SALT
Ed Snyder 6.30.72, 9.15.79.

ATOMIC ENERGY
Raymond Wilson 6.8.54.

BRICKER AMENDMENT
John P. Roche 3.17.53; **Harrop Freeman** 4.29.55.

BUDGET PRIORITIES
Ed Snyder 2.2.72, 2.2.76, 3.2.77, 3.26.79, 4.2.81.

231

CAMPAIGN/CONGRESSIONAL REFORM
Wilmer Cooper 7.6.54; Sam Levering 2.25.71.

CAPITAL PUNISHMENT
Stuart Innerst 3.14.60, 5.25.60, 5.24.61; **Bill Lunsford** 3.17.72; **Bernice Just** 5.1.81; Ruth Flower 5.5.82.

CENTRAL AMERICA
Phillip Berryman 3.11.80; **Ed Snyder** 6.14.88.

CHINA, PEOPLE'S REPUBLIC OF
Bronson Clark 2.3.66.

CIVIL DEFENSE
FCNL Stmt 3.15.57; 8.61; **Jesse Mock** 5.4.62, 8.14.62; **Edward Bevilacqua** 4.19.62; **Johan Eliot** 6.25.63; **Stuyvesant Barry** 9.12.63; **C. W. Griffin, Jr.** 12.13.63; **William Davidon** 4.21.64, 6.4.64.

CIVIL LIBERTIES
Julien Cornell 6.1.48; **Harrop Freeman** 3.30.50, 3.1.78; **William Rayhill** 7.19.54; **Ed Snyder** 5.1.59; **William Woolston** 5.12.59; **Ross Flanagan** 3.6.68; **George Sawyer** 10.30.69; **Ross Wilbur** 4.21.70; **Ruth Flower** 3.22.89.

CIVIL RIGHTS/RACE RELATIONS
Byron Haworth 2.4.48; **Frank Loescher** 5.20.49; **Mike Yarrow** 3.26.56; **David Scull** 5.25.56; **Robert Wixom** 7.10.58; **Tartt Bell** 4.10.59; **Richard Bennett** 7.19.63; **Richard W. Taylor** 7.31.63; **Noyes Collinson** 8.2.63; **Ed Anderson** 10.10.69; **James H. Harvey** 5.16.72.

CONSCIENTIOUS OBJECTORS, see also **CONSCRIPTION** Clarence Pickett 5.24.44; **Raymond Wilson** 6.17.44, 6.4.46, 3.25.50 with **Clarence Pickett**; **Julien Cornell** 6.30.47.

CONSCRIPTION/UMT/DRAFT
D. Robert Yarnall 6.7.45; **J. Henry Scattergood** 11.30.45; **Raymond Wilson** 4.4.46, 1.30.50, 2.14.52, 2.2.55, 7.8.55, 3.3.59; **Henry Cadbury** 3.30.48, 6.8.50 with **Raymond Wilson**; **Sam Levering** 4.16.48, 1.30.59; **Gilbert White** 1.29.51; **Harold Evans** 1.28.52; **Joseph P. Stokes** 4.25.53, 5.21.53; **Sam Marble** 3.1.55; **Harrop Freeman** 6.9.55; **Ed Snyder** 6.9.55, 1.26.76, 4.8.76, 3.12.79, 4.25.79, 2.27.80; **Clyde Milner** 3.1.63; **Charles Darlington** 3.12.63; **Ralph Rose** 4.14.67, 5.4.67; **Charles Harker** 10.15.69; **Lyle Tatum** 2.9.71, 3.2.71; **Jim Bristol** 5.21.79, 3.11.80; 5.7.81, 6.2.81; **Ruth Flower** 5.19.82, 2.24.83, 5.2.91, 4.27.92.

CRIMINAL JUSTICE
Ed Anderson 3.17.70; **Bernice Just** 7.21.71, 5.18.77, 2.6.78; **Harold Confer** 7.11.74, with **Stephen Angell** 5.18.76; **Mortimer S. LeCote, Jr.** 5.2.74; **Ralph Rudd**

4.18.75; **Fay "Honey" Knopp** 4.5.77, 4.27.77, 4.6.78; **Ruth Flower** 4.21.82.

DETERRENCE
Ed Snyder 11.9.81, 6.21.84.

DISARMAMENT see also **WORLD FEDERATION**
Kenneth Boulding 6.8.56.

ECONOMIC AID, see also **UN FUNDING/PEACE CORPS** **James M. Read** 1.30.48; **Delbert Replogle** 1.12.50; **Clarence Pickett** 4.3.50; **Raymond Wilson** 5.20.54, 6.22.54, 3.4.55, 5.7.56, 5.11.56, 6.24.59, 5.14.60, 6.24.60; **Warren Griffiths** 4.1.55, 4.17.55, 7.9.57, 7.31.57; **Wilmer Cooper** 7.15.55; **Ed Snyder** 6.14.56, 6.21.56, 6.5.57, 4.2.58, 7.18.58, 8.21.59, 3.30.60, 3.5.65, 2.7.66, 5.9.67, 7.11.85; **Sumner Mills** 5.29.57; **Elton Atwater** 3.14.58, 4.7.59, 5.21.59, 3.21.60; **Levinus Painter** 6.19.58; **Walter Voelker** 6.20.61; **Lee Thomas** 8.19.61; **David Scull** 4.10.62, 8.4.62, 9.7.62, 8.8.69; **William Lotspeich** 6.7.63, 6.21.63; **Fred Reeve** 11.22.63, 4.29.64, 6.24.64; **Frances Neely** 7.31.64, 11.15.67, 3.1.68, 9.24.68, 8.28.70, 3.25.81, 4.9.81; **Lyle Tatum** 9.10.65; **Robert Cory** 5.5.66, 3.22.74; **Haines Turner** 5.3.67, 6.9.67, 6.12.67; **Stacey Widdicombe, Jr.** 4.10.68, 5.14.68; **Diana Bird** 3.28.72, 6.2.72; **Larry Minear** 4.4.85, 4.10.85, 4.24.89; **Nancy Alexander** 4.14.86, 2.26.87, 4.27.88, 6.14.88, 3.28.90, 6.20.90, 7.18.90, 2.20.91, 7.9.91.

EDUCATION, Oil for
Sam Levering 4.23.47, 6.10.49, 2.23.53; **Rhoads Murphy** 2.7.52; **Miriam Levering** 3.5.53.

ENVIRONMENT/ENERGY
Frances Neely 9.19.80; **Ralph Kerman** 2.7.91, 6.12.91: DoE hearing, 3.31.92; **Nancy Alexander** 5.3.91.

EXCHANGE OF PERSONS
John Nason 2.15.46; **Gilbert White** 5.12.54; **Ed Snyder** 2.21.56, 6.25.83; **Burns Chalmers** 6.6.61.

FAMILY FARMS/RURAL DEVELOPMENT
Ed Behre 3.13.57, 4.30.58, 7.8.64; **Don Reeves** 3.14.77, 4.24.79, 7.24.79, 3.20.80; **Ruth Flower/Gretchen Hall** 3.30.88.

FOOD FOR PEACE/INTERNATIONAL/P.L.480
Raymond Wilson 5.3.50, 4.30.54, 7.8.59, 5.19.61, 5.24.61, 3.8.66, 3.9.66; **Sam Levering** 4.30.54; **Ed Behre** 7.29.59, 2.19.64, 8.12.64; **Herbert Fledderjohn** 3.13.68; **William Edgerton** 3.22.68; **Ed Snyder** 6.22.76; **Don Reeves** 7.16.79, with **Paul Tabor** 5.8.79.

FOOD STAMPS, COMMODITIES
James M. Read 4.24.47; **John H. Foster** 2.29.68; **Ed Anderson** 9.3.69; **Maria**

Pappalardo, Pamela Coe, Lorelei Means 3.27.74; **Ruth Flower** 3.24.83, 6.14.85.

GENOCIDE
Errol Elliott 2.9.50; **Ed Snyder** 4.27.70.

GREEK-TURKEY AID
Richard R. Wood 3.26.47; Henry J. Cadbury 4.3.47 as AFSC chair.

HEALTH CARE
Nina R. Ashton 1.30.52, J. Huston Westover 5.8.69; Malcolm Peterson 7.1.74, 10.29.75, 2.10.76; **Robert E. Leidigh** 3.18.76.

HOUSING
James H. Harvey 8.4.66, 8.23.67, 3.28.68.

HUMAN RIGHTS, TREATIES
Haines Turner 4.27.56; James M. Read 3.8.67; **Ed Snyder** 3.4.77, 12.19.79.

IMMIGRATION
Albert Smith Faught 2.27.46; Frank Aydelotte 7.18.47; **Lloyd Bailey** 4.21.48, 3.1.49, 7.19.49; **Rhoads Murphy** 6.2.52; **Ed Snyder** 8.9.57; **Oliver E. Stone** 7.20.61; **Richard F. Smith** 8.11.64; **James M. Read** 3.16.65, 5.18.65; **Stacey Widdicombe** 5.30.80.

INDIA
William Stuart Nelson 1.22.51; **Herbert Fledderjohn** 3.2.67.

INDIANS, see **NATIVE AMERICANS**

JAPAN
Sarah Cope Swan 6.18.59; Esther Rhoads/Raymond Wilson 6.7.60; **Raymond Wilson** 10.29.71.

JAPANESE-AMERICAN COMPENSATION
Homer Morris 5.28.47; Paul Johnson 5.21.48; **Ruth Flower** 6.17.87.

JOBS see also **WELFARE REFORM**
Eleanor Eaton 4.30.68; William Lunsford 5.5.71, 10.6.71; **Helen Ginsburg** 5.21.76.

LAW OF THE SEAS
Robert Cory 4.10.72, 3.27.73; **Sam Levering** 5.25.72, 3.13.75, 3.9.76, 5.24.76, 8.17.78; **A. Barton Lewis** 4.1.8.72.

LEGAL SERVICES
Ruth Flower 3.29.82.

MASS TRANSIT
Ross Capon 6.27.73.

MEXICO
Ruth Flower 5.22.86.

MIDDLE EAST
Paul Johnson 1.15.57; Elmore Jackson 2.4.57; John Volkmar 9.25.75, 10.2.75; John Sullivan 5.10.78; Gail Pressberg 2.25.80, 4.14.80; Frances Neely 5.11.81, 5.13.81, 4.22.82, 6.8.82, 3.8.83; Don Peretz 6.22.81, 6.28.81.

MIGRANT LABOR
David Henley 2.29.52.

MILITARY AID, see also ECONOMIC AID, MIDDLE EAST, VIETNAM
Ernest Galarza 6.30.47; Richard Wood 8.5.49; D. Robert Yarnall 8.19.49; John Plank 5.4.73; Ed Snyder 7.2.74, 9.24.76.

MILITARY SPENDING, see also BUDGET
Lawrence Apsey 5.16.63, 6.14.63; Frederick Allen Koomanoff 5.13.68, 5.6.70; Raymond Wilson/Frances Neely 7.15.68; Arnold E. True 5.69; Leonard Rodberg 3.24.71; Holland Hunter 6.10.71; Elton Atwater 3.27.72; Ed Snyder 8.10.82, 6.6.83.

NATIONAL SERVICE
Ruth Flower 4.29.87.

NATIVE AMERICANS, GENERAL
Theodore B. Hetzel 4.26.56, 3.9.66, 3.16.66; Ed Snyder 5.13.57, 5.16.57; Pam Coe/ Charles McEvers 3.11.68; Armin L. Saeger, Jr. 3.27.68; Don/Barbara Reeves 8.4.77; Don Reeves 2.9.78; Robert Bee 4.17.78, 4.19.78; Ted Zuern 4.14.80; Cindy Darcy/Mary Parks 5.11.88.

NATIVE AMERICANS, HEALTH
Ed Snyder 5.5.59; Theodore B. Hetzel 3.6.64; Bryan P. Michener 9.25.75, 4.27.76; Don Reeves/Phil Shenk 4.18.77, 4.20.77; Jan Harmon/Don Reeves 3.14.79, 8.2.79; Ted Zuern 3.25.80, 4.5.84.

NATIVE AMERICANS, RIGHTS, LAND, TREATIES
Robert Phair 5.10.57; Levinus Painter 4.13.60, 6.24.60; Walter Taylor 3.2.64; Theodore B. Hetzel 5.18.66; Alan R. Parker 4.18.75; Diane Payne 10.23.75; Dan Shaffer 3.24.80; Steve Linscheid 9.28.81, 10.30.81, 6.22.82, 7.30.82; Cindy Darcy 10.18.83, 9.11.85, 4.10.86, 7.16.86, 2.20.87, 4.7.87; Ted Zuern/Cindy Darcy 6.4.84; Steve Zehr 7.17.90; Joanna McMann 7.23.92.

NATIVE AMERICANS, RELIGIOUS FREEDOM
Cindy Darcy 6.24.85; Lawrence Hart 7.18.89; Joanna McMann/Ruth Flower 5.13.92.

NATO
Henry Cadbury/Raymond Wilson 5.11.49.

NEW ZEALAND, ANZUS
Ed Snyder 3.18.85.

NUCLEAR FREEZE
Ed Snyder 2.23.83, 6.23.83.

NUCLEAR PROLIFERATION
Raymond Wilson 6.8.54; Charles Price 5.20.57, 3.28.58; Clarence Pickett 7.2.59; Ed Snyder 2.15.66; William Huntington 7.17.68.

NUCLEAR TEST BAN
S. Arthur Watson 8.27.63; Ed Snyder 11.9.89.

PACIFIC TRUST TERRITORIES/PALAU
Raymond Wilson 5.24.62; Harrop Freeman 8.12.75; Paulette Wittwer 12.17.87.

PEACE ACADEMY
Ed Snyder 7.22.80 to U.S. Commission.

PEACE CORPS
Ruth Replogle 3.14.60; Ed Snyder 6.23.61, 8.18.61.

PEACE GARDEN
Ed Snyder 6.20.86.

PEACE TAX FUND
Peter Goldberger 8.26.88; Ruth Flower 5.21.92.

PRAYER
FCNL Statement 8.10.66; Ed Snyder 4.28.83.

POVERTY
Helen Baker 4.20.64; Cushing Dolbeare 5.22.73.

SOUTH AFRICA
Lyle Tatum/Walter Martin 3.17.66.

SOVIET UNION, see also **TRADE, ARMS CONTROL TREATIES, DETERRENCE**

Ed Snyder 2.17.67, 9.13.83, with **Seth Henry** 6.30.80; **William B. Edgerton** 6.13.68, 6.28.68.

TAX REFORM
Cushing Dolbeare 3.5.73.

TRADE, EAST-WEST, EMBARGOES
Raymond Wilson 11.22.63; **Ed Snyder** 3.5.65.

TRADE, INTERNATIONAL, RECIPROCAL
Caleb Smith 6.3.48; **Richard Wood** 5.9.50, 1.24.51, 3.1.51; **Peter Franck** 5.18.53; **Delbert Replogle** 1.21.55, 6.23.58; **Joseph Coppock** 3.9.56; **Emile Benoit** 3.7.58, 3.22.62.

TRAVEL RESTRICTIONS
George W. Marshfield 2.27.68; **Hiram Hilty** 3.27.68.

UN CHARTER REVIEW
Sam Levering 4.21.55; **Robert Cory** 4.29.65, 5.12.70; **William Huntington** 5.11.65.

UN FUNDING, see also **ECONOMIC AID**
Delbert Replogle 6.20.50; **Raymond Wilson** 3.17.54, 5.13.55, 2.19.62; **Warren Griffiths** 4.1.55, 6.17.55; **Elton Atwater** 7.18.62; **Ed Snyder** 7.12.62; **Robert Cory** 6.2.72; **Nancy Alexander** 3.14.89.

UN PEACEKEEPING, see also **MIDDLE EAST**
Ed Snyder 7.24.58; **Dorothy Hutchinson** 5.2.68.

VIETNAM/INDOCHINA, see also **MILITARY AID**
Stephen Cary 4.27.66; **Ed Snyder** 1.24.66, 12.2.70, 12.8.70, 10.31.79; **Elton Atwater** 10.27.67; **Louis Kubicka** 4.5.72; **Mike Yarrow** 4.19.72; **George McT. Kahin** 2.22.73, 3.6.75; **John Champlin** 6.11.73; **Diane M. Jones** 3.28.74, **Russell Johnson** 7.24.74; **Louis Schneider** 3. 20.75; **David W. Stickney** 5.12.75; **Wallace Collett** 9.9.75.

VOTING
Ed Anderson 2.4.70; **Ruth Flower** 4.19.88.

WAR POWERS
Ed Snyder 5.15.86.

WAR RELIEF, FOOD, ETC.
James M. Read 4.25.46, 6.19.46, 4.9.47; **James G. Vail** 8.2.46; **Claude Schotts** 6,11,47; **Raymond Wilson** 1.27.48; **Stephen Cary** 2.6.48.

WAR RELIEF, REFUGEES, UNRRA
Raymond Wilson 11.23.45; **Lloyd Bailey** 2.17.50; **William Channel/Ed Snyder** 6.7.62.

WELFARE REFORM/FAMILY ASSISTANCE
Ed Anderson 8.24.70; **Don Reeves** 11.4.77; **James Harvey** 4.18.78; **Ruth Flower** 4.22.82, 6.18.83, 3.11.87, 5.22.87.

WIRETAPPING
William Rayhill 5.12.54, 5.3.55; **Alan Hunt** 4.5.62.

WORLD COURT
Esther Holmes Jones 7.12.46; **Harold Evans** 1.27.60.

WORLD FEDERATION
Sam Levering 5.12.48, 10.12.49; 2.20.50.

YOUTH
Herbert Bergstrom 2.22.63, 3.1.63; **Robert C. Taber** 3.24.59.

Index of Persons

A

Abell, Richard 49
Abernathy, Ralph, 118
Abourezk, Senator 142
Ackley, Gardner 107
Acton, Lord 36
Adams, James L. 106
Addabbo, Joseph 64, 65, 90
Alexander, Nancy
    129, 139, 140, 153, 154, 157, 163, 233, 237
Allen, Richard 98
Amin, Idi 128
Anderson, Edward 118, 165, 232, 233 237, 238
Anderson, Jack 100
Angell, Stephen L., Jr 56, 223
Angell, Stephen W. 166, 232
Apsey, Lawrence 235
Archdale, John 10
Arias, Oscar 87
Ashley, Thomas 90
Ashton, Nina R. 234
Atwater, Elton
    49, 153, 231, 233, 235, 237
Atwater, Tim 166
Aydelotte, Frank 234

B

Bacon, Eleanor 184
Bailey, Lloyd 234, 238
Baker, Helen 236
Barber, Arthur 74
Barbour, Hugh 170
Barre, Siad 204

Barry, Stuyvesant 232
Barton, William 103
Bassett, David 112, 132
Bassett, Miyo 112
Bee, Robert 235
Behre, C. Edward 50, 59, 233
Bell, B. Tartt, 117, 232
Bell, Mark E. 185
Bello, Walden 69
Bennett, Asia 98
Bennett, Richard 232
Benoit, Emile 49,
    93, 161, 169, 237
Bergstrom, Herbert 238
Berryman, Phillip 232
Bevilacqua, Edward 232
Bingham, Jonathan 162
Bird, Diana 233
Blankfield, Ralph 56
Bliss, George 55, 67, 168
Boardman, Eugene 183
Bolling, Landrum 140
Boulding, Elise 75
Boulding, Kenneth 75,
    93, 169, 170, 233
Bray, William G. 186
Brezhnev 98, 99
Bright, John 10, 12
Bristol, Jim 110, 232
Brown, George E., Jr. 186
Bush, George 116, 172, 181, 200, 202
Byrd, Harry F., Jr. 180
Byrd, Robert O. 45

C

Cadbury, Henry
    32, 40, 42, 83, 94, 109, 146, 232, 234, 236
Califano, Joseph A., Jr. 176
Camille, Sister 203

239

Capon, Ross 235
Carter, Jimmy 38, 58, 110, 111,
    142, 147, 168, 170, 171
Cary, Stephen 237
Cavanagh, John 222
Chalmers, Burns 233
Champlin, John 237
Channel, William 238
Charles II 8
Chiperfield, Robert B. 32
Church, Frank 79
Churchill 28
Clark, Franklin 56
Clark, Bronson 232
Clark, Joseph 61
Clark, Mary 56
Clifford, Clark 85
Clinton, Bill 111, 114, 163, 181
Cobin, Martin 56
Coe, Pamela 234, 235
Coffin, Linda 27
Coffin, T. Eugene 189
Collett, Wallace 237
Collinson, Noyes 232
Condon, Edward 30
Confer, Harold 119, 166, 232
Conn, Earl L. 185
Connally, Tom 135
Cooper, Wilmer 5, 27, 31,
    54, 124, 232, 233
Coppock, Joseph 161, 237
Cornell, Julien 232
Cory, Robert 59, 139,
    171, 233, 234, 237
Cory, Sally 59
Cox, Gray 27
Cromwell, Oliver 7
Crosby, Harriett 100

D

Darcy, Cindy 121, 235, 236

Darlington, Charles 109, 223, 232
Davidon, William 232
Dellums, Ron 96,
    111, 112, 128, 197
Dennis, David W. 186
Dietz, Bill 65, 102
Dobrynin, Ambassador 99
Dodd, Thomas 47
Dolbeare, Cushing 236, 237
Douglas, Paul 12, 186, 188
Drucker, Peter 220
Dunbar, Barrington 119

E

Eaton, Eleanor 234
Edgerton, William B. 98, 233, 237
Einstein, Albert 78
Eisenhower, Dwight D.
    38, 60, 73, 81, 98, 116, 139
Eldridge, Joe 141, 193
Eliot, Johan 232
Elliott, Errol 234
Ervin, Sam 64
Evans, Harold 136, 232, 238
Evers, Medger 117

F

Fager, Charles E. 132
Farr, Louise 97, 119
Fascell, Dante B. 106
Fast, Howard 203, 206
Faught, Albert Smith 234
Felton, Walter 99
Fetter, Susie 3
Fetter, Robert 3, 223
Fikes, Jay 121
Fisher, Adrian 74
Flanagan, Ross 232
Flanders, Ralph 74, 76
Fledderjohn, Herbert 233, 234
Fletcher, Jim 119

Flower, Ruth
  4, 64, 107, 110, 113,
  115, 116, 119, 143, 166,
  172, 173, 175, 232-238
Ford, Gerald 38, 58, 111, 147
Forsythe, David 182, 195
Forsythe, Edwin 186
Forsythe, Peter 50
Foster, Herbert, 56
Foster, John H. 233
Foster, William 74
Foulke, Thomas A. 223
Fox, George 7, 8, 41
Franck, Peter 161, 237
Frank, Jerome 96
Franz, Marian 113, 193
Fraser, Don 141, 142
Freeman, Harrop
  109, 111, 231, 232, 236
French, Paul 15, 16
Fromm, Eric 96, 144
Fulbright, J. William 79, 97, 183
Fuson, Bill 50, 56
Fuson, Helen 56
Fuson, Marian D. 123, 223

G

Galarza, Ernest 146, 235
Gandhi 79
Gault, Charlene Hunter 200
Gey, Sandra 56
Ginsburg, Helen 234
Goldberger, Peter 236
Goldwater, Barry 58
Gorbachev, Mikhail 78, 102, 103, 104
Gottleib, Sandy 73, 81
Goulding, Paul, 56
Grace, Brewster 85
Graham, Chester 49, 54, 132

Griffin, C.W., Jr. 232
Griffiths, Warren 157, 233, 237
Gullion, Edmund 74

H

Hadley, Herbert 98
Hadley, Jeanette 4, 16, 54
Hall, Gretchen 233
Hamilton, Lee 65, 101, 102, 103
Hammarskjold, Dag 40
Hand, Learned 29
Hanstein, Kathleen, 49
Harker, Charles 34, 62, 109, 110, 117, 232
Harkin, Tom 128, 141, 142
Harmon, Jan 121, 235
Hart, Lawrence 236
Hart, Philip 110, 115
Hartmann, Arthur 102
Hartsough, David 62, 67, 78
Harvey, T. Edmund 10
Harvey, James H. 119, 232, 234, 238
Hatfield, Mark 112, 148
Haworth, Byron 49, 64, 116, 132, 232
Henley, David E. 223, 235
Henry, Seth 237
Herrick-Stare, Jeanne 123, 224
Hershey, Lewis B. 64, 110
Hetzel, Theodore B. 235
Hickenlooper, Bourke 42
Hilty, Hiram 237
Hinshaw, Robert 56
Hitler 188
Holifield, Chet 81, 83
Hollister, Barry 50
Honnold, Ed 166
Hoover, Herbert 13
Huffman, Herbert 59
Hulbert, Mark 223, 224

Humphrey, Hubert 60, 73, 74, 79, 82, 84, 85
Hunt, Alan 238
Hunt, Norman 25
Hunter, Holland 235
Huntington, William 236, 236
Hutchinson, Dorothy 49, 126, 237

I

Innerst, Stuart 115, 184, 232

J

Jack, Homer 73, 81
Jackson, Elmore 72, 139, 235
James, William 152
Johnson, Byron 61
Johnson, Jim 56
Johnson, Lyndon B. 38, 58, 82, 84, 85, 137
Johnson, Paul B. 115, 139, 234, 235
Johnson, Russell 237
Jones, Diane M. 237
Jones, Esther Holmes 135, 238
Jones, Jean 27
Jones, Rufus 12, 80
Judd, Walter 152
Just, Bernice 115, 119, 125, 232

K

Kahin, George McT. 237
Kahn, Herman 63
Kai-shek, Chiang 28
Kastenmeier, Bob 185
Keating, Kenneth B. 46
Kellam, John 16
Kennedy, John 38, 60, 70, 72, 74, 79, 84, 89
Kennedy, Robert F. 85
Kennedy, Ted 63, 142
Kenworthy, Murray S. 223
Kerman, Ralph 171, 233

Kerpen, Karen Shaw 183
Khrushchev 73, 80, 98
Kiermaier, Lockhart 186
King, Martin Luther 36, 85, 117, 165
King-Hall, Stephen 42
Klineberg, Stephen 5, 24, 27, 50, 207
Knopp, Fay 125, 233
Koomanoff, Frederick Allen 235
Kubicka, Louis 237
Kulberg, Raoul 132

L

Lall, Betty Goetz 73
Land, Richard 201
Landers, Ann 101
LaRoque, Gene R. 177
LaVoy, Diane Edwards 193
LeCote, Mortimer S., Jr. 232
Leidigh, Robert E. 234
Levering, Miriam 50, 137, 184, 233
Levering, Sam 3, 50, 109, 135, 137, 184, 223, 231-234, 237, 238
Levin, Carl 115
Lewis, A. Barton 234
Libby, Frederick 19
Lifton, Robert Jay 96
Lincoln, Abraham 43, 199
Linsheid, Steve 65, 121, 235
Lodge, John Davis 33, 40
Loescher, Frank 116, 232
Lonsdale, Kathleen 30
Lotspeich, William 233
Lunsford, William 115, 118, 165, 232, 234

M

MacNeil, Robin 201
Macmillan 73

Index of Persons

Mang, Bob 184
Mang, Pamela 184
Mansfield, Mike 79, 94
Marble, Samuel 109, 232
Marshall, Burke 111
Marshfield, George W. 237
Martin, Walter 236
Martin, William 132
Mason, Dorothy 50
Maxfield, William 49
McCloy, John J. 72, 73, 74
McCoy, George, 54
McEvers, Charles 235
McGhee, George 150
McGovern, George 58, 74, 142, 181, 185, 195
McHale, John 221
McKinney, Cynthia 148
McMann, Joanna 121, 235, 236
McNamara, Robert 84, 111
McNeil, Stephen 5, 27, 50
Means, Lorelei 234
Mendl, Wolf 133
Mesner, Cliff 40
Mesner, Warren 119
Meyer, Bill 61
Michener, Bryan 120, 121, 235
Miller, Chris 156
Miller, Edward 186
Mills, Lena 56
Mills, Lowell 56
Mills, Sumner 223, 233
Milner, Clyde 109, 232
Minault, Sylvain 162
Minear, Larry 233
Mitchell, John 154
Mitchell, Clarence 118
Mock, Jesse 232
Mondale, Walter 181
Moriuchi, Tak 115
Morris, Homer 115, 234
Morris, Laura Nell 27
Morse, Wayne 115, 146
Moynihan, Daniel 173
Mundt, Karl 98
Murphy, Rhoads 233, 234
Mussolini 188

N

Nason, John 97, 233
Neely, Frances 4, 78, 89, 92, 94, 139, 140, 145, 162, 169, 170, 233, 235
Neff, Ted 56
Nelson, William Stuart 234
Nicolopoulos, John A. 103
Niles, Mary Cushing 50, 167
Nixon, Richard 13, 38, 58, 60, 85, 86, 181, 189, 190, 186
Nnoka, Barbara Grant 3, 27, 94
Nugent, Michael J. 181
Nye, Nancy 4, 56, 140

O

Oldham, Alison 4, 56, 60, 65, 87, 142
Oliver, John 64
O'Neill, Tip 94
Osbourne, Winslow 30
Osgood, Charles 76

P

Packard, Caroline, 99
Painter, Levinus 233, 235
Pappalardo, Maria, 233-234
Parker, Alan R. 235
Parks, Mary 235
Pastore, John 145
Payne, Diane 120, 121, 235
Pease, Joseph 9, 10
Penn, William 7, 8, 23, 24, 124
Peretz, Don 127, 235

Perot, Ross 181
Persons, Sandy 74
Peterson, Malcolm 234
Phair, Robert 235
Pickett, Clarence
    80, 81, 151, 152, 153, 232, 233, 236
Pierre, Andrew J. 164
Piotrow, Phyllis 185
Plank, John 235
Post, Richard 83
Powell, Colin 103
Powers, Jonathan 42
Pressberg, Gail 235
Price, Charles 74, 236

R

Rayhill, William 49, 232, 238
Read, James M. 49, 233, 234, 237
Reagan, Ronald 38, 70, 95, 98, 102, 103, 122, 167, 172, 181
Reeve, Fred 233
Reeves, Barbara 235
Reeves, Don
    5, 27, 119, 120, 121, 151, 156, 163, 166, 171, 223, 233, 235, 238
Replogle, Delbert 150, 161, 223, 233, 237
Replogle, Ruth 152, 185, 236
Reuss, Henry 152, 185
Rhoads, Richard H. 223
Rhoads, Esther 234
Richardson, Eliot 184
Roberts, Adam 42
Robinson, Ted 119
Roche, John P. 231
Rodberg, Leonard 235
Romero, Archbishop 87
Roosevelt 28
Roosevelt, Eleanor 140

Rose, Ralph
    109, 110, 116, 223, 232
Rosenberg, Jean 163
Rosenthal, Ben 112
Rounds, John 49
Rowny, Edward 98
Rudd, Carolyn 123, 224
Rudd, Ralph 49, 109, 223, 232
Rusk, Dean 84

S

Saeger, Armin L., Jr. 235
Salzberg, John 141
Satterthwaite, Cameron 56
Satterthwaite, Willis H. 223
Sawyer, George 50, 119, 232
Scattergood, J. Henry 109, 232
Schindler, Alexander 201
Schlitt., Marge 56
Schneider, Louis 237
Schotts, Claude 237
Schoultz, Lars, 144, 195
Schultz, Robert C. 27
Schumacher, E. F. 158
Schutt, Walter 223
Schweiker, Richard 187
Scott, Hugh 187
Scull, David 50, 116, 117, 132, 232, 233
Seaver, Ben 231
Sevareid, Eric 101
Shaffer, Dan 65, 235
Sharp, Gene 42
Shaw, Catherine 107, 147
Shenk, Phil 120, 121, 235
Shillitoe, Thomas 9
Shirk, Melissa 121
Shultz, George 102, 103
Smith, Caleb 161, 237
Smith, Richard F. 49, 234
Snyder, Bonnie 27, 96

Snyder, Ed *
Snyder, William 27
Sorenson, Ted 89
Sparkman, John 74
Stafford, Robert T. 106
Stalin 28, 188
Stassen, Harold 74
Stevenson, Adlai 60
Stewart, Annalee 73
Stickney, David W. 237
Stokes, Joseph P. 232
Stone, Jeremy 81
Stone, Oliver E. 49, 234
Stout, Alice 4
Sullivan, John 147, 235
Swan, Sarah Cope 234
Swomley, John 109
Symington, Stuart 64

T

Taber, Robert C. 238
Tabor, Paul 233
Tatum, Arlo 49
Tatum, Lyle
    49, 109, 180, 232, 233, 236
Taylor, Richard W. 27,
    117, 133, 232
Taylor, Walter 235
Thomas, Cecil 183
Thomas, Lee 233
Thomas, Trevor 81, 115
Thompson, Richard 119
Tirk, Marguerite 56
Tirk, Richard 56
Tischbein, Harry 56
Tjossem, Ardith 56
Tolles, Frederick B. 6, 8, 10, 11, 13
Trevelyn, George M. 44
Trowbridge, Buell 195
True, Arnold E. 235
Truman, Harry 80, 150

Turner, Haines 233, 234
Tutu, Desmond 129

V

Vail, James 206, 237
Vallentine, Jo 68
VanZandt, James, 61
Vasev, Vladillen 98
Voelker, Walter 233
Volk, Joe
    3, 5, 34, 82, 95, 130, 148, 197.
    201, 203
Volkmar, John 127, 235
Voris, Floyd 4

W

Wadsworth, James 74
Wahrmund, Catherine 56
Wahrmund, Robert 56
Walker, Della 56
Wardlaw, Ada 93
Watford, Clyde 50, 56
Watford, Lilian 4, 50, 56, 123, 223
Watson, George 54
Watson, S. Arthur 236
Westover, J .Huston 234
White, Gilbert 97, 232, 233
White, Ralph 96
Widdicombe, Stacey 49, 233, 234
Wilbur, Ross 232
Wilkinson, Harold 68
Willoughby, George 49
Wilson, Olive 123, 223
Wilson, Raymond *
Wittwer, Paulette 236
Wixom, Robert 117, 232
Wood, Richard R. 94, 234,
    235, 237
Woods, Rose Mary, 189

Woolman, John
    44, 117, 179, 188, 200, 206
Woolston, William 232

Y

Yarnall, D. Robert 109, 232, 235
Yarrow, Clarence H. "Mike" 116,
    232, 237

Z

Zablocki, Clement 183
Zehr, Steve 121, 235
Ziegler, Harmon 195
Zuern, Ted 121, 235

* Numerous listings

Not indexed: names appearing under photos, names on pages i-xi, and names of employees on pages 224-229.

Index of Subjects

A

A Quaker Action Group 66
A.A.R.P 212
Abortion
    19, 38, 52, 167, 168, 209
Abraham Lincoln 43, 199
Absolutist and relativist 7
ACDA. *See* Disarmament
Act of Affirmation 9
Act of Toleration 9
Afghanistan 100, 110, 128
African Americans
    108, 116, 119, 211
African National Congress 129
Afro-Asian bloc 138
AFSC 66, 88, 98, 118, 150,
    183, 201, 205. *See also* American Friends Service Committee
AFSC delegation to Cambodia 86
AFSC Quang Ngai center 85
Age of Quietism 9
"Aging" of America 208, 211
Agricultural Seminars 54, 58
Aid to Red China 185
Aid to the contras 88
AIDS 163
"Amazing Grace" 44
American Baptist Churches 88
American Family 166, 212
American Friends Service Committee 14, 31, 66. *See also* AFSC
American Indian Religious Freedom Act 114
American Legion 47
Americans with disabilities 143

Amin's Uganda 128
Amnesty 111, 231
Anarchy 125, 130
Angola. 129
Ann Arbor, Michigan, Friends
    Meeting; 112
Ann Landers 101
Anti-communism 29, 98
Apartheid 128
Arms Transfer Working Group 148
Australian Friends 68
Australian Quaker Senator 68
Avoid term "defense" spending 106

B

Balance of power 94
Board on Peace and Social Concerns,
    Five Years Meeting 152
Bombing of Hiroshima 80
Bosnia-Herzegovina 199
Boundaries of life 209
Boycotts. *See* Economic sanctions
Bread for the World 2, 152
Bricker Amendment 231
Broader view of national security 91
Budget of the U.S. Government
    91, 177
Budget Priorities 4, 91, 178, 231
    Budget making process 92
Build a good society here at home
    71
Bulletin of Atomic Scientists 97
Burke-Wadsworth Bill 15

C

California FCL 54
Calvinist tradition 7
Cambodia 86, 199
Campaign finance reform 39, 232
Capital punishment *See* Death
    penalty

247

Central America 86, 232
Central America Working Group
    87, 142, 191
Central City, Nebraska, Friends
    Meeting 119
China
    52, 127, 129, 137, 183, 185, 190, 232
Church of the Brethren 88, 142
Church Women United 142
CIA 34, 102
Citizens Budget Campaign 191
Civil Defense 81, 232
Civil disobedience 67
Civil liberties 29, 232
Civil rights 38, 116, 131, 188, 232
Civil Rights Act of 1964 117
Clergy and Laity Concerned 142
Coalition for a New Foreign and
    Military Policy 87,
    92 142, 191
Coalition on National Priorities and
    Military Policy 92, 94, 191
Coalition to Stop Funding the War
    191
Coalition to Support WCARRD
    156
Coalitions 22, 191
Coalitions--FCNL related 192
"Code of Conduct on Arms Sales"
    95, 148
Cold War 1, 28, 34, 78, 219
"Commission to Study Non-
    Violence" 41
Common Cause 40, 165
Communicate resolve 91
Communist influence in peace
    demonstrations 30
Comprehensive energy policy
    legislation 172
Comprehensive test ban treaty 81
Compromise 10, 11, 12, 194
Compulsory reserve 109

Congress, Role of 37
Congressional Black Caucus
    92, 118, 178
"Connally Reservation" 136
Conscientious Objectors
    15, 28, 32, 64, 72, 108, 110,
    112, 232. *See also* Conscription
Conscription
    108, 109, 148, 181, 232. *See
    also* Draft Registration
Consequences 43, 45
Consumer Education Council on
    World Trade 162
Contadora peace process 87
"Contras" 87
Council of Washington Representa-
    tives on the UN 139
Criminal justice issues
    125, 166, 232
Cuba 127
Cuban missile crisis 79
Czechoslovakia 136

D

Dallas Morning News 103
Death Penalty 114, 115, 166, 232
Deep forces at work in the nation
    166
Demographic Revolutions 208
Demonstrations 67
Desegregation in the District of
    Columbia 116
Deterrence 91, 96, 99, 103, 233,
    236
Deterrence by Fear or Friendship?
    95
Disarmament 233
    Arms Control and Disarmament
        Agency
        38, 74, 82, 93, 185, 231
    Arms control treaties 74, 81, 236

Index of Subjects

Limited test ban 76, 81, 236
SALT 231
General and complete
  38, 72, 75, 93, 105
  Flanders-Sparkman Senate
    Resolution 74
  Unilateral 41, 42, 52
"Disarmament and Your Job" 93
Disarmament Information Service
  73
Divine lobbyist 13
Doctrine of nuclear deterrence 96
Domestic Economic and Social
  Development 165
  Food and hunger 166
  Full employment
    166, 175, 215, 234
  Health 166, 177
  Lack of policy clarity 178
  Safety net 175
Draft. *See* Conscription
Draft Registration 109, 110
Drastic change in personal and
  national values 159
Dumbarton Oaks Proposals 134

E

Early Quaker Precedents 7
Earned Income Tax Credit 176
East Whittier Friends Church 189
Economic and Social Development
  (Internat'l) 149, 150, 233
  1972: Moment of Truth? 158
  Constant FCNL Themes 151
  Debt burden 153
  FCNL witnesses 149
  Food and hunger 151, 205
  Limits to growth? 157
  Need for adequate capital 153
  UN programs 151, 153, 237
Economic gap 71
Economic issues 52

Economic pressures 104
Economic sanctions 108
"Economic Warfare and People..."
  133
Effects of Nuclear War 83
Egypt 147
El Salvador 87
Ending Poverty 174
"Enemies" 96
English Reform Bill of 1832 9
Environment
  159, 168, 200, 218, 220, 233
  "Energy and Nuclear Policy
    Statement" 168
  Impact of development 156
  Sustainable development 157
  Appeal to Reagan and Breschnev
    103
Episcopal Church 88, 120
Equal Rights Amendment 124
Evil 40, 41, 200
"Evil empire." 99
"Exchange for Peace Resolution" 65,
  101, 102
Exchange of Persons 71, 97, 233

F

Family Farms/Rural Development
  233
FBI 31
FCNL
  1955 Reorganization Plan 49, 55
  Beginnings 1, 14, 15, 28
  Committees
    Executive
      19, 29, 30, 190, 201
    General 19, 21, 30, 66, 69
    Nominating 19
    Policy 46, 49, 167, 169, 170
  Futures Committee 207
  Interns 5, 59

249

Legislative priorities
   51, 171, 197
Publications
   Visions of a Warless World 69
   "How-to" series 36, 45
   Presidential candidates compared 58
   "That Yellow Sheet" 56, 64
Seeking consensus
   2, 4, 17, 19, 47, 51, 53
   Disclaimer 21, 46
   Statement of Legislative Policy
     19, 41, 48, 53, 68
FCNL and Electoral Politics 60
FCNL as Catalyst 191
FCNL's approach to national security 71
FCNL's "Human Rights Secretary" and lobbyist 165
"Federal World Government" 135
Federation of American Scientists 74, 81
Fellowship of Reconciliation 61, 132
Field secretaries 55, 56
"Findley" amendment 99
Five Years Meeting 11, 54, 58, 132
Florida Avenue Meeting 16, 28
Food for Peace 185, 233
Food Stamps 233
Former Yugoslavia 129, 200
Friend-in-Washington 84, 98, 117, 120, 140, 172, 183
Friends abroad 67
Friends Committee on Gay and Lesbian Concerns 66
Friends Committee on Unity with Nature 66
Friends General Conference 67
Friends Meeting of Washington 189. *See also* Florida Avenue Meeting

Friends Peace Witness 1960 67
Friends Service Council of London 31, 68, 103
Friends United Meeting 54
Friends Witness for World Order 67
Friends World Committee for Consultation 67, 98, 162
"Frozen Fund" 109

G

Gender neutral language 123
Generational and interethnic equity 212
Genocide Convention 140, 234
Ghosts of Munich and Pearl Harbor 70
"Gleanings from Quaker Dialogues" 170
Global Economy 217
God's guidance 44
Graduated Reciprocated International Tension-reduction (GRIT) 76
Grass-roots cooperation 63
Gray v. Sanders, 45
Greece 32, 94
Greek-Turkey Aid 234

H

Harkin amendment 128, 141
Health care reform 4, 234
High priced lobbyists 39
Hispanics and Asians 211
Historic Peace Churches 113, 193
"Holy Experiment" 7, 10, 124
Hope 83, 144
House Republican Research Committee 57
Housing 234
"How to Work in Politics" 61

Human Rights 38, 140
  Carter's Role 142
  Covenants 141, 234
  Final Act of the CSCE 141
  Relation to Indochina anti-war movement 142
  "To Link or Not to Link?" 143
  Universal Declaration on Human Rights 140
Human Rights Working Group 142, 191
"Humanitarian" aid to contras 88
"Humanitarian Military Intervention" 125, 130, 201

I

Ideals and actions 84
Illinois-Wisconsin FCL 54
Immigration laws 210, 234
Impeachment of Nixon 190
Impounding literature 30
In Place of War 42
India 131, 234
Indochina war 34, 84, 86, 110. See also Vietnam War
Indonesia 147
Institute for Soviet American Relations 100
Interfaith Action for Economic Justice 173
International institutions of law and order 71
International policing 125
International Society of Political Psychology 96
Interreligious Task Force on U.S. Food Policy 171, 191
Iowa Yearly Meeting Conservative 29
Iran 140, 147
Iran-Iraq 147

Iran-Contra 34
Iraq 128, 129, 133, 140
Irrational and nonrational forces 96
Israel 138, 139, 147

J

Japan 28, 234
Japanese American Citizens' League 115, 116
Japanese Americans 108, 115, 234
Jerusalem 197
Jesuit Social Ministries 88, 120, 142
Jesus 1, 7, 41, 129, 193, 199, 208
Joint Committee on Atomic Energy 81
Judgment and Mystery 43
Judiciary, Role of 38
Just and enforceable world law 125
"Just war" 71, 202

K

Kenya 67
Khmer Rouge 86
Korea 29, 76, 131
Korean War 126

L

Law of the Seas 38, 50, 137, 184, 190, 234
Lebanon 131, 140, 147
Legal Services 234
Legitimate use of force 108
London Yearly Meeting 10
Long Term vs. Short Term 75
"Love-hate" relationship toward government 124
Lutheran Church 88, 120
Lyng v. Northwest 114

M

MacNeil-Lehrer News Hour 200, 203
Mansfield's 1973 amendment to cut overseas manpower 94
Mass Transit 235
McCarthyism 29
McCloy-Zorin Agreement 73
Meeting contacts 55
Meeting for Sufferings 8
Mennonites 3, 113, 120, 193, 201
Mennonite Central Committee (MCC) 120, 205
Methodist Board of Peace and World Order 79
Mexico 235
Middle East 139, 235
   1957 Eisenhower Doctrine 139
   1979 Camp David agreement 148
   Arms shipments 139, 147
   "Middle East Forums" 140
   Palestine refugees 140, 150
   U.S. military action 140
Middle Period of Quakerism 8
Migrant Labor 235
Military aid, training, and sales 83, 145, 235
   1978 Conventional Arms Transfer (CAT) talks 148
   International Military Education and Training 147
   U.S.-Soviet Conflicts in the Developing World 148
Military spending 89, 178, 219, 235
   Difficulty in quantifying 90
Military-industrial-academic complex 39, 92
Monday Arms Control Lobby 191
Most Friends are not anarchists 124
Multilateral nuclear force (MLF) 81
Mundt-Nixon bill 30
My Lai 40

N

NAFTA, the North American Free Trade Agreement 163
Namibia 129
Naming the Problem 184
Nation-state system 94
National Campaign for a Peace Tax Fund 193
National Committee on U.S.-China Relations 183, 184
National Committee to Abolish the Federal Death Penalty 115
National Council Against Conscription 109
National Council of Churches 142, 183
National Council to Repeal the Draft 110, 191
National Origins Quota Act of 1921 209
"national security" 71, 95
"National service" 111, 235
Native American Free Exercise of Religion Act 114
Native Americans 3, 108, 119
   Alaska Native Land Claims 119
   Gambling 122, 197
   General legislation 122, 123, 235
   Indian Health Care Improvement Act 120, 122, 235
   Kinzua dam 119
   Legislative priorities 119, 120, 121
   Particular tribes 122
   "Report on Indian Legislation" 119

Index of Subjects

Treaty rights and self determination 122, 235, 236
Vocational training and sanitary facilities 119
Nebraska Yearly Meeting 119
NETWORK, a Catholic nuns lobby 88, 193
New England Yearly Meeting 83
New work ethic 176
New York Times 31
New Zealand 236
Nicaragua 87, 136
"No new taxes" 34
Nobel Peace Prize 31, 87
Non-Proliferation Treaty 82
Nonviolence 40, 206
Nonviolent actions 131
Nonviolent resistance 42, 70, 131, 194
North Atlantic Treaty Organization (NATO) 94, 236
North Carolina 10, 78
North Korea 127
Nuclear arms race 28, 80
Nuclear delivery systems 82
Nuclear Factor 78, 231
"nuclear freeze" resolution 82, 236
"nuclear pacifists" 71

O

Oil for Education 233
Olympic boycott 128
On the Beach 81
"One person-one vote" 39
"One world" 28
Oregon v. Smith 114
Orme Dam in Arizona 65

P

Pacific Trust Territories/Palau 236

Pacifism 29, 32, 70, 79, 105, 180, 182
Pacifist dilemmas 130
Palestine Liberation Organization, 138
Panama 131
"Pay Any Price" 89
Peace Academy 75, 106, 236
Peace Agency 75
Peace Brigades International 66
Peace candidates 61
Peace Corps 38, 152, 185, 233, 236
Peace Garden 236
Peace Tax Fund bill 113, 148, 236
Peace Testimony 40, 197, 198, 200
People's Republic of China, *See* China
Persian Gulf 111, 147
Philadelphia Yearly Meeting 10, 11, 197, 198, 199
Philippines 147
"pocketbook issues" 93
Point IV 149, 150
Police 124
Political process 36, 38
Political will 104
Poll tax 28, 116
Poor People's Campaign 117
"Population and Family Planning" 167
Population growth 154, 159, 208, 217
Pornography 52
"poverty effort" 154
Power of evil 40
Prayer in public schools 38, 113, 114, 236
Presbyterian Church (USA) 88, 120
President, Role of 38
Pressure tactics 22
Projecting Power Abroad 83

253

Puritan tradition 7

Q

Quaker International Affairs Representative 85
Quaker Leadership Seminars 59
Quaker Team at the UN 59, 66, 82, 137
"Quakerism and Politics" 6
Quakers in Congress 186
"Questionnaires for Candidates" 61

R

Racism 166
Reciprocal Trade Program 161
Reduce U.S. troops in Europe 94
Reformed Church 120
Religious Freedom 113
Religious Freedom Restoration Act (RFRA) 114
Republican Convention Platform subcommittees 165
Reykjavik summit 103
Rhode Island 10
Rhodesian chrome 128
Right to vote 117
Role of police 108, 124
Rump Parliament 8
"Rural development" 156
Rwanda 197

S

Sanctions 124, 125, 127, 129, 130, 132
SANE, National Committee for a Sane Nuclear Policy 73, 81
Saudi Arabia 147, 194
Scandinavian resistance to Nazism 131
Scapegoating 96

Scattergood School 29
Schools 214
Scientific and technical exchanges 100
"Search for Peace in the Middle East" 140
Secular culture 29, 31
"selective objector" 110
Selective service 109. *See also* Conscription
Seminars 58
Senate Subcommittee on Disarmament 93
Sexual orientation 52
Shift from Resources to Knowledge 215
Singapore 85
"Small Is Beautiful" 158, 181
Somalia 130, 131, 199, 200, 204
Some Dilemmas of Pacifist Lobbying 133
South Africa 128, 236
South Korea 147
Sovereignty 94, 134
Soviet Embassy 29
Soviet Union 34, 77, 78, 79, 80, 97, 127, 128, 183, 236
 1985 change in leadership 104
Starnes Rider 72, 109
State FCL committees 54
Statement of Legislative Policy, see FCNL
Steadfastness 4
Stockholm 1981 Quaker conference 97
Strategic Arms Limitation Treaties, SALT 82
"Structural adjustments" 154
Struggle against racism and poverty 34
Substance abuse 52

Index of Subjects

"Substantial agreement" 53
Suez 136
Survival 91
"Surviving Together" 100, 103

T

Task Force on a New Global Economic and Political Order 169
Tax exempt status 14
Tax resistance 113
Taxation and the Distribution of Wealth and Income in the USA 168, 170, 173
Taxes 237
"Terrorism–Bringing the War Home." 106
"The Big Hand in Your Pocket" 93
"This Life We Take" 115
Three unprecedented developments in human history 28
"too far out to be effective" 118
Trade
   Code of Conduct for Transnational Corporations 163
   "Free" or "freer" trade 161
   Geneva Codes of Trading Conduct 162
   Reciprocal trade testimony 237
   Trade Adjustment Assistance 162
   UN Conference on Trade and Development 160
TRADE, An Essential Ingredient 160
Trade, East/West 237
"Transfer amendment" 92
Travel Restrictions 237
True "pro-family" policy 214
True security 4
Turkey 32, 94, 234

U

U.S-Cuba 84
U.S. Catholic Conference 88
U.S. Institute of Peace 75
U.S.-Soviet cooperative projects 103
U.S.-Soviet exchanges 99, 100
U.S.-Soviet Working Group 101, 103
UN 34. *See also* United Nations
UN Association 79
UN Charter 134
UN Charter Review 237
UN Conference on Environment and Development (UNCED) 157
UN Conference on Trade and Development 162
UN Development Program 57
UN Education and Advocacy Group 139
UN Emergency Force 126
UN Funding 233, 237
UN Peacekeeping 126, 127, 131, 219, 237
UN Police 126
Un-American Activities Committee 30
UNESCO 95, 138
UNIFIL 127
Unilateral Initiatives 76. *See also* Disarmament: Unilateral
UNITA rebels 129
Unitarian Universalist Association 88
United Church of Christ 88, 120
United Methodist Church 88, 120, 142
United Nations 28, 136 *See also* UN
   Failure to support 136

255

FCNL, a prime advocate 137, 139
United Nations Association 139
United Nations Police Organization 126
United Society of Friends Women 120
United World Federalists 74, 135
Universal military training 14
Universal military training (UMT.). *See* Conscription
"Unmitigated Condemnation" 80
Unresolved "Challenges" 51
"utopianism" 42

V

Vietnam 84, 127, 131. *See also* Indochina war
Vietnam War 62, 148, 165, 187, 237
Vision 42
Visions of a Warless World 60
Voting records 57
Voting Rights 237

W

War Powers Resolution 86, 237
War Problems Committee 15
War Relief 237, 238
Washington Friends Joint Peace Committee 132
Washington Interreligious Staff Council 191
Washington Office on Latin America (WOLA) 193
Watergate 34, 190
"Weaknesses of United States Deterrence Policy" 97
Welfare reform 173, 234, 236, 238
Western Europe 28

"What If..." 182
"Why Does Not the Process of Disarmament Begin?" 97
William Penn House 23, 59, 118, 128, 171
wiretapping 238
Witness for Peace 88
Women 211
  In the Life of FCNL 123
  Population growth 155
  Married women into the labor force 213
  Rural development 156
Women Strike for Peace 30
Women's International League for Peace and Freedom 74, 126
"Work" and compensation 177
World Bank 154, 156, 160
World Council of Churches 67
World Court 135, 136, 238
World Federalism 126, 238
World law 72
World Peace Tax Fund 112
Worship 2, 5

Y

Young Friends Committee of North America 132
Youth 238
Youth Seminars 59
Yugoslavia 130